THE EIGHT
CRYSTAL
ALLIANCES

The Group of 5 Crystals Series

Crystals and Stones: A Complete Guide to Their Healing Properties

Publications by Paume de Saint-Germain Publishing

The Lion's Roar: The Master from Montreal, Klaire D. Roy, 2008

New Tantrism, Klaire D. Roy, 2008

Tantric Training in the Age of Ray 7, Klaire D. Roy, 2008

New Tantrism: Introductory Themes, Klaire D. Roy, 2007

Conclave of the Cryptic 7, Volume I, Klaire D. Roy, 2007

The Spiritual Science of Essential Yoga: Techniques of Meditation, Mantrams, and Invocations, Volume I, Sri Adi Dadi, compiled by Martine G. Fortier, 2004.

Publications by North Atlantic Books

The Book of Stones: Who They Are and What They Teach, Robert Simmons and Naisha Ahsian

Stones of the New Consciousness: Healing, Awakening and Co-creating with Crystals, Minerals and Gems, Robert Simmons

The Mysterious Story of X7: Exploring the Spritual Nature of Matter, Anonymous, Robert Sardello, Sir George Trevelyan, and Anne K. Edwards

Steps on the Stone Path: Working with Crystals and Minerals as a Spiritual Practice, Robert Sardello

THE EIGHT CRYSTAL ALLIANCES

THE INFLUENCE OF STONES ON THE PERSONALITY

THE GROUP OF 5

Paume de Saint-Germain Publishing
Montreal, Quebec, Canada

North Atlantic Books
Berkeley, California

Published by   and
North Atlantic Books   Paume de Saint-Germain Publishing
P.O. Box 12327   235 Rene Levesque Blvd. East, Suite 310
Berkeley, California 94712   Montreal, Quebec, H2X 1N8 Canada

Translated from the original French by Jill Capri
Cover design by Lucie Robitaille, Lucie Létourneau, Susan Quasha
Book design by Lucie Robitaille, Lucie Létourneau
Photography by B. Simhananda,
 and Gaétan A. Brouillard, © Lux Æterna
Printed in the United States of America

The Eight Crystal Alliances: The Influence of Stones on the Personality is sponsored by the Society for the Study of Native Arts and Sciences, a nonprofit educational corporation whose goals are to develop an educational and cross-cultural perspective linking various scientific, social, and artistic fields; to nurture a holistic view of arts, sciences, humanities, and healing; and to publish and distribute literature on the relationship of mind, body, and nature.

North Atlantic Books' publications are available through most bookstores. For further information, visit our website at www.northatlanticbooks.com or call 800-733-3000.

Library of Congress Cataloging-in-Publication Data

Influence des pierres. English.
  The eight crystal alliances : the influence of stones on the personality /
The Group of 5 ; [translated from the original French by Jill Capri].
      p. cm.
  Summary: "Provides tools for understanding the spiritual nature of crystals and stones and how certain minerals can faciliate human development and transformation. Describes eight types of human personality and their corresponding relationships, or 'alliances' with various crystals that can support the full flowering and development of the soul"--Provided by publisher.
  Includes bibliographical references.
  ISBN-13: 978-1-55643-964-3
  ISBN-10: 1-55643-964-4
  1. Crystals--Psychic aspects. I. 5, The Group of. II. Capri, Jill. III. Title.
  BF1442.C78I5413 2011
  133'.2548--dc22
                            2011015828

1 2 3 4 5 6 7 8 9 United 16 15 14 13 12 11

To Dadi, our Source of Inspiration

We dedicate this book to Dadi Darshan Dharma, our precious guide in this present incarnation. He has transmitted to us his love for the mysterious kingdom of stones and crystals, and has shown us how to work in their company with respect and authenticity.

We also thank all our friends and patients who have allowed us to deepen our knowledge of this wondrous mineral kingdom that contains vast mysteries, which we hope one day to reveal.

CONTENTS

Foreword

This book was first conceived during a group study on geometric alliances carried out by therapists from the Medicine Buddha Mandala Institute in Montreal. Working together, we discovered these alliances and tested them on ourselves and on individuals who came to us for lithotherapy treatments. They have now become an inextricable part of our day-to-day lives. We see these alliances everywhere and are pleased to recognize them because they constitute a remarkable tool for self-knowledge and change.

The study of the geometric alliances is now an essential component of the first level of the lithotherapy program offered at the Medicine Buddha Mandala Institute. This book was written by the institute's therapists, who joined forces to bring the project to life.

We would like to thank Michael Gienger for his work, *Crystal Power, Crystal Healing: The Complete Handbook,* which explains the crystal systems that inspired and guided us in preparing this publication on the geometric alliances as we now use them. His book remains a primary reference for us in our practice as lithotherapists.

Since this book is intended as a nonscientific expression of this approach, we focused our attention mainly on the human aspect of these geometric alliances. Its style and structure are simple yet effective to ensure that the subject matter is easily accessible to all readers.

We sincerely hope you will enjoy reading it as much as we enjoyed writing it.

Klaire D. Roy
Director, Medicine Buddha Mandala Institute, Montreal

INTRODUCTION

Since the early twentieth century, psychologists have proposed numerous theories to explain the human personality. Despite the vast differences in their ideas, most describe personality as a set of traits and modes of thought and behavior that can be used as a basis for defining, recognizing, and gaining insight into individuals and their motivations.

Today, growing numbers of psychologists and therapists from various schools of thought look to the study of the individual as a whole as the key to a true understanding of human nature. Often called "holistic," these approaches take into account not only the role of personality in our development and growth but also the other elements that make up our being, such as our physical body, thoughts, emotions, and soul.

The study and application of the characteristics of geometric alliances help us develop the many facets of our being by compelling us to seek a cure, a change, or a transformation. This approach is particularly valuable in that it encourages us to delve into the depths of our being to draw on the abilities, knowledge, and qualities inherent in our true nature. We are then more likely to live in harmony with our potential and adopt modes of thought and behavior that supersede the rigid confines of personality.

Studying the eight geometric alliances equips us with a wonderful tool for enriching our understanding of what and who we really are, based on natural principles of energy that closely link the human and mineral realms. The knowledge we gain illuminates the mysterious kinship between these two realms, a vital connection that we have just begun to discover.

These alliances can be of great assistance when we feel a deep desire to change since, as crucial as this desire may be, it cannot effect change on its own.

The specific energies of stones set off an energy modification process than can affect our etheric body and in turn all the other bodies that make up our being. In other words, the power of stones can trigger an enduring and profound transformation by infusing our being with higher vibration frequencies.

THE EIGHT GEOMETRIC ALLIANCES

A geometric alliance is the specific geometric pattern or system in which atoms and molecules are arranged. These basic blueprints never change, meaning that a given mineral maintains the same clearly defined structure. There are seven basic geometric forms in the mineral realm; each fills an entire space in an orderly manner without leaving any gaps. These forms are cubes, hexagons, parallelograms, rectangles, rhombuses, trapeziums, and triangles, which in turn give rise to a corresponding geometric alliance: cubic, hexagonal, monoclinic, quadratic, rhombic, triclinic, and trigonal.

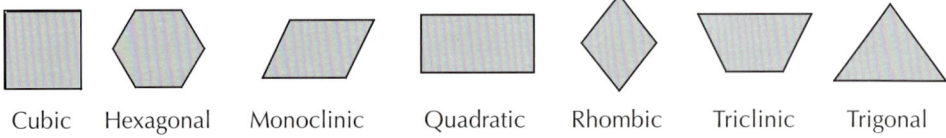

Cubic   Hexagonal   Monoclinic   Quadratic   Rhombic   Triclinic   Trigonal

All crystal atoms on the planet cluster into one of these shapes. When we talk about the geometric forms underlying mineral formation, we mean the way the atoms bind together rather than their actual shape or the outer form of the stone seen with the naked eye.

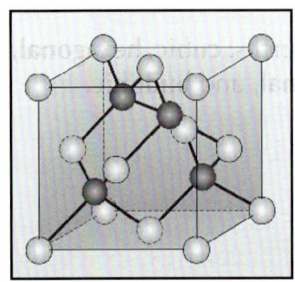

Atoms bind together to form a cubic structure.

Source: *Encyclopædia Universalis*

4

The quadratic alliance, for instance, is based on the rectangle, even though a quadratic stone may not necessarily be rectangular in shape.

As every rule seems to have an exception, in this case it is the eighth geometric alliance, which is not generally acknowledged by geologists or included with the others. Why? Because the atoms of the stones associated with it lack a specific geometric form. For that reason it is called "buddhic," or amorphous, the latter term being somewhat inappropriate in our view given its dynamic nature. The molecules of these stones bind together so rapidly that their atoms are forced together without having the opportunity to form a specific geometric shape. One example is obsidian, which is volcanic in origin and is formed by rapidly cooling lava. An initially molten mass solidifies to form this strangely glass-like stone.

Symbol of the buddhic alliance

GEOMETRIC ALLIANCES AND FORMATION PROCESSES

Stones and crystals are allies from the mineral realm that we can use to assist us in three different ways: first, according to their geometric alliance; second, according to the processes that formed them; and lastly, through our knowledge of their respective properties.

1. GEOMETRIC ALLIANCES

As indicated above, there are eight geometric alliances: **cubic, hexagonal, monoclinic, quadratic, rhombic, triclinic, trigonal,** and **buddhic.**

The properties or "lifestyles" of each are reflected in the various aspects of our daily lives. These common traits color our day-to-day reality, our perceptions and conceptions, our communications with others, our actions, and even our ways of dealing with and expressing our emotions. In general, one particular alliance, which we choose through observing and imitating one of our parents, exerts a strong influence over our lives. Thus it is not the alliance that chooses us, but we who choose it.

However, other alliances can also impact how we act and react to certain external stimuli, depending on our focalization. For example, someone could be extremely disciplined and organized at work because of the influence of the cubic alliance and yet be very casual in his or her love life due to the influence of the buddhic alliance. In this instance, the cubic system acts on the mental level, while the buddhic system affects the emotions.

By carefully studying each alliance, we can determine the one to which we belong. We then possess a vital key to enhanced self-knowledge and awareness. Through this study we can also discover which stones can be useful to us, regardless of whether or not they are part of our own geometric alliance.

In practice, here's how we can benefit from knowledge about the lifestyles of these alliances in our daily lives. Using stones from the geometric alliance that represents us encourages us to positively focus on the qualities associated with it. In short, they can help us transform our bad habits and negative tendencies into positive qualities and virtues.

A sense of order is so important for people living a cubic lifestyle that when everything isn't structured and organized exactly as they wish, their life becomes chaotic. Nothing works! Stones from this alliance can help cubic personalities develop a sense of order that will be useful to them and to others, yet not be absolutely indispensible to their happiness and day-to-day functioning. Fluorite has proven to be an excellent stone for eliminating inflexible attitudes and narrow-mindedness, bringing order and clarifying confused thoughts.

Once they have achieved a balanced sense of order and organization, cubic individuals may decide to use stones from other geometric alliances to develop additional or complementary qualities that will enable them to evolve further. They may choose to work with a stone from the buddhic system with very different properties. Moldavite, for instance, encourages spontaneity, inspires original ideas, and grants access to a higher spiritual dimension. Cubic personalities could then develop a new faculty that could be described as "ordered spontaneity."

2. Formation processes

Rocks are formed according to three generally recognized processes: **magmatic, sedimentary,** and **metamorphic.**

The atoms of all stones carry the experience and wisdom of hundreds of thousands of years of formation and transformation. According to how a stone itself was formed and developed, i.e., through a magmatic, sedimentary, or metamorphic process, it can sustain us in our own development and transformation. By identifying the type of situation we are experiencing or will have to experience, we can chose to work with stones that were formed through a similar process. They can thus sustain us in overcoming certain obstacles and integrating difficult situations or experiences.

The role of magmatic stones is to bring us closer to our true inner potential—potential that can be compared to the magma that is the core element in their composition.

Labradorite is a magmatic stone associated with the triclinic alliance. It helps dispel illusions, stimulate intuition, retrieve forgotten memories, and clearly identify the source and motivation of our true intentions and objectives. This stone can be very beneficial when we sense we are losing contact with our inner self and feel the need to rediscover our true nature.

As its name suggests, fire opal, another buddhic stone, awakens our inner fire and inspires risk taking. We all know that it always takes courage to make a profound change. Fire opal stimulates the adrenal glands, promotes dynamism, and encourages us to take action (although it can sometimes make us more volatile).

As for sedimentary stones, they enhance our understanding of the events that have shaped and molded our lives, forging the being we have become today. They can help us transform our vision of life and of ourselves so that we can continually adapt to our environment.

Pietersite is a sedimentary stone belonging to the trigonal alliance. It promotes mastery over the emotions and inner peace in periods of chaotic change. This stone clarifies confused thoughts and can release us from outworn habits we no longer need.

Metamorphic stones can sustain us when have to make a major and seemingly impossible change in our lives. Since these stones have themselves been transformed by heat and pressure, they can assist us in making profound, sometimes radical changes when we are unable to make them on our own.

Take, for example, the buddhic alliance stone, Tibetan tektite. It can guide us to the heart of a problem and help us understand its true cause to take the necessary steps to resolve it. It possesses a particularly high energy vibration and confers strength, courage, and the will to make significant changes in our lives.

Garnet, which belongs to the cubic alliance, encourages dynamism and promotes action and perseverance. It revitalizes and regenerates, boosts self-confidence, and transforms crises into challenges. Sometimes called the "disciple's stone," it can also assist in overcoming opposition and dissolving obsolete behaviors.

3. Stones and their respective properties

Knowledge of the respective properties of stones obviously forms the foundation of any therapeutic approach. This knowledge, based on the stones' chemical composition, color, qualities, vibration, and role, enables therapists to specifically target their treatment.

Specific stones for each individual

Every stone has therapeutic properties that can sustain us throughout our lives. The potential of each derives from the affinity between us and the stone, which is determined not only by the geometric alliance that influences us but also by the specific events that mark our destiny.

In the event of a serious illness, for example, someone who is associated with the buddhic alliance will receive strong support from moldavite, which can spark profound inner change since it belongs to the same alliance. Other stones whose therapeutic properties enhance overall well-being can also be sustaining.

The more carefully the stones are chosen, i.e. through close attention to the harmony or kinship between the stone and the person, the greater their effect will be.

Become an active participant in your own transformation

When using stones for therapeutic purposes, it is important to remember that we must be active participants in our own cure. Actively committing ourselves means agreeing to work on certain fundamental truths that characterize us, learning to understand them, and then engaging in a purifying process.

For instance, we can decide to use peridot, a magmatic stone from the cubic alliance, to alleviate liver problems linked to repressed anger. Working with peridot can eliminate this anger over time and improve our well-being. Peridot also facilitates introspection to allow us to resolve what is troubling us. We can then forgive ourselves and others, for which our liver will only thank us. Of course this process may take several weeks or even months, but change will occur if we persevere and truly desire it.

This book is an invitation to gain greater self-understanding through the various geometric alliances whose powerful envoys we encounter each and every day. It doesn't matter if we are skeptical about their influence; their work will be in no way diminished by our resistance, doubts, or beliefs.

This is a marvelous, safe, and simple-to-use tool that will help everyone who is sincerely eager to transform themselves to better understand who they really are and better live this life we so cherish.

INVOCATION

We could not give life to these pages without including an invocation on stones. It was written by Dadi Darshan Dharma as a tribute to the mineral kingdom. We recite it regularly, since it invites us never to forget that stones and crystals are great work companions that sustain us daily in the duty we are accomplishing toward humanity. They reveal themselves as perfect servants, devoted and thoughtful, that give their energy and power so that people may better meet their challenges in the diverse domains of their existence.

I

Kinship of the Stone

IN THE BEGINNING two Sacred Loadstones from the Great Central Sun
Broke reverently into the Void of Cosmos and coming irresistibly together,

Brought to birth within its One Clap the sound of the Rainbow into Creation.

And it was upon the same Mythical Moment of mysterious Mystical Twine
That a lonely and lovely gemstone was instantly Agni-ized as planet Earth.

And chosen it was to be paramountly perched as a brilliant Blue Pearl
upon the deep indigo Necklace of Infinity.

And therewith began the Kinship of the Stone with the humming Harmony
of the Spheres.

II

Upon This Stone ...

OF OLD, STONES WERE said to be the shattered bones of the gods.

He who won the Hermetic Stone epitomized Divine Power and Perfect Love.

He who accessed the Philosopher's Stone possessed the Truth and banished all Ignorance.

It was upon tablets of stone that were writ in flame the Ten Commandments by the finger of the Nameless One.

And there was placed beside each commandment a glowing gem, each being dropped selectively into the deep sapphire sea of a man's Being.

And there issued forth in the Medieval era the Wondrous Work of the Alchemical Stone; and there was the Singing Stone of the Wise Man; and there was the Knight Templar of the Golden Stone, riding his steed of righteousness into the 'terra incognita' of the Masonic Square.

And there was the quintessential quest for the gem-studded, oracular chalice of the Holy Grail, enfolding the living waters and loving attar of life eternal.

And there was, and is, the Kaaba Monolith of mystical and traditional Islam, once blissfully white, and now blackened over eons by the bittersweet tears of longsuffering pilgrims and the salacious stain of sin.

And lead, to the Egyptians, led unerringly to the skeleton of Saturn; and iron was about the muscled marrow of Mars, and silver gave shine to the Moon, and antimony bravely braced up the Earth.

And of shining stone and jubilant gem was the glow and the glory of the once Great Pyramid.

And each planet of the Zodiac is gem potentized, and each constellation is gem consecrated, and each of the Seven Solar Men stands gem-authorized before the Diamond Throne of the Lord of Shamballa.

And that mythical stone, the "Heliogabalus," also black, was said to be especially sacred to the Sun.

Conjecture claims (perhaps) that it was teleported down Jacob's Ladder, and became the infamous Black Rock pillow, upon which this extraordinary Servant of God laid his head in rest every eve.

And which now, in occult and humble fashion, adorns the seat of the eminent coronation chair in the Abbey of Westminster.

And finally it was once said (not so long ago) that: "Upon this stone, I shall build my Church ...," and thus again, was re-affirmed the sacred kinship of stone and Spirit.

III

Stones

STONES BREATHE DEEPLY in patient beauty and grow in studied symmetry.

Slowly, they exhale their light in perfect and unreserved service to all,
Whether the all be that of the universe, or a planet, or simply the kingdom
of mineral, plant, animal, or man.

Stones are spiritual carriers of the principle of growth, of elevation, of
evolution.

They arouse the winds of change to cast their vibratile incorporeality
upon the samsaric consciousness.

Slowly, slowly, stones correct all wrong thinking and do their best to amplify
the philosophic perspective;

And empower do they, the imprisoned small-self, to have Divine concourse
with the bright awesomeness of the Soul.

IV

Gemstones

A GEMSTONE'S HEART beats slowly, pulses highly, and never forgets the lowly.

A gemstone's roots are elemental but devic in essence, and earthly-bent in daily task.

A gemstone comes from the light, is made of light, and is a bearer of light to World upon worlds of shadow and distress, doubt and despair, woe and wrong.

A gemstone is the eye of the sky casting a pure look through the dust of conflict and pain.

A gemstone is the distillation of heaven's Love aesthetically cast in crystalline concentration upon all human cry and call.

To pick up and pocket a gemstone is to self-create a covenant for conversion, commutation and change.

To pick up and pocket a gemstone is to decide to truncate and temper all struggle and strife.

To pick up and pocket a gemstone is to beckon a holy helper to come renew our resolve (and restore our strength).

To pick up and pocket a gemstone is to honor the hand of the mineral kingdom and to dine with the Divine in variegated hues of adamantine Light.

V

Blessed Be the Stone

BLESSED BE THE STONE ... for in it is to be found the Gem of God.

BLESSED BE THE STONE ... for in it is grounded the Brilliance of God.

BLESSED BE THE STONE ... for in it is built the Beauty of God.

BLESSED BE THE STONE ... for in it is shaped the Geometry of God.

BLESSED BE THE STONE ... for in it is organized the Chemistry of God.

BLESSED BE THE STONE ... for in it is set the Adamantine Word of God.

BLESSED BE THE STONE ... for in it is held the Wisdom of God.

BLESSED BE THE STONE ... for in it is housed the Harmony of God.

BLESSED BE THE STONE ... for in it is honoured the Healing Angel of God.

BLESSED BE THE STONE ... for in it is affixed the Mercy of God.

BLESSED BE THE STONE ... for in it is crouched the Grace of God.

BLESSED BE THE STONE ... for in it is fructified the Benevolence of God.

BLESSED BE THE STONE ... for in it is inspirited the Intelligence of God.

BLESSED BE THE STONE ... for in it is forged the Power of God.

BLESSED BE THE STONE ... for in it is matrixed the Love of God.

BLESSED BE THE STONE ... for in it is substantiated the Science of God.

BLESSED BE THE STONE ... for in it is conjured the Magnificent Magus of God.

BLESSED BE THE STONE ... for in it is humanized the Light of God.

BLESSED BE THE STONE ... for in it is dreamt the Dream of God.

BLESSED BE THE STONE ... for in it is inscribed the Plan of God.

BLESSED BE THE STONE ... for in it is encoded the Purpose of God.

BLESSED BE THE STONE ... for in it is envisioned Man's Service to God.

BLESSED BE THE STONE ... for in it is salaamed Man's Devotion to HIM.

Dadi Darshan Dharma
October 20–21, 2004
April 22, 2008

Crystals and Stones
Formation Processes

This chapter explains the relationship between the science of rock formation and the influence these different formation processes may have on human behavior. We will first examine how nature produces magmatic, sedimentary, and metamorphic rock. Then, since we know that each type of formation process influences us in different areas of our lives, we will briefly explore their impact on the human spirit.

How stones and crystals are formed

The Planet Earth evolved roughly 4.57 billion years ago from a disk-shaped mass of dust and gas released by the sun. Its volcanic activity produced a primordial atmosphere consisting of vast quantities of water vapor. After undergoing a fusion process, its outer layer cooled to form a solid crust when water began accumulating in the atmosphere. Oceans were formed by the condensation of this vapor combined with ice delivered by comets colliding with the Earth.

GEOLOGICAL STRUCTURE

The Earth is made up of a number of inner, almost concentric, layers, as follows:

1. The solid continental and oceanic crusts, which constitute only one percent of the Earth's volume. The continental crust varies in thickness from 18.6 miles to 62 miles beneath mountain ranges and is mainly made up of granitic rocks (silicon and aluminum), sometimes overlain by sedimentary rocks. The oceanic crust is relatively thin, generally around 3 miles in depth, and is essentially composed of basaltic rocks (silicon and magnesium).

2. Just beneath the Earth's crust lies the upper mantle, which is about 400 miles thick and is primarily comprised of rocks such as peridotite (olivine, pyroxene, garnet). At a temperature of 2,000 degrees Fahrenheit, it has a higher viscosity than the lower mantle.

3. The lower mantle, which has a temperature of 3,600 degrees and extends to a depth of 1,400 miles, displays the properties of an elastic solid and is extremely hot and highly viscous. Together, the upper and lower mantles constitute eighty-four percent of the Earth's volume.

4. The liquid outer core is close to 1,370 miles thick and is essentially composed of iron and nickel. Due to its temperature, around 7,200 degrees, its viscosity is similar to that of water. The Earth's magnetism is said to derive from the convection currents within the liquid core.

5. The solid inner core, which is 807 miles thick, is mainly composed of metal. It remains solid due to massive pressure, despite temperatures of close to 9,000 degrees.

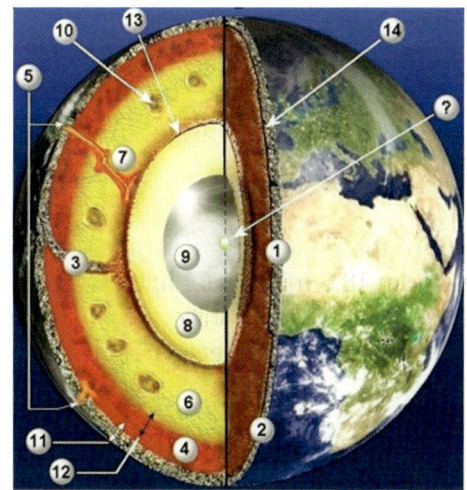

The Structure of the Earth
Source: Wikipedia.org

1. Solid continental crust
2. Solid oceanic crust
3. Subduction zone where the plates descend into the mantle
4. Upper mantle
5. Eruptions in the active volcanic zones
6. Lower mantle, with the properties of an elastic solid
7. Plume of hotter material rising from the outer core boundary
8. Liquid outer core
9. Solid inner core
10. Mantle convection cells
11. Lithosphere, crust, and upper mantle, 62 to 124 miles thick
12. Asthenosphere: deeper part of the upper mantle
13. Gutenberg discontinuity: core-mantle transition zone
14. Mohorovicic discontinuity: crust-mantle transition zone

Chemical composition

The Earth's mass is chiefly made up of iron (32%), oxygen (30%, oxides), silicon (15%, silicates), magnesium (14%), sulfur (3%), nickel (2%), calcium (1.5%), and aluminum (1.4%), plus other trace metals. Heavier metals like iron (89% of the Earth's solid core), nickel (6%), and sulfur (4.5%) tend to sink toward the center of the Earth. Some forty-seven percent of the Earth's crust consists of lighter-weight elements, mainly silicon, aluminum, iron, calcium, magnesium, potassium, and sodium oxides, which float on top of layers of denser rock similarly to the way ice floes float on the ocean's surface.

Convection currents and tectonic plates

The Earth's crust or lithosphere is broken into plates of varying thickness. Convection currents within the underlying upper mantle move these plates in different directions.

Convection is the transfer of heat due to movement (currents) in a fluid. For example, in a pan of boiling water, the water particles at the bottom expand, become less dense, and rise toward the surface due to buoyancy forces, while the water closer to the surface cools down and sinks back toward the bottom, creating a circulating motion. The Atlantic Ocean's Gulf Stream is an example of a convection current on a broad scale. As it travels north from the Gulf of Mexico, the warm water at the ocean's surface cools dramatically on contact with the polar ice cap. The resulting increase in salinity and decrease in temperature cause it to sink to the bottom of the ocean and then return toward the Gulf of Mexico. Thus, the release of heat from the Earth's core creates convection movements in all layers of the planet.

The Earth's mantle is composed of extremely hot elastic rocks, at a temperature of 2,000 degrees, that flow on geological timescales of several million years, producing a very slow rotating movement. The pressure generated on the lithosphere by the convection movement in the mantle causes the tectonic plates to drift, separating the continents, forming mountains, and creating earthquakes and volcanic eruptions.

TYPES OF ROCKS

Rocks may be classified into three major groups according to how they were formed:

(a) **Magmatic rocks,** also called igneous or eruptive rocks, form when magma cools and solidifies, with or without the complete crystallization of the minerals of which it is comprised. When such rocks solidify deep within the Earth, they are called plutonic rocks, while those formed at the surface are called volcanic (extrusive or effusive) rocks.

(b) **Sedimentary rocks** are formed on the Earth's surface or in bodies of water when various materials are layered by erosive agents like water and wind.

(c) **Metamorphic rocks** are formed when sedimentary or magmatic rocks recrystallize in response to growing heat and pressure within the Earth's crust or on contact with other extremely hot rocks.

MAGMATIC OR IGNEOUS ROCKS

The following factors play an important role in magmatic rock formation: the composition of the magma, pressure, the space needed for the crystals to develop, and the time it takes for the molten rock to cool.

Magmatic rocks are produced from a molten liquid that is so hot it is luminous. This liquid is called magma. Its composition will determine the type of rock that will be formed on the Earth's surface, i.e., a mineral, such as amethyst, or a rock composed of several minerals, such as granite.

There are two types of magmatic rocks: vulcanites, which are formed at the Earth's surface; and plutonites, whose name derives from Pluto, the lord of the underworld, which are formed deep down in the Earth. The major difference between the two is the length of time it takes them to cool. Lava cooling on the Earth's surface can take only a few hours or days to solidify, while the cooling process in the depths of the Earth can last thousands of years.

A) Vulcanites

The cooling process begins when the magma erupts and comes into contact with the air. If the lava takes several days to solidify, minute crystals are formed as it hardens. However, if the lava cools quickly, which happens when it comes into contact with water, for example, the crystallization process will be very different. The dramatic temperature shock prevents crystals from forming, and the lava solidifies in a glass-like form, producing stones like obsidian.

B) Plutonites

The formation of plutonites differs from that of vulcanites in that the magma remains under the Earth's surface, acting directly on the size of the crystals that are formed. Because the heat underground is constant and extremely high, the magma solidifies slowly over thousands of years. The crystals thus have the time they need to separate and form according to their chemical elements.

Therapeutic benefits of magmatic rocks

From the moment of our birth, we possess an inner force that surpasses our understanding. This force is our true identity, just as magma is the essence of magmatic rock. As humans, we develop along a specific evolutionary trajectory, as do members of the animal, plant, and mineral kingdoms. Our inner force influences what we are—our gender, race, parents, and abilities, and determines certain character traits.

When we are children, our primary goal is to learn about life and develop skills like learning to walk, run, talk, read, and count. At this stage, we learn very quickly since we are still connected to our true essence, where these predispositions reside. This force is to humans as magma is to stone. In other words, these faculties are not developed, they are innate.

Over time, we mature and are no longer attuned to this inner force, choosing to follow what seems to us the more logical path mapped out by our intellect. When we are young we simply learn lessons; as we grow older we attempt to understand and analyze them, which can sometime lead to a lack of creativity and narrow-mindedness, making us rigid and "crystallized." Of course, the brain is able to learn, but being Cartesian in nature, it can be a very limited tool. It functions well in the areas it knows because it has created its own reference points that help it navigate these areas. However, when we are faced with a new subject or have to be spontaneously creative, our brain, without any of these benchmarks to rely on, has to rise to new challenges.

Magmatic rocks can be effective tools to help us reconnect with our inner force. They cannot change the innate predispositions of our being, but they can help us tap into and integrate them. These stones are excellent companions when we have to develop a latent ability or are confronted with new situations. We need to use our brain in today's world, but it is a limited instrument. Using magmatic stones can enhance and complement our own effectiveness.

Particular attention should be paid to black magmatic stones. Having lived many years, some very peacefully, others less so, these stones can bring to the surface dark memories embedded in our being. Little by little, these memories will have to be purified. Rather than fear these stones, we should use them wisely and discerningly so that they can accomplish their work without unduly upsetting our balance. It is advisable to use them with other stones that will support us in dissipating the darkness we have carried through many lives.

Pressure is also a key element in maintaining conditions in the subterranean world, since it is a driving force. Without pressure, magma would stagnate, remaining static and lifeless. All these riches would be lost forever, buried underground beyond our grasp. Since the magma would lack this driving force, the geological equivalent of the human will, it would never reach the surface or erupt. There would be no volcanic eruptions, and life on Earth would be seriously at risk. The same principle can be applied to human beings. We must have the will to develop and supply the necessary effort to do so. Pressure is to magma what will is to human beings. It is will that produces the driving force or synergy we need to attain our goals. Just as magma becomes active under pressure, our goals are actuated by our will. Without it, unsuspected treasures will remain locked deep within our being and never rise to the surface.

Sedimentary rocks

Nothing in this world is eternal; everything is transient. Rocks on the Earth's surface are eroded by the rain, snow, wind, sun, frost, and thaw that change their composition and cause them to disintegrate. Over a period that can be as long as several thousand years, they are slowly transformed. During the erosion process, some minerals break away and other minerals are formed.

We can observe this process in nature: sediment that is broken off from the parent rock by erosion is transported by water (streams, rivers, and so on), wind, and ice. As long as the water and wind are in motion, they carry the sediment along with them. When they slow down, it can no longer continue on its course. Lakes, deltas, rivers, and oceans are environments conducive to the formation of sedimentary rocks since their flow is relatively calm. First the coarser and then the lighter sediment settles in riverbeds and on the bottom of lakes and sea floors. After thousands of years, it compacts to form sedimentary rocks.

Therapeutic benefits of sedimentary rocks

As mentioned earlier, from the moment we are born, we possess certain natural predispositions, just as rock contains certain minerals that are bound together after the lava has cooled. This is not a perpetual state. All human beings are affected by their environment, as sedimentary rocks are affected by erosion. From our childhood on, certain episodes, experiences, or beliefs permeate our conscience, leaving scars that may sometimes be so deep-seated they remain with us for the rest of our lives. Metaphorically, we too are weathered by erosion.

We spend our lives immersed in an environment that has repercussions on our present and on our future. These physical, biological, sociological, and chemical conditions critically influence us, some in positive ways that encourage growth, others in negative ways that cause suffering and resistance to life.

Our parents educate us and teach us about life so that we can become healthy human beings. According to their own intrinsic values and beliefs, they show us what is good and what is not. When we are young, we are unable to distinguish truth from falsehood, and we trust those around us to guide us. In some cases, we live through distressing situations and block off these so-called past experiences. Unconsciously, we don't want to repeat them because we know they will make us suffer. These lessons and experiences will play a decisive role in our lives since they will be the lenses through which we will view it.

Too often, these lenses can become rigid beliefs, forcing us into a limited view of life. They condition our being, which is unfortunate as they are often distorted, blurring our vision. In turn, this vision can cause great suffering when we refuse to adjust it to the various situations we face. We resist change because it frightens us. We become, as it were, crystallized, incapable of adapting to certain conditions because we fear pain or renewal. The underlying cause of this suffering is resistance to change, the fear of shedding these lenses, beliefs, or experiences that control us. Giving up the way we see things can be terrifying as it often means we have to lower barriers that we have erected to protect ourselves from danger.

Sedimentary stones can help us better connect and adapt to our environment. Produced by erosion, they have been weathered by their surrounding environment and have lost, as it were, a part of themselves. From this long transformation process, new minerals have emerged. These stones have the power to draw out the inevitably harmful residue left by our past experiences and lessons learned. Although it may seem difficult, we must discard these old habits to align our view of life with our environment. These stones can be our servants and support us in letting go of what we no longer need.

Sedimentary stones are also useful in crisis situations, which are usually directly linked to our environment. They can mitigate critical states by restoring calm and proposing a new perspective.

In most cases, it is not life itself that is problematic, but the way we perceive it. For example, some may see a simple argument as the end of the world, while for others it is merely an opportunity to discover their personal failings.

All the problems arising from our immediate environment influence us and can cause us sorrow. Sedimentary stones have the power to awaken a new vision and help us live in harmony with everything life places in our path.

METAMORPHIC ROCKS

Let's take a closer look at the Earth's upper mantle and its deeper, more turbulent levels. This underworld is dominated by two factors: extreme heat and pressure, which both inexorably transform the surrounding matter.

When rock near the magma is subjected to high temperatures and intense pressure, it becomes unstable and undergoes a fundamental transformation. Its crystals are rearranged and restructured. All magmatic, sedimentary, and metamorphic rocks undergo some form of transition. Those affected by heat and pressure are literally transformed.

Heat raises the temperature of the rock, "baking" it as it were. If the temperature is high enough, the rock's inner structure will be altered. Under the action of pressure, its inner structure is compressed. As a result, the crystals are forced to occupy as little space as possible and bond together. Sometimes the pressure is so intense that certain substances are squeezed out of the rock. If neighboring rock is subject to the same process, these substances are pressed together to form new, more resistant minerals. Chemical elements of the same nature tend to come together because their atomic attraction is stronger than the attraction between unlike elements. This explains mineral deposits in mines.

Interestingly, even though a rock may be subjected to high temperatures during the metamorphic process, it is prevented from melting by pressure. During this process, everything that does not withstand the tremendous pressure and high temperatures is transformed into more resistant matter.

REGIONAL METAMORPHISM

Metamorphism may occur on a broad scale, affecting entire areas. This is called regional metamorphism, which usually occurs when two continental plates meet, as the model of the Earth illustrates (p. 23). The lighter plate will slightly rise, creating mountain ranges like the Rockies, the Andes, and the Himalayas. The denser plate will sink under the lighter plate and be increasingly subject to the heat and pressure of the magma as it descends into the mantle. The nearer it is to the depths of the Earth, the greater the metamorphism.

CONTACT METAMORPHISM

During volcanic or plutonic eruptions, adjacent rocks, which are cold in comparison to the magma, are affected by the extreme heat. Under such high temperatures, these rocks are "baked" and altered, and they become metamorphic.

THERAPEUTIC BENEFITS OF METAMORPHIC ROCKS

Although most people are under the impression that the Earth's interior is static, it is actually in constant movement and flux. From this process, new, more resistant minerals are born. Does this same process apply to human beings? Are we really sincere with ourselves and with others? We can either be honest or else we can pretend that we are happy, that we feel good about ourselves and are proud of our achievements. Of course it is possible to conceal our true feelings, but can we continue to carry on this pretense from one life to the next? As pleasant as it may be to live in this haze of superficiality, beneath it a shadow remains. We all know we are not always genuine, that something is preventing us from attaining perfection. At times we want to feel better about ourselves but are unsure of how to go about it. By seeking a way out, removing our blinders, and facing the truth, we will be able to change and achieve an authentic transformation that may shake us to the very core of our being.

Since metamorphic stones have been transformed by pressure and heat, they have the potential to rescue us and guide us toward a sometimes radical change. They can help unveil certain facets of our being that remain hidden from us and from others. We will emerge from this process transformed. The pressure and heat that have tested metamorphic rocks symbolize an unease within us that can often persist for years or even entire lifetimes. We must be honest with ourselves so that we can offer the best of ourselves to others.

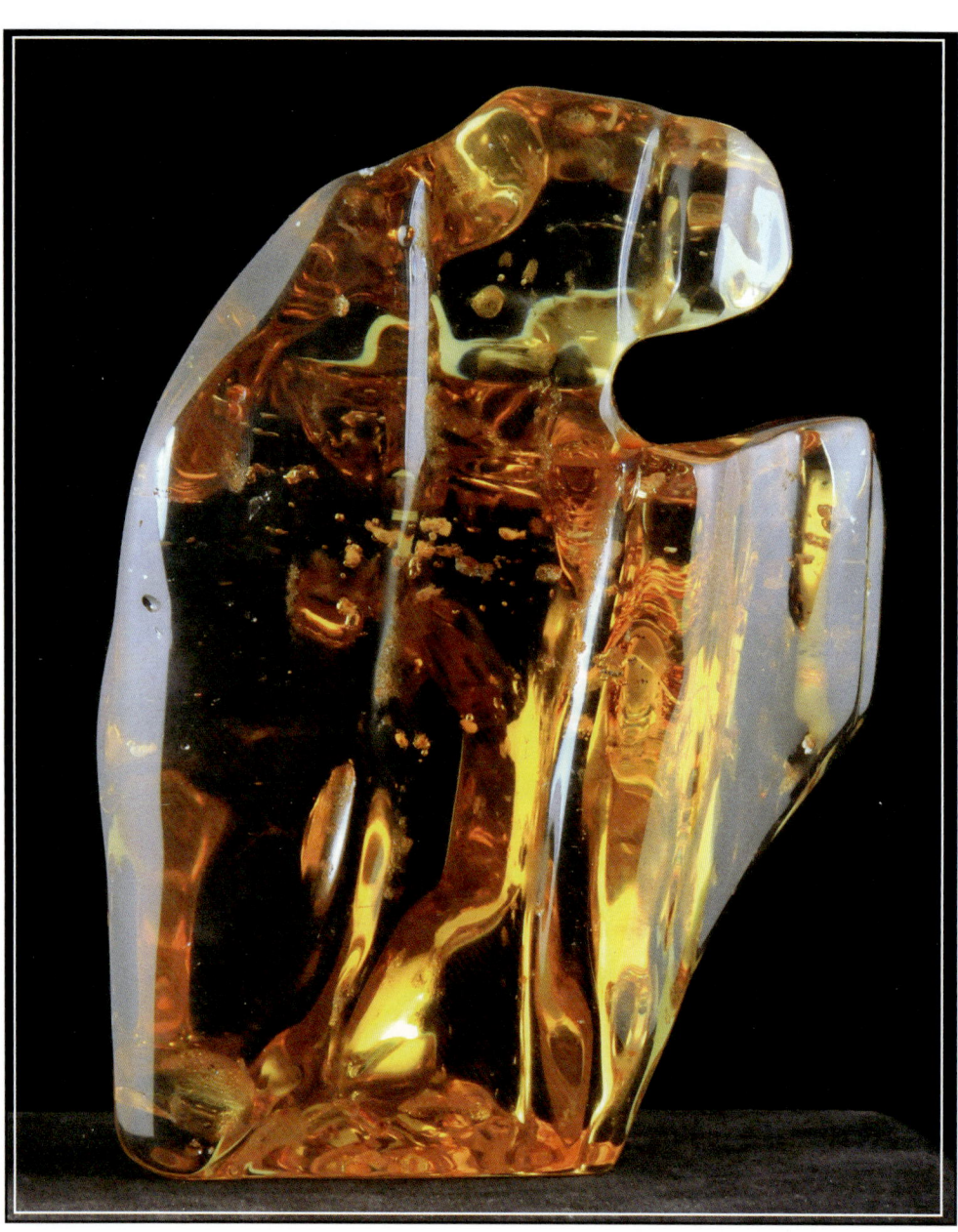

Choosing a stone

The first question we need to ask when we want to work with a stone is, what type of rock formation best corresponds to our needs? The answer will help determine the source of the problem to be resolved. If we use a type of formation that is appropriate to the solution sought, the desired effects will quickly become apparent since stones are able to transmit what they have experienced.

When it's hard to identify the source of our problems, it's almost impossible to determine the appropriate type of rock formation. That's when stones like apatite, amazonite, aventurine, and pyrite, which contain the three formation principles, can be very useful. These stones can help raise the veil masking the reasons for our turmoil and become precious allies in helping eliminate them, enabling us to rediscover peace and harmony.

It's important to carefully select the companions that will support us in what we have to accomplish. Some will be more effective in maintaining our physical health while others will stabilize our emotions, giving us the strength to face the challenges life brings us.

Stones and crystals can operate on a number of levels. They can alleviate physical pain, reduce existential angst, and guide us along our spiritual path. Beauty shouldn't be the only criteria since beauty isn't always synonymous with effectiveness.

Factors influencing stone and crystal prices

Many factors influence the price of a stone or crystal. First, the authenticity of the piece will play an important role in the use we'll make of it. An artificial turquoise, created in a laboratory, will not be as efficient as a real turquoise. So be wary of imitations: although certainly less expensive, they'll also be less effective.

The purity of the piece is an equally important factor to consider when purchasing a stone or crystal. The more crystalline it is, the greater its capacity to convey light. It will transmit its therapeutic particularities in less time and will increase our chances of success. The rarity of a stone or crystal directly influences its worth, hence its price. So, a crystal from Tibet will be more expensive than a crystal from Arkansas. The originality of a piece and the extent of its beauty are often considered criteria of rarity, which increase the value of a stone or crystal.

Dimensions of a stone or crystal

The choice of the dimensions of a stone or crystal depends on the use we want to make of it. In therapy, we tend to choose smaller pieces that will be comfortable for the body. In daily life, certain pieces are ideally worn as jewelry. The dimensions and location—on the neck, finger, directly on the skin, or in the pocket—have a direct impact on the desired effect at the place where we want it to be produced. As a decorative piece, or to harmonize and increase the energy and light of a given area, it is advisable to favor more imposing pieces like geodes or quartz clusters, which can be placed in a room such as an office or any other location.

Care of stones and crystals

Stones and crystals are precious friends; owing to their high sensitivity, proper care requires a particular vigilance that necessitates specific treatment. Ignoring this rule can lead to the destruction of these companions. When in doubt, it is better to refrain and wait to be certain as to the approach to be used. However, we have found two methods that are efficient and without danger: incense and an amethyst or quartz cluster.

Regarding incense, just pass it over the stone or crystal for a few minutes. Reciting a mantra may increase the purifying effects. The choice of a mantra is a personal one, but "om" has proven to be as potent as a more elaborate mantra.

The use of a quartz or amethyst cluster is easy: it is simply a matter of letting the piece rest on the cluster for a few hours. The quartz or amethyst cluster will clean and charge the piece by injecting it with a supplementary energy dose that will render it more effective. Several other cleaning methods are also available. However, we wish to reiterate that vigilance is important, since a bad choice can be fatal to your companion. Do not hesitate to consult books or to contact a specialist for advice on the best method to use for the stone or crystal you want to clean.

BEST-KNOWN CLEANING METHODS

· sunlight, ideal for all quartz

· moonlight, preferred by kyanite

· fresh cold water, adored by the majority of stones and crystals

· salt, to be used with caution

· earth, in certain cases, particularly if a crystal is very damaged

· snow, as a replacement for cold water

BEST-KNOWN RECHARGING METHODS

· quartz cluster

· sunlight

· moonlight

· cold water

· incense

· mantras

Methods of cleaning and recharging may differ, and one may not necessarily include the other. For example, salt may clean but not recharge a stone.

USING STONES AND CRYSTALS IN PERSONAL THERAPY

We can wear a stone or crystal as jewelry or directly on the body. Ideally, precious and semiprecious stones must touch the skin, but not all quartz families, among them crystals such as amethyst, citrine, and others, require contact with the skin. These crystals and stones can be worn on our bodies in cotton or linen pouches or simply slipped in our pockets. For maximum efficiency, the piece must be located as close as possible to the area we wish to treat. It is better to wear one stone or crystal at a time; however, in certain cases, wearing a few pieces simultaneously can also be beneficial.

The length of time a stone or crystal should be worn differs depending on the purpose and result desired; it can vary from a few minutes to a few hours. Generally, when worn as jewelry, we should let the stone or crystal rest for the night after we remove it. If we wear a crystal such as a citrine on our skin for a specific benefit (for example, to facilitate digestion) in general, the crystal should not be worn for more than a few hours. It is our duty to be attentive to our body and its reactions.[1]

---

[1] The Group of 5, *Crystals and Stones: A Complete Guide to their Healing Properties* (Berkeley, CA: North Atlantic Books, and Montreal: Paume de Saint-Germain Publishing, 2010).

THE ORDER AND ORGANIZATION (RATIONAL) FILIATION

CUBIC ALLIANCE

LEAVING NOTHING TO CHANCE

Keyword: control.

Strengths: ability to see the big picture, efficient, fearless, logical, organized, ritualistic, structured.

Weaknesses: calculating, conservative, dislike of the unexpected, lack of flexibility and spontaneity, impatient, insecure, quick-tempered, solitary, unwilling to be guided by feelings.

Stones, minerals and metals: argentite, betafite, boji, boleite, chromite, cobaltite, copper, cuprite, diamond, fluorite, galena, garnet, gold, halite, hauynite, Isis/Osiris, lapis lazuli, lazurite, magnetite, periclase, platinum, pyrite, silver, sodalite, sphalerite, spinel.

Focus: mental.

Professions and trades: accountant, architect, cartographer, pharmacist, physician, police officer, secretary, soldier, surgeon.

Polarity: masculine.

Ailments: backache, high blood pressure, illnesses caused by bad habits (alcohol, tobacco, food, etc.).

Dress: conservative, understated.

Well-known personalities: Rabbit in *Winnie the Pooh,* Jack Nicholson's character in *As Good as It Gets,* Queen Elizabeth II (very formal), Richard Gere (always well-dressed, always drinks the same kind of white wine, etc.), Captain Von Trapp in *The Sound of Music.*

While the inner geometric structure of the cubic alliance is square, it can also be in the form of a rhombidodecahedron, octahedron, tetrahedron, dodecahedron, pentagon, and so on. The cubic lifestyle is a structured and orderly one where everything runs according to schedule. For individuals belonging to this alliance, there's no such thing as chance; order reigns in the material world around them and in their relationships.

It's easy to recognize the desk of someone influenced by the cubic alliance because there's a place for everything and everything is in its place. The pencils gleam in their pencil-holder; each piece of paper is carefully filed away in the file cabinet. The books on the desk are arranged according to author or subject and lined up like soldiers in neat rows. The to-do list is well in evidence, and what has been completed has either been disposed of or put in a safe place.

When in a negative mindset, the cubics see themselves and life as follows:

- I'm insecure.

- Life is too unpredictable.

- So I have to control everything.

Life is too unpredictable; I need to create order

To make sure that everything is under control, cubic personalities structure every area of their lives, from the way they dress to the way they drive and even the way they organize the fridge. Everything has to be in its own specific place. Their need for order reassures them and saves them time. They even carry this need over into their love life, which they control to make it as predictable as possible.

Peter is a prosperous businessman. When he's working on his computer, he saves his important work every five minutes because he can't risk losing any part of a file. What's more, since he knows that there's always room for error when things can't be tangibly controlled, he also makes copies that he keeps in a safe place. His work is so vital to him that he can't run the risk of losing a single document. His time is too valuable, and he always aims for perfection.

Fluorite can be a crucial stone for Peter. Placed on his desk, it will help him maintain order and efficiently process the information he receives. It can also give him self-confidence and reduce his mental fatigue.

> *Everything is uncertain, temporal and temporary.*
> *Naturally this inevitable reality frightens us,*
> *so much so that we seek to control change*
> *rather than simply surf its waves.*
>
> D.D.D.

A place for everything and everything in its place

At home and at work, cubic personalities know exactly where to find what they need to make their day run smoothly. If, by some misfortune, their quart of milk or their favorite drink isn't in its usual place, they immediately become annoyed. Their entire day could be ruined because this lack of order brings temporary chaos to their perfectly planning. They dislike the unexpected and hate surprises, both good and bad.

I'm always in control of myself, and I control my surroundings

Diane, a "perfect" secretary whose self-image is crucial to her, has been invited out to a restaurant. She has no idea that her friends have organized a surprise birthday party for her and are waiting for her there. She arrives, casually dressed, wearing very little makeup and feeling very tired. Her first reaction is anger because she feels trapped and not at her best. She tries to hide her feelings but her stony expression gives her away. It takes her a few hours to relax and enjoy her friends' company.

Wearing **lapis lazuli** would be a great help to Diane because it would encourage her to relax and realize that unexpected surprises aren't all that bad. It would help her become aware of her individual worth and reduce her fear of being judged, of not being perfect, and of not being in charge at all times.

Cubic personalities want to control the world around them and are totally unaware that it controls them, triggering every least action and thought. As a result, each second of their day is structured, leaving room only for regularly programmed behavior. They eat their meals at certain times, brush their teeth with a particular brand of toothpaste, always put the tube back in the same place, wear the same style of clothing day in and day out, drive the same make of car, and make love according to a strict schedule. Anything unforeseen instantly produces anxiety. Their day planner is their bible where they record almost every appointment and date. They're always punctual or always arrive five to ten minutes late, which they see as a form of punctuality. They plan well in advance and do everything they can to make sure these plans materialize.

> *Everything in life is fleeting and unforeseeable.*
> *Instead of letting events distress us,*
> *let's learn to master our feelings and thoughts.*
>
> D.D.D.

Planning is crucial

Individuals influenced by the cubic alliance are incapable of acting spontaneously since they always want to know the outcome of their actions in advance. They like to plan everything and make lists to make sure that nothing is forgotten. For example, if they're taking a trip, they'll map out their route ahead of time and choose their suitcase for its practicality rather than its appearance. Efficiency is what counts. They detest the unexpected and are furious if their luggage gets lost.

Paul, a young veterinarian who spent his vacation in Paris, is returning home via London, which he had visited before travelling on to Paris. At Charles de Gaulle Airport, the passenger agent tells him his luggage is overweight and he has to pay a supplement. Furious, Paul explains that since he's only passing through London on his way back home to Chicago, he's allowed to take two suitcases because it's an international flight. The discussion heats up and Paul ends up losing his temper. Finally, another passenger steps in and helps. Paul and the agent really listen and understand what the other is saying.

Wearing a **diamond** would have helped Paul put things into perspective, understand the situation, and evaluate the consequences of his actions. However, when worn unconsciously, a diamond can act as a catalyst and increase the desire for control. Paul would always have to be on his guard, as this metamorphic stone can bring out the best or the worst in the wearer.

Logic rules

Cubic personalities need to see the big picture in every situation in their lives. They love order and do everything in their power to eliminate disorder. They believe in efficiency and favor processes they consider to be rational, generally preferring to benefit from the results of an experiment rather than actually experiment themselves.

Since they are logical thinkers it's usually very easy for them to systematically research the underlying causes of events. Their thinking is precise and exact, and their attention to detail can strengthen their position in a conflict situation. Extremely cautious by nature, cubic individuals have to see the cause-and-effect relationship in all situations and instantly reject any unfounded points of view. The only risks they take are calculated ones.

Furthermore, cubic personalities don't like to be at the mercy of their feelings, which can take them into uncertain and uncharted waters. Since they always want to be in control, they are on the defensive as soon as they are in danger of revealing feelings that could tarnish their image of strength and self-control.

Garnet can sustain cubic personalities through crises and help them overcome their bad habits. However, it can also increase aggressiveness as well as reduce it. As a metamorphic stone, garnet can be effective in periods where radical changes have to be made since it provides the energy and strength to inspire such change. Nonetheless, when worn continually and without a deep desire for transformation, it can lead to frustration, fuel aggressiveness, and increase the need for control.

Dress and diet

Cubic personalities usually prefer dark colors and wear their clothes until they're practically worn out. While they dislike being the focus of attention, they also want to make a good impression. Their clothing is of good quality, understated, and comfortable.

Individuals belonging to this alliance prefer to eat food they think is healthy. In fact, they can sometimes become almost obsessive about it.

They'll scrutinize the list of contents of a box of cereal to make sure it contains the best possible ingredients. They'll even travel several miles out of their way to buy fruit from a store or market they think carries the best produce. Because they fear illness, they take vitamins and food supplements to keep their body fit and "under control."

Peter's wife, Lucy, has had to watch him eat the same kind of cereal every single day they've been together for the last 10 years. She has often attempted to convince him to try something else, but she's wasting her breath. Peter has always been satisfied with this cereal, and he's sticking to it.

Bojis, which are sedimentary stones, could be excellent for Peter as they would help him understand how events from his past have influenced his need to eat this particular type of cereal. They could help him realize that other food can also meet his body's nutritional and energy needs. Bojis can put his faith in this "perfect" cereal into perspective, and encourage him to try more variety in life.

Gaining a few pounds can be catastrophic for cubic personalities, and when they do, they work hard to shed them as quickly as possible. They diet and exercise to get back into perfect shape. Should this prove to be impossible, they can become depressed, sometimes even for the rest of their lives.

Unfortunately both good and bad habits are equally strong in cubic personalities. They can become slaves to bad habits that in turn become the main cause of any illnesses they contract. A poor diet, an unhealthy lifestyle, tobacco, and alcohol are all bad habits they cling to regardless of opposition, sometimes even risking their health and their very lives. They might even prefer to die rather than to change. Their bad habits often stem from out-of-control feelings or their need to overperform. That's when fast food too frequently becomes the answer to all their problems. They'll eat on the run to make sure they don't waste any of the precious minutes they've noted in their day planner.

Control, control, and more control

One of the greatest weaknesses of cubic personalities is their inflexibility. Because of their need for security and control, they attach too much importance to reason and logic. They'll suppress their intuition and feelings to the point that they're no longer aware of them. They can become cold and distant for fear of appearing weak and vulnerable.

Cubic personalities' mental faculties are their main weapon in their struggle against change and in sustaining their way of thinking. They'll have built up solid arguments that prevent them from seeing any other possibilities. Since they have great observation skills, they can pinpoint the exact moment when their words will have the most devastating effect and use them to stun the other person into a disoriented silence.

Cubic individuals can become prisoners of their thought patterns because they can't see any other way to act. Highly manipulative, they can even interpret certain situations to their own advantage. In extreme cases, they won't hesitate to use any means at their disposal to impose their point of view. Their desire to maintain the established order can sometimes lead to unnecessary complications. One of their mottoes is, "Why make things simple when we can make them more complicated … and without risk?" Their rules and laws become even more problematic when they grant them so much importance that they are only able live according to set patterns.

Joanne is a forty-something divorcée with no children. Her entire world has collapsed because she can't imagine living alone. Her value system has taken a serious beating. Married at age eighteen, she has always depended on being part of a couple, considering her value as a woman to be based on being loved and involved in a relationship. Without a man in her life, she thinks she's worthless and insignificant.

Wearing a **lapis lazuli** would help Joanne face the truth, and especially discover her own strengths and worth. **Sodalite** would enable her to let go of her preconceived ideas.

Cubic personalities see any unexpected change as a threat and every criticism as a personal attack. Unable to conceive that they could be loved for themselves rather than for their accomplishments, they become suspicious or depressed. Their thinking becomes polarized and they see only faults, problems, failures, and danger. They rely on logic alone to gather information that conforms to their perceptions and distances them from their emotions. Any offers of help make them suspicious. They can decide that everyone is against them and then build their patterns of thought and action into a fortress they think will be a safe haven. They cut themselves off from others, feel sorry for themselves, and end up thinking that no one loves or understands them.

By adhering to certain modes of thought and behavior, cubic personalities repeat the same mistake over and over again—the mistake of wasting their lives. This initial mistake can lead to problems of all kinds. For instance, they can refuse effective alternative therapies even though they may be seriously ill; avoid consulting a doctor despite recurring pain; insist on always eating the same things because they don't see any point in changing; drive when they've had too much to drink because they still think they're in control; and work until they're burned out, putting their income and professional status ahead of their health. They cling to their preconceptions, refusing any change.

> *Sometimes it's easier to stumble over a detail*
> *than to face a serious problem.*
> D.D.D.

When in a positive mindset, the cubics see themselves and life as follows:

- I feel safe.

- I have confidence in life.

- And I love the challenges life places in my path.

The Soul doesn't seek perfection.
It is always in the process of becoming.

D.D.D.

A BALANCED CUBIC PERSONALITY

Making order work for themselves and for others

Cubic personalities can develop positively as well as negatively. For example, a cubic lifestyle can enhance their qualities, expand their vision, and help them achieve great things because of their ability to see the big picture. These qualities can be very useful for anyone working in a large organization or learning a complex computer program, for example.

When they are in this positive mode, cubic personalities see themselves as vital components of a grand plan. They become the ideal companions, both professionally and personally. Others can rely on them and their resourcefulness. Where they used to remain fixated on certain concepts, they can now cut right through them or adapt them. They open up and are prepared to consider new options, new experiences. They expand their learning capacity—a quality that is typical of the cubic alliance.

As advocates for order with the gift of a broad and balanced vision, and as informed and conscientious thinkers capable of great efficiency, cubic personalities can use their talents to serve others, optimize performance, and produce unhoped-for results at work. As a result, they often hold key positions in the organizations where they work.

For those influenced by the cubic alliance, success is a law of nature. Every action is carried out in full knowledge of what is at stake. Every problem becomes a challenge, an opportunity to learn or to develop.

In their positive aspect, cubic individuals manage their emotions more effectively and let them "breathe." They aren't ashamed to cry, and they appreciate little surprises and tokens of affection from their friends. They are more flexible, conciliatory, and better team players within teams based on mutual respect.

AFFIRMATIONS[1]

"Everyone has his place and everything is in its place!"

"I am a Creative Craftsman in the Temple of Ritual(ized) Renewal."

STRENGTHS TO CULTIVATE[2]

May I empower myself with:

His beauty
« *Saundarya* » OM AH HUM   JAH HUM BAH HOH   « *Saundarya* »

Serenity
« *Sama* »   OM AH HUM   JAH HUM BAH HOH   « *Sama* »

Detachment
« *Vairagya* » OM AH HUM   JAH HUM BAH HOH   « *Vairagya* »

See "The Forty-five Great Empowerments of the Soul," page 173

MEDITATION

See "Circulation of the Light," page 163

---

[1] Etbonan Karta, "Seven Studies of the Soul's Earthly Pilgrimage of Service upon the Seven Cosmic-Physical Rays," *The Divine Concordance of Light: A Handbook from Heaven to Progression Earth, the Seven Rays of God* (Montreal: Magnificent Magus Publications, 2000).

[2] Sri Adi Dadi, *The Spiritual Science of Essential Yoga*, Volume II (Montreal: Orange Palm Publications, forthcoming). © All rights reserved.

INVOCATION[1]

Soul-ar Progression Three
Upon Ray VII
"That Watcher in the East"

WE STATION OURSELVES

Upon the Way of the Word Creative.
And from out of the south, north and west,

Do we pilgrims rise to face the East.

And the Temple Doors of the Lord
Are opened by that Watcher in the East,

By that Whirling Sphere and Guardian of the Magic Word.

"And steady and centered do we stand
In the closed Mystic Pentagram.

Steady and centered do we stand infolded and
Illumined by the Face of the Master in the East."

And in Ritual-ruling and Ceremony-cast,

Do we all face the Test of Transmuting

The Pentagramic Potencies and Tetrahedronic Lines of Force,

Into bright Fiery Rings of Power, and of Flame, and Light.

"Let us link lastingly the Within and Without,
And seek to establish the Magic on earth,

Of only those Forms aligned, imbued and ordered
With the Great and Holy Spirit of the One God,

As is sought by the Plan, and Envisioned by Man."

E. K.

---

[1] Karta, "Seven Studies."

Cubic stones

Best-known stones

boji(s): *sedimentary* (iron sulfide)

diamond: *metamorphic* (carbon)

fluorite: *magmatic* (calcium fluoride)

garnet: *metamorphic* (aluminum, calcium iron silicate)

halite: *sedimentary* (sodium chloride)

lapis lazuli: *metamorphic* (sodium aluminum silicate with sulfur and chlorine)

magnetite: *magmatic, metamorphic* (magnetic iron oxide)

pyrite: *magmatic, metamorphic, sedimentary* (iron disulfide)

sodalite: *magmatic* (sodium aluminum silicate with chlorine)

bojis   diamond   fluorite

garnet   halite   lapis-lazuli

magnetite   pyrite   sodalite

The Goal-Oriented (Efficiency) Filiation

Hexagonal Alliance

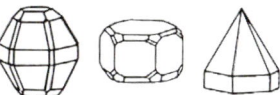

Going for the Goal

Keyword: efficiency.

Strengths: determined, efficient, quick to react, responsible.

Weaknesses: hard-hearted, impatient, individualist, narrow vision, stressed, suppresses emotions.

Stones, minerals, and metals: aquamarine, apatite, golden beryl (heliodor), pink beryl (morganite), red beryl (bixbite), transparent or colorless beryl (goshenite), emerald, graphite, sugilite, vanadinite, zincite.

Focus: mental.

Professions and trades: manager, executive secretary, firefighter, lifeguard, production manager.

Polarity: masculine.

Ailments: exhaustion, gout, heart attack, heartburn, hypoglycemia, rheumatism, stroke.

Dress: ready-to-wear, comfortable clothing.

Well-known personalities: Helena Petrovna Blavatsky; Tom Cruise's character in *The Last Samurai;* Inspector Gadget; William Wallace, Mel Gibson's character in *Braveheart;* Alexander the Great; Florence Nightingale; Miranda, Meryl Streep's character in *The Devil Wears Prada.*

The inner geometric structure of this alliance is composed of hexagons. Of the seven geometric forms, the hexagon has the smallest perimeter in relation to surface area enclosed. This form symbolizes one of the major character traits of individuals associated with this alliance—their efficiency. In fact, bees build their honeycombs in this pattern in order to make the most of the limited space available.

When in a negative mindset, the hexagonals see themselves and life as follows:

- I'm in a hurry.

- Others are too slow.

- I therefore have to act alone.

Time is precious

Hexagonal personalities make the most of their resources to secure the best possible results. Because it's so crucial for them to reach their goals, their actions are direct and straightforward. Time is precious to them; there's never a minute to waste. They'll always take the shortest route, and once they've set off on this path, no detours are allowed. Nothing can distract them or deflect them from their goal. And as soon as they've attained their objective, a new challenge is usually already waiting in the wings.

It's easy to recognize hexagonal personalities since they can't sit still for long. They're always on the go, and even when they appear to be inactive physically, their mind is always racing.

A magmatic stone like **beryl** can have a beneficial effect for hexagonal personalities because it can help them maintain their balance and tap into their full potential. It also shows them what they need to do and then helps them do it. It is, moreover, the ideal stone for managing stress. Beryl also inspires hexagonal personalities to seek their goals in ways that complement the recommended methods.

The goal is what matters

Since the end is more important than the means, hexagonal personalities don't waste time on trivial details. Before they take their first step, they thoroughly analyze each situation and prepare their plan. Their thinking is clear and analytical. They're quick to understand and they're determined. Whatever their goal, they work tirelessly to reach it. Individuals associated with this alliance are considered to be strong-willed "doers." The fact that they never lose sight of their objective gives them the strength they need to carry on, no matter what obstacle is placed in their path. Hexagonal personalities are career-oriented, driven to succeed, and proud of their achievements.

Amelia works efficiently and quickly. She always meets her tight deadlines well ahead of time. Julie has recently joined the company, and Amelia has been asked to train her. Unfortunately, Julie doesn't work as fast as Amelia and lacks the experience to be as efficient. Amelia becomes less productive and starts handing in her reports late. She becomes impatient and intolerant. Since diplomacy isn't one of her strong points, she assigns Julie to filing, without giving her the chance to learn, and then finishes the job herself.

Hexagonal personalities typically lack long-term vision, which prevents Amelia from seeing Julie's potential. All she can think about is the work that's piling up and the deadlines being missed—a situation that is inconceivable to her.

Amelia has to learn how to be a better communicator and accept that everyone works at their own pace. She needs to be more humane in her attitude toward others. In this case, an **aquamarine** could be of considerable assistance to Amelia. It could help her understand how important it is to communicate properly, as well as make her less impatient, more aware of others, calmer, and less uptight. As a magmatic stone, aquamarine stimulates the inner capacity to see the broader picture over the long term.

Hexagonal personalities are faithful to their fundamental beliefs. However, when they encounter something new that can help them reach their goal more quickly, they are well able to switch tactics in the blink of an eye. They are thorough and even run the risk of being overly meticulous, not because they get bogged down in details but because they need to make sure that the details are ones they think are important. In general, the best is barely good enough for hexagonal personalities.

Emotions are an obstacle

Hexagonal personalities are first and foremost rational beings. They pay little attention to their feelings, which can sometimes be very intense. If their emotions risk getting in the way of what they want to accomplish, they are immediately able to distance themselves. In short, they can overcome anything.

Sylvia works in an accounting firm. It's now the month of April, which is a very busy period because of the preparation of tax returns. In order to meet her deadlines, Sylvia works overtime. But then her mother passes away. Because she doesn't have time to take care of the funeral arrangements or, even more importantly, to grieve, she leaves everything up to her brothers and sisters.

Hexagonal personalities don't see themselves as romantics. They live in their minds, seldom in their hearts. Since they fear that their emotions will cause them to lose control, they remain detached from others and from circumstances. On the rare occasions when they do let themselves get emotionally involved, they keep a tight lid on their feelings.

Apatite, a stone that promotes communication and personal expression, can be a valuable stone for hexagonal personalities. Because it is magmatic, sedimentary, and metamorphic, it can be used at all stages of life. It facilitates personal contacts, calms the spirit, and eases distress.

Alone and free

People influenced by this alliance are individualists. They feel trapped when others tell them what to do. They know what they want, accept no impediments, and aspire to decision-making positions, seldom being satisfied to remain in the lower ranks of an organization. They need to be recognized as being the best and even indispensible. For them, ruling from behind the scenes ensures they hold onto the reins of power far longer.

Take Jack, for example. He's a supervisor who marches to the beat of his own drum and pays scant attention to any advice he's given. He has five employees under him and knows how to get the best out of those who can help him complete his projects. However, he's pretty tough on one employee because he thinks he's too slow or perhaps because he simply doesn't like him.

When Jack's bosses ask him to hand in a report the next day, he prefers to work with his two most efficient employees and not involve the others. He'll do the rest of the job himself. He agrees to work overtime, which doesn't really bother him. Producing a good report on time is his priority.

Because they are always wearing blinders, hexagonal personalities can cause considerable damage around them. Team work doesn't come naturally to them. Although they are able to accept others' ideas, these ideas have to conform to their perspective. They are hard on themselves, but they're also just as hard on others. They have no sympathy for anyone who doesn't want to get ahead or work at their pace.

Hexagonal personalities leave their mark wherever they go. In a very short time, they can make themselves indispensable. They quickly earn their superiors' trust because of their efficiency, which means they can work according to their own rules and may even be given carte blanche. However, they can become trapped by their behavior because they don't allow themselves any time to relax or enjoy life.

> *Hell is living in the grip of time, without God.*
> *Heaven is living within God without time.*
> D.D.D.

Lifestyle

Physically, those associated with the hexagonal alliance have to be resilient to do their work properly. They take care of their health, and their diet enables them to function well, unless something important becomes a priority and requires all their attention. If a deadline is approaching, they can easily skip breakfast and grab a bite at their desk for lunch. They see this as normal rather than as a sacrifice. However, it would never occur to them to go on a fast for several days or weeks or take a vacation at a health spa. What a waste of time that would be! Sometimes they even cut short their vacation or use it to go on a course to improve their performance.

The main causes of illness among hexagonal individuals are overwork, self-neglect, and the excessive demands they place on themselves. Although they may suffer physically, they don't think it's important. They prefer to take a pill to help them sleep or to ease stomach pain. They have to keep functioning at any cost. If they're forced to take a sick day, they're chomping at the bit to get back to work, disregarding the risk of a relapse or a chronic illness.

An **emerald** can be beneficial for hexagonal personalities since it encourages inspiration and grants infinite patience. It ensures physical, emotional, and mental balance and eliminates negativity by inspiring positive action. This stone reinforces the immune system and promotes healing. It brings clarity, enhances foresight, and facilitates teamwork by fostering mutual understanding.

Dangers and repercussions

Countless dangers lie in wait for hexagonal personalities. Fixating on a single goal with never a glance to the left or right limits their vision, reinforcing the feeling that they never have enough time. They become increasingly harried, impatient, and stressed out. They miss out on the positive opportunities that life offers because their lack of vision prevents them from even seeing them.

Relying on the strength of their willpower, hexagonal individuals never think about the consequences of their lifestyle until the day comes when their energy reserves are depleted and they are incapable of coping with the consequences of their actions. And so they face a crisis. As soon as they have attained a major goal, they fall apart, unable to furnish the effort to reach another objective. Suddenly something vital is missing from their lives: a goal, a task, a sense of being useful or playing a key role.

Those influenced by the hexagonal alliance always need to have a goal in front of them rather than the memory of past achievements. That's one of the reasons they seldom celebrate success. This fear of emptiness, of having nothing to do or to strive for, is so strong that they instantly start looking for a new project instead of resting or relaxing. Because it's so important for them to feel useful, they then become obsessed with meeting this new objective. Fanaticism is always dangerous since it means that they overlook their own needs, which are sooner or later imposed on others. In the end, what hexagonal personalities consider the art of living is transformed into a lack of respect and fanaticism. In extreme cases, this fanaticism can even endanger their own lives or the lives of others.

Naturally, not all personalities of the hexagonal alliance are so extreme. From an early age, hexagonal individuals acquire experiences that present them with clues signaling the need to change and to be prepared to question their goals. These experiences help them understand that the closer they get to the mountaintop, the clearer their vision. They realize that the view from a distance isn't necessarily the same as the view from the summit. Their new outlook gives them the chance to adjust their vision, allowing them to head off in a new direction and establish a new goal.

When in a positive mindset, the hexagonals see themselves and life as follows:

- I'm quick to act.

- Not everyone has the same rhythm.

- Therefore, I will adapt and work with the best others can offer.

A BALANCED HEXAGONAL PERSONALITY

Making efficiency look easy

The key for hexagonal individuals to develop and find their way lies in their inner certainty of being able to reach their goal, a natural trait of their personality. Once they realize this, they can relax and become less demanding with themselves and with others because they know deep down that they have the ability to attain their goal. Then and only then will they be able to let go. This relaxed attitude will guarantee success more surely than any efforts they could deploy. Obviously, hexagonal personalities will continue to play active leading roles, but the way they play them will be different.

Freed from their blinders and feeling safe, they can then move forward in leaps and bounds. They realize the importance of teamwork and become less individualistic. Tolerance and acceptance of others are now part of their way of operating. And finally, thanks to these experiences, they understand that the path is the goal.

> *All roads lead to God.*
> *However, the best road is the one that*
> *takes us where we need to go.*
> D.D.D.

AFFIRMATION[1]

"I stand solitary strung with the Many upon the Path of Purpose."

STRENGTHS TO CULTIVATE[2]

May I empower myself with:

Actionless action (effortless effort/nonkarmic deeds)
« *Naishkarma* »   OM AH HUMJAH HUM BAH HOH   « NAISHKARMA »

Emptiness
« *Shunyata* »   OM AH HUM JAH HUM BAH HOH   « *Shunyata* »

No worry
« *Chintamanisiddhi* » OM AH HUM JAH HUM BAH HOH   « *Chintamanisiddhi* »

See "The Forty-five Great Empowerments of the Soul," page 173

MEDITATION

See "The Eye of the Hurricane," page 164

---

[1] Karta, "Seven Studies."

[2] Sri Adi Dadi, *Spiritual Science of Essential Yoga*, Volume II.

INVOCATION[1]

Invoking the Blessings of Christ

Let not my life know a stranger, but only a Friend in Thee.

Let not my life know separateness, but only the Unity of Thee.

Let not my life know another, other than myself seeing my neighbor through Eyes of Thee.

Let not my life know love, other than that Love coming unconditionally down through Thee.

Let not my life know the many, without the Complete Oneness of Fusion with Thee.
Let not my life know the bountiful, without the brotherly and sisterly sharing of the Wealth of Thee.

Let not my life know desire, other than first adoring Thee, revering Thee, and desiring only Thee.
Let not my life know knowledge, other than through the wisdom of my heart aflame with the Fire of Thee

Let not my life know government, without Thy spirit and Thy sense of karmic justice.
Let not my life know politics, without Thy Palm of Goodwill equally directed toward all peoples.

Let not my life know eloquence, without my telling of Thy Truth, and of the Way It Is, upon Thy Path.
Let not my life know art, without Thy Brush of Beauty in my hands, highlighting the Canvas of Creation.

Let not my life know anger, but only Thy Greatest Calm, and Thy Highest-born Tranquility.
Let not my life know violence, but only Thy Most Perfect Peace and Thy Gentlest Baraka Blessings.

Let not my life know myself, except through my soul's Light and Thy Mind's Knowing.
Let not my life know song, except through the Vach's Soundless Voicing of Thy Shabd.

Let not my life know action, other than under the direction and the scepter of Thy Guiding Will.
Let not my life know freedom, other than the True Liberation of humbly serving Thy purpose and Thy Plan.

Let not my life know life, except as Life flowing through Thee loving all, loving Thee, and loving me.

E.K.

Hexagonal stones

Best-known stones

apatite: *magmatic, sedimentary, metamorphic* (calcium phosphate with fluorine and chlorine)

aquamarine: *magmatic* (beryllium aluminum silicate)

golden beryl (heliodor): *magmatic* (beryllium aluminum silicate)

pink beryl (morganite): *magmatic* (beryllium aluminum silicate)

red beryl (bixbite): *magmatic* (beryllium aluminum silicate)

transparent or colorless beryl (goshenite): *magmatic* (beryllium aluminum silicate)

emerald: *magmatic, metamorphic* (beryllium aluminum silicate)

graphite: *metamorphic* (carbon)

sugilite: *magmatic* (potassium sodium lithium iron manganese aluminum)

vanadinite: *sedimentary* (vanadium oxide and lead chloride)

zincite: *metamorphic* (zinc oxide)

apatite

aquamarine

golden beryl

pink beryl

red beryl

transparent beryl

emerald

graphite

sugilite

vanadinite

zincite

Interestingly, the best-known hexagonal stones contain aluminum, which possesses valuable properties that can help realign certain negative aspects of the hexagonal personality.

ALUMINUM

In addition, aluminum can help diminish feelings of mental disturbance, a potential danger for hexagonal personalities because they fear emptiness, which they experience as not having a goal to attain or a task to complete. It also promotes the ability to express emotions, something that is very difficult for hexagonal personalities. It breaks down the barriers of individualism and encourages the abandonment of certain attitudes, fostering a broader vision. Furthermore, aluminum stimulates the desire for diversity and change, making it easier to target multiple objectives.

Aluminum can also help in cases of loss of identity, guiding us toward our true being and our true tasks and goals in life. It also promotes a sense of reality, objectivity, and presence of mind, removing the blinders and creating a feeling of security. It also inspires the discernment necessary to resist the temptations of modern illusions and assists us in confronting them.

On the physical level, aluminum sustains the acid-base balance and alleviates hyperacidity-related disorders by reducing excess acidity in the stomach. It stimulates the absorption of iron in the intestine and stabilizes nerve conduction. Aluminum also provides support for generalized weakness, reduced perception or mobility, and paralysis.

THE FEELING-EMOTIONAL (SENSITIVITY) FILIATION

MONOCLINIC ALLIANCE

FROM THE OUTSIDE IN

Keyword: doubt.

Strengths: aware of one's own and others' needs, calm, confident, courageous, humble, intuitive, tolerant of the self and others, visionary, well-balanced, wise.

Weaknesses: distanced from one's own and others' needs, judgmental, lacking discrimination, naive, oversensitive, perfectionist, pessimistic, proud, self-centered, unreliable, unstable.

Stones, minerals, and metals: azurite, azurite-malachite, charoite, chrysocolla, epidote, gem silica, howlite, jade, kunzite, lepidolite, malachite, moonstone, selenite, seraphinite, serpentine.

Focus: emotional.

Professions and trades: arts, dramatic arts, consultant, diplomat, host, mediator.

Polarity: feminine.

Ailments: adrenal gland and kidney dysfunctions, depression, digestive system disorders, hormonal imbalance, menopausal disorders, painful menstruation, panic attacks, PMS-related hormonal imbalance, stress-related problems, toxins in bodily and organ tissues.

Dress: varied and unpredictable.

Well-known personalities: Céline Dion, Dalida, Howard Hughes, Marilyn Monroe, Michael Jackson.

The inner structure of monoclinic stones is in the shape of a parallelogram, which can easily tip to one side or remain in a stable position. In a similar fashion, monoclinic personalities can be subject to mood swings, although they are less dramatic than those experienced by triclinic personalities who, being influenced by the trapezium shape, are able to totally reverse their position in response to a sudden emotional change.

People associated with the monoclinic system tend to be natural worriers. They doubt their strengths and have a deep-seated fear of failure. This built-in insecurity dominates their daily lives, sometimes causing severe distress that is hard to disguise.

When in a negative mindset, the monoclinics see themselves and life as follows:

- I'm useless without guidance, acceptance, or gratification from others.

- Life is made up of punishments and rewards, acceptance and rejection; it can't be trusted.

- I therefore have to struggle to avoid rejection and punishment and to be accepted and rewarded.

What you see is what you get

While triclinic personalities can sink into depression for no apparent reason, the mood swings of people living a monoclinic lifestyle are easy to predict since they are naturally and constantly affected by their external environment. They fear punishment, rejection, and abandonment and seek recognition, praise, and acceptance.

Since monoclinic personalities' self-worth depends entirely on what they see in others' eyes, they are exceptionally sensitive to other people's moods, feelings and thoughts, and are always trying to adapt to them. Although it's easy enough to anticipate their downward spiral into discouragement, it's almost impossible to predict their day-to-day behavior, which can be upsetting and disconcerting for those close to them.

Lynn is often exasperated by her husband David's erratic behavior. For example, he'll wear a conservative three-piece suit to a spring picnic, but Bermuda shorts and a short-sleeved T-shirt to her mother's birthday dinner. Or his sleep will be deep and undisturbed for a few nights, and then he'll wake up in the middle of the night, get up, watch television, or be glued to the computer screen. He'll buy sophisticated exercise equipment that he can't afford, use it twice (once at 2 AM) and then give it away to his neighbor who has had his eye on it for some time. Then again, if he realizes that he's half an hour late for a business lunch, he'll cancel the appointment on the pretext that something has suddenly come up. Some mornings he'll enjoy making a fantastic breakfast for the entire family, while on others he'll quickly down a glass of juice and then sneak out while the rest of the house is still sleeping.

Kunzite can calm and balance the emotions, which would be good for David. It could also clear his mind, develop his concentration and make him more receptive to others and their needs.

Monoclinic personalities are very easily influenced by others. They change with the wind and have no problem suddenly abandoning an idea they've been passionately defending, which undermines their credibility and reliability. This behavior leaves their friends and families wondering who they really are, but there's no real answer to that question because monoclinic personalities don't know themselves.

People influenced by this alliance are terrified of making a mistake, failing, or making a wrong decision. They're generally lost in a daze as they futilely weigh the pros and cons of their decisions and the potential impact on themselves and their environment.

Tony and Alice have been living together for years, and no one knows better than Tony the cost of asking his girlfriend a simple question. After a delicious dinner one summer evening, Tony asks Alice if she'd like a cup of coffee. He asks her twice, and when she doesn't answer he assumes she doesn't want one. So he just makes one cup and drinks it while it's hot. Fifteen minutes later, he hears Alice say, "yes, OK," but he doesn't know what she's agreeing to. "OK what?" Tony asks. "I'll have a cup of coffee," she replies. Tony good-naturedly suggests she make it herself since she couldn't be bothered to answer him before, even though he really wants to know the reason for her silence. In reality, all that time Alice was weighing the pros and cons of the question, i.e., whether she should have a cup of coffee or not. Would it keep her awake or affect her health? Should she only have half a cup and add milk? Would there be enough coffee left for breakfast? All these practical questions were swirling around in her head.

Malachite could help Alice by encouraging her to take risks and break her old habits. It could increase her powers of observation and enable her to understand the needs of those close to her as she lets herself be guided by her innate sensitivity.

An agonizing internal dialogue is always going on in the minds of monoclinic personalities, impeding their decision-making and turning it into a long and excruciating process. They'll even let other people make their most personal decisions for them because they think that's what will make everyone happy. Being dominated by others prevents them from hearing their inner voice. And this means that they make mistakes, which is, ironically, exactly what they were trying to avoid in the first place. People living this lifestyle can be somewhat naive and even be exploited by others, who won't hesitate to take advantage of their lack of discrimination.

Carol regularly visits a local clairvoyant who, for a modest fee, gives her specific advice about important day-to-day decisions and makes predictions about the future. One of these sessions proves to be very interesting; she predicts Carol will meet the man of her dreams, someone from another country who's tall, dark, and has an exotic accent. A year and a half later, Carol is teaching English in Chile. One sultry summer evening in a small town near Santiago, she meets a tall, dark Mexican who charms her with his Spanish accent. She remembers the clairvoyant's predictions and rushes headlong into a relationship that turns out to be very destructive. This man is far from being the ideal partner. Instead of listening to her intuition and taking the time to really get to know him, she throws herself at this stranger and ends up wasting a year of her life.

Lepidolite, which contains lithium, could assist Carol and encourage her to break away from this emotional and mental dependence by neutralizing her obsessive thoughts and anxieties. By liberating her from the influence of others, lepidolite could stabilize her emotions and enable her to act wisely.

Creating conflict

Because they're so insecure, monoclinic personalities are extremely sensitive to any form of criticism, even when it's constructive. Their friends and family may feel apprehensive and uneasy around them, not daring to express their opinions because they don't want to hurt these supersensitive souls. A simple misunderstanding is enough to throw them into a state that is absolutely incomprehensible to others. For example, if someone makes an innocent remark about their new shoes, they could rush out and take them back or even become extremely depressed. And yet a second later, a thoughtful compliment could trigger a radiant smile and a glow of happiness.

People influenced by this alliance can work themselves into a state of mind where they see nothing but criticism, whether it's real or not. Their excessive reaction to the smallest comment makes others uncomfortable and drives them away. Feeding on this fear of rejection, and since they see themselves as inadequate and imperfect, they imagine that everyone is avoiding them.

The attitude of monoclinic personalities can also cause conflict through the confusion they create and their lack of communication. By trying to avoid errors and meet expectations in a constantly changing and unpredictable environment, they themselves become changeable and unpredictable. People begin to have doubts about them and view them as neurotic and unscrupulous. Unbeknownst to them, others start to put a negative spin on their behavior and react to their apparent lack of credibility. Monoclinic personalities are seen as a disconcerting anomaly because they can't be labeled or defined. Little by little, the atmosphere around them becomes tense and awkward, and confusion sets in.

Although people associated with the monoclinic system are aware of the friction around them, their fear prevents them from confronting it. They leave others in ignorance, not daring to reveal their true motivations, which are far from ill-intentioned. Unlike cubic or even triclinic personalities, monoclinics try to adapt to the needs of the moment, to live according to their instincts and feelings. Their major weakness is their excessive attachment to the external world, which stems from their inaccurate interpretation of life as filtered through their senses. Driven by fear that distorts their view and causes them to repress their feelings, they end up swimming against the tide of life. They can't see things as they really are or recognize their own emotions, despite the fact that these impulses are unsuccessfully attempting to guide them through what they view as an apparently imperfect world.

Out in the cold

Monoclinic personalities may feel so doomed to failure that whatever they attempt ends in disaster. They feel rejected and criticized in every area of their lives. They have the impression that they're never good enough and convince themselves that no one appreciates them.

Unlike the depression afflicting triclinic personalities, a monoclinic descent into melancholy is predictable for reasons that are obvious to everyone. Seeking help is the key that can unlock the door of their personal prison. Their need for love and acceptance can lead them to welcome the assistance offered. When the misunderstandings are finally cleared up, and small successes give them a boost, then a friend can step in and help them slowly rebuild their self-confidence.

When in a positive mindset, the monoclinics see themselves and life as follows:

- I'm fundamentally worthy and internally grounded.

- Life is a testing ground.

- I therefore have to carefully and judiciously steer my course.

A BALANCED MONOCLINIC PERSONALITY

Impeccability versus perfection

People living the monoclinic lifestyle must consciously cultivate genuine humility; then they will be able to learn from their mistakes. Their desire to be perfect springs from their proud and anxious ego, which desperately craves attention and acceptance in an unreliable and illusory world. They seek continuity through rewards and recognition because they unconsciously believe in their own immortality. They forget that everything is impermanent, in constant flux and perpetual movement. Attempting to be above it all is an unrealistic goal that causes them a great deal of suffering. They need to learn that they can't always win.

They must also realize that what they see as a loss may turn out to be a gain in terms of personal growth and development.

> *Learn to be Kind to your imperfections*
> *and to become impeccably Imperfect.*[1]
> D.D.D.

When they realize that they can rise above their surroundings, monoclinic personalities take risks in the heat of the moment. That's when they'll encounter increasing success in situations they previously avoided. They realize that it's better to act and even to make the occasional mistake than to remain paralyzed and inert as they were when they inaccurately viewed the world from behind their fortress walls. They seriously think about their mistakes, learn their lessons without judging themselves or others, and then pick up their feet and continue on their chosen path. They listen objectively to constructive criticism and seek the opinion of their peers because they recognize that several ideas are better than one. They develop wisdom and insight, knowing how to tune in to their inner voice that leads them to more genuine action. They can tell which comments will help them improve and grow and which they would be wise to ignore. They realize that they themselves are a work in progress, or "perfectly imperfect."

> *Dare to be successful, failure after failure.*[2]
> D.D.D.

Using Their Intuition

Although in their negative isolationist mode, monoclinic personalities are loners obsessed with the world's opinion, ironically they are also most likely to develop a strong inner perception that will enable them to sail smoothly through the troubled waters of life. While triclinic personalities have to learn to develop faith in a superior power, monoclinics have to cultivate their impeccable intuition. They learn to intuitively avoid words

---

[1] D.D.D., *Knots of Eternity: Paradoxes from Dadi to Daughter,* Volume I (Montreal: Orange Palm Publications, 2007).

[2] D.D.D., *Knots of Eternity.*

76

and actions that can trigger conflict and failure and can thus dissipate confusion even before it arises. No longer governed by the desperate need to succeed and please, they "know" which plans to put into action and which to avoid. Their timing is perfect, and they surprise those around them with the accuracy of their internal clock.

> *Dare to be faultless in fault;*
> *and full of fault even though faultless.*[1]
>
> D.D.D.

From then on, the need to be seen as perfect propels them to act impeccably and in harmony, sustained by an innate code of universal ethics as they face the many challenges that arise. They humbly recognize their own and others' worth and know that such basic humanitarian understanding transcends the rocky road they perceived through their five senses. Their motto becomes "Life is never as it seems." These words transform their perception of themselves and give them confidence.

---

[1] D.D.D., *Knots of Eternity.*

AFFIRMATIONS[1]

"I am Soul, Soul is me.
I am Soul, Soul are we."

"I am the Divine Dweller who dwells in
the Holy Habitat of the High Self."

STRENGTHS TO CULTIVATE[2]

May I empower myself with:

Spiritual listening
« *Sravana* »   OM AH HUM   JAH HUM BAH HOH   « *Sravana* »

Spiritual pondering (deep thinking and reflection)
« *Manana* »   OM AH HUM   JAH HUM BAH HOH   « *Manana* »

Discrimination
« *Viveka* »   OM AH HUM   JAH HUM BAH HOH   « *Viveka* »

See "The Forty-five Great Empowerments of the Soul," page 173

MEDITATION

See "Circulation of the Light," page 163

---

[1] Karta, "Seven Studies."

[2] Sri Adi Dadi, *Spiritual Science of Essential Yoga*, Volume II.

Invocation[1]

Soul-ar Progression Four
Upon Ray IV

"The Bull's Eye of Unitive Resolution"

WE STATION OURSELVES

And retreat from the rub and test of frictionized experience, and pull away from the lash

And the clash of all opposing forces, and put away finally, the delusive toys of the Mayic life.

And we shoot out the Consciousness with the expert Eye of the Marksman, *into the Bull's Eye of Unitive Resolution.*

"Balanced are we thus, upon the Center Point of Contrasting Contrarieties, and stable are we upon the Comparable Pairs,
As under the Banner of Synthesis, we unfurl in a great outburst of Living Art, the flying flag of the Glorious Symmetry of God.

United we stand under His One sky in Beauty of Form and in Peace of Soul, and celebrate do we
The Christed Chord of Love, in invoking forth into our Heart, the Humming Harmony of the Spheres."

E.K.

---

[1] Karta, "Seven Studies."

Monoclinic stones

Best-known stones

azurite: *sedimentary* (basic copper carbonate)

azurite-malachite: *sedimentary* (basic copper carbonate)

charoite: *metamorphic* (hydrated potassium sodium calcium silicate)

chrysocolla: *sedimentary* (hydrated copper silicate)

epidote: *magmatic, metamorphic* (structurally complex calcium aluminum iron silicate hydroxide)

gem silica: *sedimentary* (hydrated copper silicate and silicon oxide)

howlite: *sedimentary* (calcium borosilicate hydroxide)

jade (nephrite): *metamorphic* (basic calcium magnesium iron silicate)

kunzite: *magmatic* (lithium aluminum silicate)

lepidolite: *magmatic* (potassium lithium aluminum silicate fluoride hydroxide)

malachite: *sedimentary* (basic copper carbonate)

moonstone: *magmatic* (potassium aluminum silicate)

selenite: *sedimentary* (hydrated calcium sulfate)

seraphinite: *metamorphic, sedimentary* (magnesium iron aluminum silicate hydroxide)

serpentine: *metamorphic* (basic magnesium silicate)

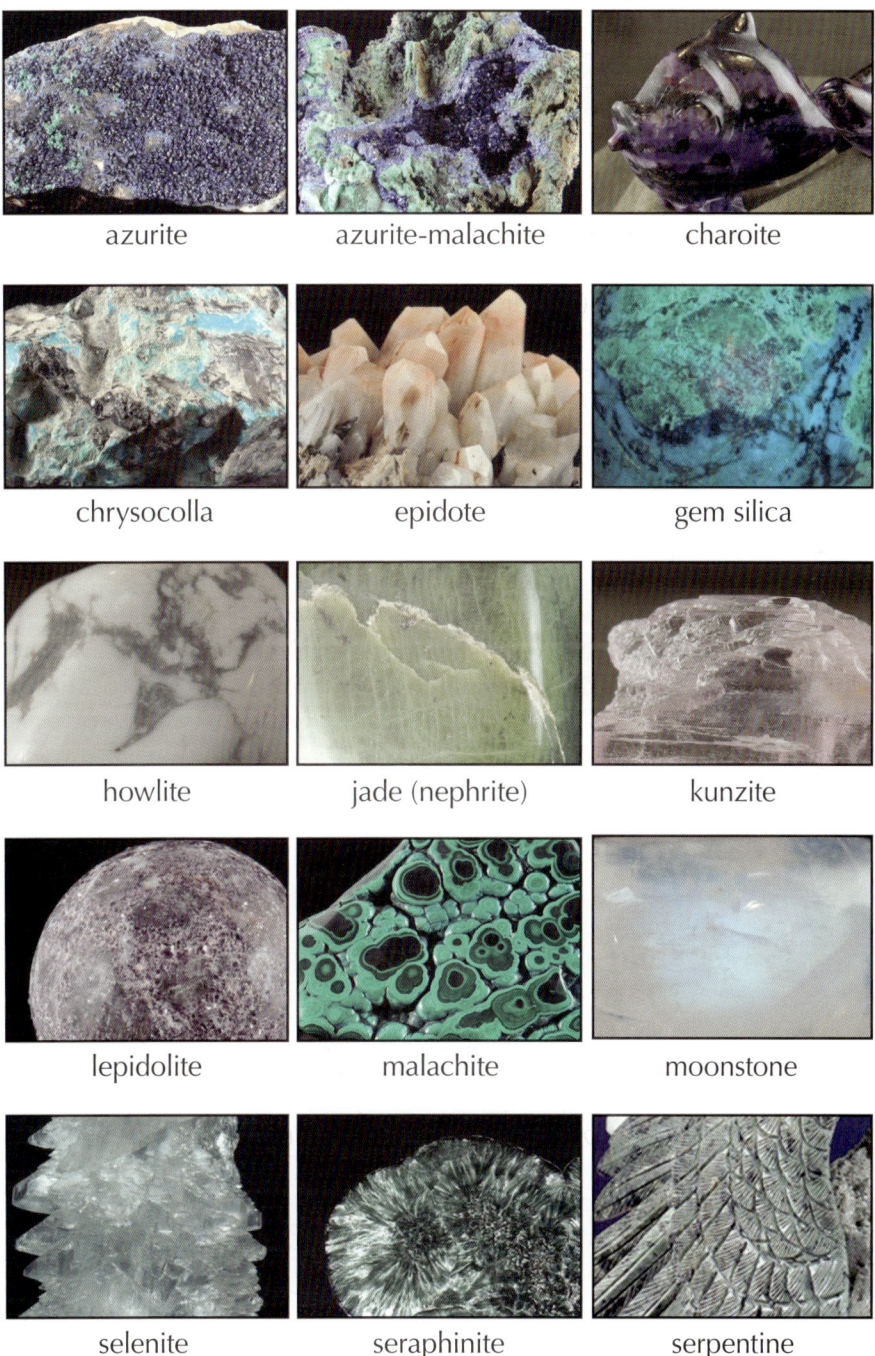

azurite   azurite-malachite   charoite

chrysocolla   epidote   gem silica

howlite   jade (nephrite)   kunzite

lepidolite   malachite   moonstone

selenite   seraphinite   serpentine

CALCIUM

Calcium is the element that is most predominant in monoclinic stones. Interestingly, some stones, such as kunzite and lepidolite, also contain traces of lithium.

Calcium increases receptivity to the environment and encourages discrimination in making choices. It stabilizes the emotions, reduces anxiety, and boosts motivation and self-confidence. It alleviates mental confusion and promotes clarity and openness to new perspectives. It is also an excellent biocatalyst for calcium and mineral deficiencies, osteoporosis, fractures, and rickets, and it is an effective antispasmodic. Calcium is often prescribed to support growth as well as during pregnancy and breast-feeding.

LITHIUM

Lithium, which is the least dense of all solid elements, is a white alkaline metal. Lithium salts are prescribed in psychiatry to alleviate nervous and behavioral disorders, cases of adaptation, anxiety in anticipation of an activity or event, and bipolar disorders or depression. It encourages humility, flexibility, and adaptability, and it teaches us to be true to ourselves. Lithium can alleviate skin disorders that are nervous in origin and help combat insomnia.

The Energy Manipulation (Situational) Filiation

Quadratic Alliance

Who Am I?

Keyword: indefinable.

Strengths: adaptable, creative imagination, instinctively analytical, openness to change, seeker of truth.

Weaknesses: conceals the truth, dishonest, hides behind a role, liar, unpredictable, unstable, unreliable.

Stones, minerals, and metals: apophyllite, chalcopyrite, rutile, vesuvianite (idocrase), wulfenite, zircon.

Focus: emotional.

Professions and trades: actor, lawyer, philosopher, politician, psychologist, researcher, salesperson.

Polarity: feminine.

Ailments: depression, schizophrenia.

Dress: all styles, depending on the role to be played.

Well-known personalities: Jim Carrey's character in *Liar, Liar*; John Forbes Nash Jr., Russell Crowe's character in *A Beautiful Mind*; Frank Abagnale, Leonardo DiCaprio's character in *Catch Me If You Can*; fictional characters Sherlock Holmes, Superman, Spider-Man, Batman, and James Bond.

The quadratic lifestyle is symbolized by a rectangle, a four-sided figure similar to the cubic configuration. On the surface the two may appear alike and their lifestyles may seem similar, but at heart the quadratic personality is quite different. Cubic personalities are very confident, organized, and in control, whereas quadratic personalities simply give the impression of being in control and sure of themselves. In reality, their decisions are spontaneous and generally triggered by strong emotions.

When in a negative mindset, the quadratics see themselves and life as follows:

- I'm someone who plays a role.

- People around me are confused.

- Therefore I'm always in control.

Two faces

Quadratic personalities aren't what they seem. On the surface, they appear to be stable and reliable, which is far from the truth. You'd swear that they're always in control because they always seem to be on top of everything. Yet there's no doubt that nothing turns out the way they think it will or the way they've planned. For instance, they will enthusiastically embrace a project and then shelve it a minute later because they haven't properly estimated the time needed to complete it or simply because they've changed their mind. While all this chopping and changing doesn't bother them at all, their family and friends find it quite disconcerting.

George is always busy making plans. A friend who edits a travel magazine asks him to write an article about Africa, a place that has always fascinated him. He immediately swings into high gear, searching for anything that could be useful to him. He starts writing, but after one or two chapters he receives an unexpected invitation to take a trip. So he abruptly changes track and drops the article, becoming totally absorbed in preparations for this new adventure.

People influenced by the quadratic alliance have problems with advance planning. Because they always find someone or something else that appeals to them, they'll stop whatever they're doing and switch directions. Even though they may have a thousand and one plans in mind, they seldom translate them into reality unless they're in their positive mindset.

Apophyllite can encourage quadratic personalities to examine their behavior and prevent them from being sidetracked from finishing what they've started. This magmatic stone can help them discover their potential, unblock their suppressed emotions, and support them in times of uncertainty.

Fascination with the new and unknown

Unlike those living the hexagonal lifestyle, quadratic personalities can't sustain enthusiasm for anything over the long term. Their constant need to be stimulated explains their horror of routine. They're too fond of change and the unknown to be able to maintain a steady pace. They'll impulsively decide to drop a project because they're not getting any more out of it or just because they've lost interest. Although their unpredictability is perplexing to those around them, they're always able to explain their motivations and feelings logically and defend their new opinions. This ability can enhance their personal development because it allows them to radically change their point of view, head off in a new direction, and discover new experiences.

Appearances

People living this lifestyle hate to be hemmed in. What's more, they always find a convincing way to make sure they look good in any situation. They have a foolproof solution for always seeming to be right. Rarely do they admit they've made a mistake, and they won't hesitate to tell a bold-faced lie or invent a convincing story to pull the wool over other people's eyes and fool themselves as well. This is how they create their own new reality.

Thirteen-year-old Jack decides to skip school because he doesn't want to take an exam he hasn't prepared for. He writes a note explaining that he won't be able to take the exam for some time and forges his mother's signature. He plays his part well and manages to convince the principal with apparent ease. His acting and his attitude are perfect. Quadratic personalities are skilled manipulators and liars. Members of the other alliances may try to imitate them, but they'll never be as successful.

Rutile, or the "light of the sun," is a stone that confers hope. It can teach quadratic personalities to be frank and honest by dissipating their unspoken fears and raising their self-esteem. This magmatic stone can bring out their full potential and improve their physical, emotional, and spiritual balance.

> *Real transformation is impossible*
> *if we hide our true face.*
> D.D.D.

An impenetrable facade

In principle, quadratic personalities are always very sure of themselves. They're the ones who decide whether or not they'll confide in anyone else. In a given situation, they feel compelled to hide their feelings and moods and act according to the needs of the moment. They can lie, double-cross, or even adopt a new identity, all for the sake of appearance.

People living the quadratic lifestyle pay particular attention to their physical bodies and make sure they highlight their positive features while concealing their negative ones. Their appearance is always changing. In some circumstances, they think nothing of cutting their hair or changing its color, gaining or losing weight, or even completely altering the way they dress. But because of all this pretense they run the risk of losing their way and their identity. This in turn makes them dishonest, even with people close to them. They bottle up their feelings and cut themselves off from others, even though they may seem friendly and sociable on the surface. This duality can cause them a great deal of anxiety. If they don't share their suffering, they can secretly harbor suicidal thoughts and even put them into action rather than be unmasked, through the fear of revealing their true selves. Because they've built up an impenetrable facade and everything they do is based on appearances, it's easy for quadratic personalities to live a double life with a second partner, with no one being any the wiser.

Jonathan is the head of a large corporation in Chicago and is also in charge of a branch office in Milwaukee. His job requires him to travel between the two cities every other week. In Chicago, he lives with Sophie and his two children. Two years ago, he met Sylvia at a cocktail party in Milwaukee and ever since has been living with her whenever he's in the area. He's content with Sophie and his two children in Chicago;

in Milwaukee he enjoys his passionate life with Sylvia. He thinks this situation is normal and has no qualms about its morality. He's happy with both women, and both are happy with him. They have no idea he's living a double life.

Commitment

Quadratic personalities always maintain the illusion that they're free to act as they please. That's one of the main reasons they have problems committing to a spiritual life in the company of an inspirational guide, especially if the guide suggests changing behavior patterns that impede their development. They'll often decide not to change and head off in a totally different direction. Yet, in some way, this decision is diametrically opposed to their lifestyle: they like change, but not profound change that would force them to be honest with themselves and with others.

Dan decides to follow a spiritual path with a guide. Obviously, it's impossible to hide anything from an authentic Master. At first everything is fine, but after a while Dan has to make a more serious commitment to the route he has chosen. That's when he realizes that his life isn't as enjoyable as he'd like it to be, which causes problems with his life partner. This turns out to be the perfect opportunity for him to blame his problems on his guide and disengage himself from his spiritual commitment. So that he won't feel guilty, he justifies his decision to drop out by accusing his guide of manipulating him instead of admitting that he doesn't really want to change.

Wulfenite could be a great help to Dan and to anyone living a lie. This sedimentary stone is extremely useful in conflict situations since it encourages us to accept our negative side. It allows us to perceive, accept, and gradually integrate the darker side of our nature. Wulfenite can also be used to promote contact with its soul group.

Anything's better than losing face

When people living the quadratic lifestyle are exposed and can't escape by telling a lie or creating a false reality, they're totally lost and fall to pieces. Losing face is very destructive for them. Suddenly ashamed, they belittle themselves and no longer see their good qualities. They feel worthless.

That's when quadratic personalities can become aggressive and vindictive. Another facet of their personality can also emerge: they may punish themselves and sometimes even self-destruct, fleeing reality and seeking refuge in another world. Schizophrenia—a psychosis characterized by loss of contact with reality—is common among quadratic personalities and is a good example of this escape mechanism. Schizophrenics create their own ever-perfect worlds because they can't face true "reality."

Quadratic personalities are so afraid that someone will get the better of them that they feel compelled to dominate everyone around them. Yet this attitude adds to their loneliness. They need to understand that their behavior locks them into an artificial reality that prevents them from enjoying a wealth of new experiences.

Greg needs to feel different from other people. In a way, he wants to be above the crowd. As an experienced therapist, he firmly believes he can cure any patient. Even though he's burned out, his need to perform is stronger than his exhaustion. He doesn't understand that he can't save everyone. Because of this need, he absolutely has to be recognized in order to function. Yet the image he projects causes him to forget who he really is.

Greg's behavior masks his extreme vulnerability, his fear of being wrong and being seen as imperfect. Quadratic personalities want to become indispensable because being valued gives them a feeling of self-worth.

Vesuvianite, a metamorphic stone of change, can release suppressed emotions. It calms fears, opens the mind, banishes negative thoughts, and stimulates the need to discover who we really are.

When in a positive mindset, the quadratics see themselves and life as follows:

- I'm someone who can cope with anything.

- Others can rely on me at all times.

- So I can show them an entirely new reality.

A BALANCED QUADRATIC PERSONALITY

A new and truthful face emerges

Quadratic personalities can reach a point where they no longer want to conceal anything. They become tired of maintaining a facade and are ready to move on to a new stage in their lives. Superficial satisfaction no longer suffices. That's when they can use their spontaneity and analytical strengths in a positive way, turning them into tools to help them discover the reality behind the appearance. Encouraged by these feelings, they are able to question their behavior and throw themselves into new experiences in their search for the truth.

They're then ready to get to the heart of things, lower their barriers, and remove their masks. They're also prepared to discover the deeper meaning and hidden values of life. This new attitude motivates them, provides daily satisfaction, and brings them intense inner happiness.

> *If we don't seek out the lie,*
> *we can never know the truth.*
> D.D.D.

AFFIRMATION[1]

"The Truth of the matter is that Truth matters."

STRENGTHS TO CULTIVATE[2]

May I empower myself with:

Truth
« *Satyam* »   OM AH HUM   JAH HUM BAH HOH   « *Satyam* »

Righteous Living
« *Dharma* »   OM AH HUM   JAH HUM BAH HOH   « *Dharma* »

Purity
« *Soucha* »   OM AH HUM   JAH HUM BAH HOH   « *Soucha* »

See "The Forty-five Great Empowerments of the Soul," page 173

MEDITATION

See "Circulation of the Light," page 163

---

[1] Karta, "Seven Studies."

[2] Sri Adi Dadi, *Spiritual Science of Essential Yoga*, Volume II.

INVOCATION[1]

Innocence
(Affirmation)

I am the Love Child of the lovely Morning Star,

Beaming bright its Wisdom-light from heaven afar.

I am the Innocence of Spirit's Purity Blue,

Mirrored in the mist of the morning-glory dew.

E.K.

Quadratic stones

Best-known stones

apophyllite: *magmatic* (complex hydrous calcium potassium silicate containing fluorine)

chalcopyrite: *magmatic, metamorphic, sedimentary* (copper iron sulfide)

rutile: *magmatic* (titanium oxide)

vesuvianite (idocrase): *metamorphic* (complex calcium magnesium iron aluminum silicate)

wulfenite: *sedimentary* (lead molybdate)

zircon: *magmatic* (zirconium silicate)

Like the personalities that belong to this alliance, these stones are indefinable. There is no one predominant element in their composition.

apophyllite   chalcopyrite   rutile

vesuvianite   wulfenite   zircon

The Sympathy and Empathy (Service) Filiation

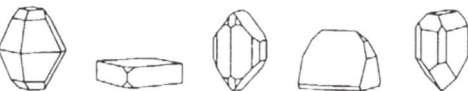

Rhombic Alliance

Life Is a Never-ending Routine

Keyword: permanence.

Strengths: adaptable, caring, committed, discreet, empathetic, enthusiastic, generous, good listener, helpful, modest, persevering, possesses balance and harmony, receptive, self-effacing, sensible, thorough.

Weaknesses: dependent, dissatisfied, easily influenced and led, insecure, prone to exhaustion, self-destructive, too altruistic.

Stones, minerals, and metals: alexandrite, andalusite, aragonite, barite (barytine), cat's eye (cymophane), celestite, chiastolite, chrysoberyl, danburite, iolite, marcasite, peridot (olivine or chrysolite), prehnite, stibnite, sulfur, tanzanite (blue zoisite), topaz, variscite, zoisite.

Focus: emotional.

Professions and trades: assistant or second in command, nurse, researcher, secretary, therapist, volunteer.

Polarity: feminine.

Ailments: arthritis, brittle nails and hair, constipation, liver problems, low blood pressure, osteoporosis.

Dress: stylish but discreet.

Well-known personalities: Lady Bird Johnson; Jacqueline Kennedy Onassis; Piglet in *Piglet's Big Movie*; Batman's sidekick, Robin; Mother Teresa, Martha Washington.

The underlying shape of this alliance is the rhombus, which is somewhat similar to a square. However, although all squares are rhombuses, not all rhombuses are square. Like the square, the rhombus has two pairs of parallel sides of equal length. These two perpendicular diagonals bisect each other. The square is made up of right angles, which is not true of all rhombuses. On the surface, the rhombic lifestyle may seem to resemble the orderly cubic lifestyle. In reality it is a series of long monotonous periods occasionally disrupted by sudden, unexpected changes. People associated with this alliance usually see life as a chain of perpetual repetition. Since everything seems to remain exactly the same, rhombic personalities view life through a distorted lens—they depend on the constant replication that shapes their lives and are unable to make any changes.

When in a negative mindset, the rhombics see themselves and life as follows:

- I depend on events and on others.

- Life, people, and events are inevitable.

- So why would I change anything?

Time Is a constantly recurring phenomenon

Rhombic personalities believe in permanence and are convinced that everything always remains the same. Hasn't the Earth been revolving around the sun since the beginning of time? So why would their lives be any different? Because of this attitude, they don't see any point in planning for the long term, since no matter what they plan their lives depend on external events and on others.

Yet when something important crops up that changes their lives, people living this lifestyle are well able to cope. They quickly adapt to the new situation, begin a process of readjustment, and end up reestablishing a form of stability and a familiar pace of life. In short, these new changes soon become habits, which in turn become permanent. Many rhombic personalities function this way. They are able to fling themselves into new relationships or far-reaching projects and work hard at them. In this way, they create new stability and security in their lives without, however, broadening their development or their personal knowledge.

Susan has eliminated all planning from her life. Because she's firmly convinced that everything always stays the same, she thinks making plans is a futile exercise. She always makes sure that things barely change and never takes any risks. For instance, it would never occur to her to treat herself to a lavish spending spree, color her hair, wear a revealing dress, or paint her living room a bright trendy orange. She has no trouble turning down the chance of an exotic vacation because she's simply not interested. Susan much prefers to stay at home to be available in case her children, ages twenty-six and twenty-four, need her. In any event, she doesn't like to fly. She's happy with anything that's reassuring and familiar.

However, a radical and unavoidable change occurs when Susan's two children leave home within two months of each other. Of course she's upset, but she quickly throws herself into making their new homes livable—cleaning, painting walls, and sewing curtains. She does everything she can to make sure her children will be comfortable for some time to come.

Danburite is a highly spiritual stone that promotes spiritual development. It could show Susan new ways of perceiving life and expand her vision. It also supports the user's personality and can serve as a guide for navigating the world and day-to-day reality. Danburite could help Susan understand true inner permanence.

> *Comfort is the quiet crematorium of the Soul.*
> D.D.D.

All or nothing

People associated with the rhombic system live stable and orderly lives that resemble a long, gently flowing river. Their sensible, unobtrusive behavior makes their lifestyle seem almost monotonous. Absolutely nothing may happen for long periods of time, and then suddenly an external force or internal change can sweep in and turn everything upside down, creating anxiety, depression, or irascibility. Rhombic personalities often respond to crisis situations in a surprising way. Venturing well beyond their limits, they can make reckless, radical decisions, sometimes even throwing the baby out with the bathwater.

Charlotte's life is going along nicely with few unexpected highs or lows. Is she just lucky, or is it simply that it's easy for her to succeed in everything she undertakes? Her life has been pretty conventional: university, marriage, family, and work. She's been married to her husband for twenty-seven years, has worked at the same company for twenty-one years, and has been a longstanding volunteer with several community organizations. One morning, Charlotte wakes up feeling anxious and unsettled; something is missing from her life. She then spirals into a deep depression. She sees her weekend activities as a waste of time, feels overwhelmed by all her social commitments, and makes hasty decisions. She immediately quits three organizations she has been working with for years and hands in her resignation to the chair of the board of a fourth nonprofit group where she has been an active member for the past five years. Once she has made up her mind, there's no looking back.

Zoisite confers the ability to transform destructive behavior patterns into a constructive lifestyle. It stimulates creativity by helping us get in touch with our true intentions and translate our own wishes and ideas into reality. It could therefore help release Charlotte's suppressed emotions and prevent them from becoming a ticking time bomb. It could also prevent Charlotte from making radical decisions.

> *We fear our inner depths.*
> D.D.D.

Service is the key

People associated with the rhombic system live stable and orderly lives that resemble a long, gently flowing river. Their sensible, unobtrusive behavior makes their lifestyle seem almost monotonous. Absolutely nothing may happen for long periods of time, and then suddenly an external force or internal change can sweep in and turn everything upside down, creating anxiety, depression, or irascibility. Rhombic personalities often respond to crisis situations in a surprising way. Venturing well beyond their limits, they can make reckless, radical decisions, sometimes even throwing the baby out with the bathwater.

Lisa has been an assistant for twenty-one years. One of her jobs is to head up a team to organize conferences. Her team members always feel secure because they know the conference will be a success with her in charge. She assigns responsibilities, keeping the larger share for herself. She makes plans, does research, networks, works overtime, sleeps less, and sometimes even takes over her team members' jobs before they've even started.

At home, Lisa is a superwoman. Everything is always spotless. She does the housework and makes the meals to make her husband happy. If anyone drops in unannounced, she makes them feel right at home even though she hates unexpected company. She's always eager to satisfy others' needs, down to the very last detail. Yet putting their needs ahead of her own sometimes causes her a lot of stress and disappointment. She feels she has bitten off more than she can chew because she can't do everything she thinks she should to make everyone happy. She often confides to her close friends that her many responsibilities are wearing her down and making her unhappy. She realizes that she's too giving and has problems defining her own limits.

Andalusite, a stone that encourages moderation in all things, would be a considerable asset to Lisa. It would help her understand that even though self-sacrifice can be a good thing, it is never an obligation. Andalusite brings emotional stability, calms fears, and makes it easier to face reality. It also brings harmony to those who are upset by certain events or behaviors.

When in a positive mindset, the rhombics see themselves and life as follows:

- I'm aware of and in touch with my true inner essence.

- Life offers a wealth of opportunities to be shared.

- So I use this essence for others and for my own development.

A BALANCED RHOMBIC PERSONALITY

> *The work must never be a burden, nor a suffering, nor a sacrifice.*
> D.D.D.

Confidence to better serve others

For people living the rhombic lifestyle, the key to balance lies in building up their inner strength. The more confident they are of their own worth, the greater their self-respect and self-esteem. They'll then be able to express their most fundamental quality: to be of service. Rhombics are always where they're needed or where they feel their help is necessary. Since they're very good listeners and are naturally sensitive, they can quickly tune in to others' moods and adapt. Not only are these qualities supportive to others, they also enhance their own well-being and development.

Definitely not leaders, rhombic personalities are the ideal second-in-command. They excel behind the scenes, are persevering and hard-working, and make terrific coworkers, unobtrusively supplying the effort needed to attain their objectives. It's a wise leader who recruits them for his or her team.

Once they achieve stability, rhombic personalities can then rely on their inner confidence. They attain a state of tranquility, no longer fearing new experiences or searching for excitement and adventure. Then, and only then, will they be able to face the true causes of their problems and disappointments, understand their underlying mechanisms, and leave their dark side behind. These changes will occur gradually, without creating turmoil in their lives or the lives of those around them. Their self-confidence will guide them to more enlightened choices.

The world of harmony

When people belonging to the rhombic alliance achieve balance, harmony comes into their lives. Their earlier need for permanence and routine is replaced by an inner harmony that is reflected on a day-to-day basis. In other words, what seemed to be a need for cast-iron stability was only a distortion of the desired inner harmony, which they can now access because they're in touch with their true nature.

AFFIRMATION[1]

"None is Master but my-Self, who bows to none but the Master."
"May the Living Lord in me … by his Word willing …
raise all that is dead in me to (Re-newed) Life."

STRENGTHS TO CULTIVATE[2]

May I empower myself with:

Inner silence
« *Mooka (Moona)* »   OM AH HUM   JAH HUM BAH   « *Mooka (Moona)* »

Courage
« *Dhairya* »   OM AH HUM   JAH HUM BAH   « *Dhairya* »

Joy
« *Santosha* »   OM AH HUM   JAH HUM BAH   « *Santosha* »

See "The Forty-five Great Empowerments of the Soul," page 173

MEDITATION

See "Green Tara," page 66

---

[1] Karta, "Seven Studies."

[2] Sri Adi Dadi, *Spiritual Science of Essential Yoga*, Volume II.

INVOCATION[1]

True World-Servers
(Affirmation)

We are the happiness of selfless
And blessed service
To all.

We are the humility of giving
The Love, and Will of God,
Enthralled.

E.K.

Rhombic stones

Best-known stones

alexandrite: *metamorphic* (beryllium aluminum oxide)

andalusite: *magmatic, metamorphic* (aluminum silicate)

aragonite: *magmatic, sedimentary* (calcium carbonate)

barite (barytine): *magmatic, sedimentary* (barium sulfate)

cat's eye (cymophane): *magmatic, metamorphic* (beryllium aluminate)

celestite: *sedimentary* (strontium sulfate)

chiastolite: *metamorphic* (aluminum silicate with carbon inclusions)

chrysoberyl: *magmatic, metamorphic* (beryllium aluminum oxide)

danburite: *magmatic* (calcium boron silicate)

iolite: *magmatic* (magnesium aluminum silicate)

marcasite: *magmatic, sedimentary* (iron disulfide)

peridot (olivine or chrysolite): *magmatic* (iron magnesium silicate)

alexandrite   andalousite   aragonite

barite   cat's eye   celestite

chiastolite   chrysoberyl   danburite

iolite   marcasite   peridot

prehnite: *magmatic* (calcium aluminum silicate)

stibnite: *magmatic* (antimony sulfide)

sulfur: *magmatic, sedimentary* (pure sulfur)

tanzanite (blue zoisite): *metamorphic* (calcium aluminum silicate with strontium)

topaz: *magmatic* (aluminum silicate)

variscite: *sedimentary* (hydrated aluminum phosphate with iron)

zoisite: *metamorphic* (calcium aluminum silicate)

prehnite

stibnite

sulfur

tanzanite

topaz

variscite

zoizite

Essential minerals for rhombic personalities

The three most common minerals in rhombic alliance stones are, in descending order, aluminum, calcium, and iron.

ALUMINUM

From a spiritual perspective, aluminum helps us find our true identity, which is the basic challenge facing all rhombic personalities. Aluminum opens us up to discover our true mission on Earth. It can also help rhombic personalities when they are confused, since it sharpens their sense of reality, objectivity, and presence of mind. By increasing the desire for change and diversity, aluminum encourages them to shed their fixed habits and attitudes.

Aluminum has a calming effect on anxiety, tensions, and feelings of guilt. It also supports the absorption of iron in the intestine.

CALCIUM

Calcium has the rare ability to regulate and stabilize the development of the personality. If development is accelerated or seems chaotic, calcium slows down the process, whereas it speeds up development that is slowing down. By promoting balanced personality growth, it activates spiritual development. In rhombic personalities, calcium can create balance between the tendency to inertia and the desire to make spontaneous, radical changes that trigger chaos.

In addition, calcium acts on the mental level of the rhombic personalities. It encourages them to determine what they want and don't want by developing their discernment. Calcium helps dispel confusion, providing a clear vision of events that impact their lives. It also has a stabilizing effect on the emotions, promotes self-confidence, and helps eliminate fear, offsetting the negative impact of acute anxiety or sudden depression.

Calcium strengthens the heart, regulates the heartbeat, and supports blood clotting. This beneficial impact on the physical body symbolizes the need for rhombic personalities to learn to synchronize the rhythm of their lives with the heartbeat of the universe.

Calcium is also known for supporting bone formation and strengthening bones, teeth, and tissues. It is necessary for the formation of DNA and encourages cell metabolism. Lastly, calcium prevents bone diseases that sometimes affect rhombic personalities.

IRON

Iron stimulates initiative, will power, perseverance, and enthusiasm; promotes dynamism; and increases endurance. It confers vigilance, making us unchallengeable, and encourages the development of the warrior side of our nature. It can also enhance the personal power of rhombic personalities and their ability to assert themselves.

Iron can promote inner calm and deepen meditation. It is thus useful when we want to rid ourselves of painful destructive elements deep within our subconscious. It can help rhombic personalities confront their true nature and uncover the real source of their problems.

By promoting the formation of hemoglobin and red blood cells, iron ensures oxygen circulation throughout the body. It provides strength and energy and helps fight fatigue and weakness. Iron also acts on the liver and spleen and reinforces the immune system.

Furthermore, by helping to stabilize nerve conduction, iron supports the nervous system, which is often affected in rhombic individuals because of their extreme agitation and hyperactivity.

Other characteristics of rhombic stones

Like rhombic personalities themselves, rhombic stones don't attract our attention at first glance. Understated in color, they range from all shades of green to pale yellow, gray, brown, and pale blue or are colorless and, on rare occasions, pink.

Some rhombic stones, like andalusite, aragonite, and peridot, have protective powers; others, like peridot, help free us from external influences. Stones like chiastolite combat adverse outside influences and dissipate negative thoughts and feelings. Because rhombic personalities are highly sensitive, protective stones can be of great assistance to them in resisting destructive influences.

Other stones belonging to this alliance, like celestite and pink topaz, confer comfort, warmth, and maternal tenderness. Supported in this way, rhombic personalities can develop maternal affection and unconditional self-acceptance, and they can experience genuine well-being. Once they can love themselves unconditionally, they can then extend this love to others.

THE CONFLICT-HARMONY (ROLLER COASTER) FILIATION

TRICLINIC ALLIANCE

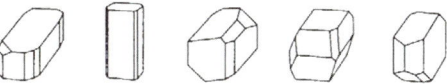

EXPECTING THE UNEXPECTED

Keywords: incompetent/competent; unstable/stable.

Strengths: adaptable, attuned to the rhythms of life, creative, flexible, intuitive, goes with the flow, psychic, resourceful, stable.

Weaknesses: feels victimized, feels weak and powerless, lacks confidence, moody, unstable.

Stones and minerals: amazonite, kyanite (cyanite or disthene), labradorite (spectrolite), larimar (pectolite, dolphin stone), rhodonite, sunstone, turquoise.

Focus: emotional.

Professions and trades: adviser/consultant, artist, craftsperson, healer, resource person, self-employed worker.

Polarity: feminine.

Ailments: arthritis, colds, depression, bipolar disorders, digestive disorders, physical or emotional sensitivity to atmospheric pollutants, stress-related problems, weak immune system—few defenses against germs, rheumatism, and sore throats.

Dress: generally mirrors their mood, seldom thought out in advance.

Personalities: Mr. Bean, Michelangelo, Jackson Pollock, Vincent van Gogh.

The trapezium forms the base of the triclinic structure. On one side it is so stable and solid that nothing can tip it over. When turned upside down, however, it becomes unstable and could easily collapse. Reflecting this shape, the lifestyle of triclinic personalities is naturally unpredictable and ever-changing. One day, they may suddenly feel extraordinarily creative, while the next they won't have a single spark of motivation. When they're on a creative roll, they feel they could conquer the world, but a second later, they can feel lost and desperate, like a child who has been punished too often. Their mood swings are erratic and can abruptly plunge them into a deep depression for no apparent reason. In fact, there are times when triclinic personalities sometimes find it impossible to control their lives or their emotional state.

When in a negative mindset, the triclinics see themselves and life as follows:

- I'm powerless, defenseless, a victim of others, of life, and of my own emotions.

- Life is unpredictable, can't be trusted, and can't be controlled.

- I must therefore protect myself by being elusive, withdrawing, and attacking and blaming others.

These attitudes have taught triclinic personalities that the unexpected is always just around the corner. Since anything is possible, why should they bother planning anything? Nothing happens the way they want it to in any event.

Karen decides to take a chance and reserves airline tickets to the Canary Islands for the following month. She's thrilled about this trip and is already imagining the great time she'll have. But all of a sudden a hidden fear surfaces, a little voice warns her to be careful because something could happen to ruin her plans. Although this fear is often unconscious, it's still strong enough to make her uncomfortable. Karen stops talking about her trip, works even harder, and tries to avoid her friends because she doesn't feel like talking. The very next morning, her boss informs her that she'll have to postpone her vacation because a huge contract has just landed on his desk. Karen bursts out of his office, vowing to herself that she'll never plan a vacation again, even though she definitely needs one.

Larimar, also known as pectolite and dolphin stone, is a triclinic stone that could be very useful to Karen. It could help her become more detached from the material side of life and enhance her understanding of her place in the world. It is also known for dissolving martyr complexes.

Beyond control, beyond reason

Triclinic personalities' mood swings can be disconcerting and bewildering for their families and friends, who never know why they'll suddenly disappear or what they'll be thinking from one day to the next. Trying to follow their thought processes soon becomes exasperating and distressing.

People belonging to this alliance can feel they have no control over their lives, and this feeling fuels their greatest fear.

When the members of Martin's family get together, they usually spend their time passionately debating any issue at hand. Even though it's all in good fun, they objectively analyze each and every opinion, and their arguments are intended to knock their opponents off balance. Although it's never clear who has made the best case or won their point, one thing is obvious: Martin always manages to slip away for hours without anyone really understanding why. That's how triclinic personalities act: veering from stability to instability. Is Martin too uncomfortable with all this friction? Does he feel he has lost control of the situation? Is he suddenly unable to justify his point of view?

Rhodonite can help eliminate anxiety and bring clarity to chaos. Since it also confers calm assurance in all situations, promotes positive interpersonal relations, and encourages attention to others, it could be a very helpful stone for Martin.

Where there's a will, there's a way

When they're in their negative mode, triclinic personalities see themselves as totally lacking in willpower, unable to accept what they can't change or to change what they can. They feel like martyrs or victims of circumstance and complain that life is unfair. They're convinced that others control their fate and are responsible for their misfortune. Claiming that they can't get what they want, they become paranoid and feel misunderstood. Because they believe the whole world is against them, they think they have to manage on their own. As a result, they feel humiliated and become passive-aggressive and depressed. They hit bottom, cut themselves off from the world, and almost seem to enjoy wallowing in their dismay. Their despair affects everyone around them and reflects their refusal to take control of their lives and find happiness. Their lack of confidence in others stops them from asking for or accepting any help offered. However, true to their nature and thanks to their inherently strong willpower, they are able to persuade themselves that they have to emerge from this dark cloud. So they pull themselves together, flex their muscles, fling open their windows and doors, and once more venture forth into the light of day.

Beware of opening an umbrella indoors

Bad luck seems to pursue people living this lifestyle, reinforcing their impression that they are powerless and have no control over their lives.

Frank works in a garage, where Paul, one of his coworkers, is often skeptical about his friend's alleged bad luck. Paul has a typically cubic personality, which means that everything is always in its rightful place. He has blithely followed his daily routine for years now; he's never late and always finishes work at the same time.

Unlike Paul, Frank has a fantastic morning, whistling cheerfully while he works. Seeing no problems or worries on the horizon, he thinks he'll probably be able to go home early. And then, for no apparent reason, his energy levels, which were so high in the morning, seem to have plummeted by the afternoon. He's constantly dropping his tools, and a major piece of equipment inexplicably breaks down. Because he has to finish the job, he'll have to work overtime. I shouldn't have been so upbeat this morning, he thinks helplessly. It just brought me bad luck for the rest of the day. As for Paul, he simply nods his head and leaves at five on the dot—just like he does every other day of the week.

Is Frank really unlucky, or did he unconsciously sabotage his afternoon to relieve the pressure? Was his morning just too good to be true? Triclinic personalities are often suspicious of good days because they know they never last. Ironically, they sometimes actually create problems, delays, and disarray so that they can more effectively control their environment. The unknown can be terrifying, and the inevitable wait for something to happen can be extremely stressful. In these cases, as the saying goes, it's best to keep friends close and enemies closer.

Like a sponge

Individuals associated with this structure are often extremely sensitive to the energy of those around them. They frequently absorb this energy or unconsciously react to it. And so what may appear to be bad luck, a feeling of instability or sudden sadness or depression, can in fact be the result of indiscriminately absorbing too much energy from others. Fear of being negatively influenced or victimized can make triclinic personalities overly cautious, which in turn drives them to withdraw or turn inward.

Turquoise is a good guide for the unknown. It provides protection and encourages independence. It is also considered to ward off attacks, accidents, and the negative energies that seem to influence triclinic personalities more than they should.

There's never enough time

People influenced by this alliance often have a contentious relationship with time when they're out of step with themselves and their environment. So if things don't work out the way they've planned, they'll miss appointments, be late for romantic dinners, or find themselves fighting their way through frustrating and unexpected traffic jams. Even though they've left home with time to spare, mysterious circumstances beyond their control prevent them from reaching their destination. But instead of simply accepting that the traffic is heavy that day and making a quick phone call to explain they'll be late, they view the situation as an intolerable obstacle, and add it to the list of reasons why they're having such a bad day.

When in a positive mindset, the triclinics see themselves and life as follows:

- I'm a responsible and powerful participant in the game of life, in perfect harmony with the environment and myself.

- Life is an unpredictable adventure.

- I must therefore open up to its many possibilities.

A BALANCED TRICLINIC PERSONALITY

> *Learn to carry the angel within you down to the pits of manifest Hell.*[1]
>
> D.D.D.

The first lesson triclinic personalities have to learn is to accept what life offers them, to go with the flow, without drowning in deep waters. They need to understand that they aren't in control and never will be. A force higher than their own aspirations is at work.

Whatever happens, the green light is within

In Buddhist philosophy, all things are impermanent, transient, and in a constant state of flux. Human suffering and conflicts are rooted in the desire to hold onto a moment, an event, a person, or an object. This philosophy teaches us that in order to attain true and long-lasting stability and joy, we must accept that we can lose everything at any time. It also teaches us that we have to stop seesawing back and forth between happiness, which occurs when our desires are satisfied, and distress, which occurs when they are not. Triclinic personalities need to understand the abstract concept that happiness comes from within.

> *Learn to be detached from attachment,*
> *and more importantly, not attached to detachment.*[2]
>
> D.D.D.

People living this lifestyle will discover their personal strength and power by detaching themselves from their excessive attraction to the external world. This attraction often replaces attention to the call of the higher self, the soul. In the words of Carl Jung, "A sense of wider meaning to one's own existence is what raises a man above merely getting and spending. If he lacks this sense, he is lost and miserable."[3] Triclinic personalities

---

[1] D.D.D., *Knots of Eternity.*

[2] D.D.D., *Knots of Eternity.*

[3] C. G. Jung, *Man and His Symbols* (Garden City, NY: Doubleday, 1964).

have to shift their attention from pain and pleasure, acquisition and loss to the recognition of the higher and broader meaning of their existence and suffering.

> *Dare to be securely insecure.*[1]
> D.D.D.

With time, I'll find my rightful place

In their positive development, triclinic individuals have no real expectations about the future because they live in the present moment. They glide through time and space offering little resistance. They know that all experiences provide an opportunity to learn, to deepen the meaning of life, to burn their karma, and to test their strength and resourcefulness. Little by little, they come to understand that action is generated by a force higher and superior to their own. They then begin to submit their own will to the will of this greater force. Gradually, they come to feel fulfilled, calm, and happy, no matter what the situation.

They no longer feel personally targeted and responsible for what life brings them since they recognize that the experience they face mirrors their own consciousness. Capable and responsible, they come up with creative solutions to their own problems and even, when necessary, to the problems of others. They live in perfect harmony with life and learn to ignore their desires and pain, to think of others, and to contribute to their well-being. They have become fluid, flexible, lighthearted, and adaptable.

---

[1] D.D.D., *Knots of Eternity*.

With time and practice, triclinic personalities can live in harmony with the present moment, with murmurs from the invisible world, with the call of the spirit and their higher self. They develop impeccable intuition and can even become clairvoyant. A supersensitive and fragile ego can be transmuted into a well-balanced and mature individual, with one foot solidly anchored in the inner world, the other solidly grounded in the external. In short, they can at last create perfect balance within themselves.

AFFIRMATIONS[1]

"Lord would you wipe the tears from my eyes
so that my Soul may see."

"Life is my laboratory of Labor leading me to the Light of Liberty."

STRENGTHS TO CULTIVATE[2]

May I empower myself with:

Faith
« *Sraddha* »   OM AH HUM   JAH HUM BAH HOH   « *Sraddha* »

Desirelessness (for the joys of this and other worlds)
« *Ihamutraphalabhog VAIRAGA* »   OM AH HUM   JAH HUM BAH HOH
« *Ihamutraphalabhog Vairaga* »

Strength
« *Bala* »   OM AH HUM   JAH HUM BAH HOH   « *Bala* »

See "The Forty-five Great Empowerments of the Soul," page 173

MEDITATION

See "The Eye of the Hurricane," page 164

---

[1] Karta, "Seven Studies."

[2] Sri Adi Dadi, *Spiritual Science of Essential Yoga*, Volume II.

INVOCATIONS

"Skywalks!"[1]

"I Am the Light
within the Light,
brightening Abright
with perfect Godsight
the skywalks of my Life."

or

Soul-ar Progression One
Upon Ray IV[2]

"An Infinite Point of Peace"

WE STATION OURSELVES

Upon an Infinite Point of Peace.
Laying forever still the waters of war and strife.

*"Let then Harmony rule United the above and below,
The higher and lower, the form and the formless.*

*Let the Angel and the Warrior meet and merge as ONE,
Into the LIGHT, in Beauty and in Love."*

E.K.

---

[1] Karta, "Seven Studies."

[2] Karta, "Seven Studies."

Triclinic stones

Best-known stones

amazonite: *magmatic, metamorphic, sedimentary* (potassium aluminum silicate)

kyanite (cyanite, disthene): *metamorphic* (aluminum silicate)

labradorite (spectrolite): *magmatic* (aluminum calcium silicate)

larimar (pectolite, dolphin stone): *magmatic, vulcanite—hydrothermal formation in volcanic rock* (complex sodium calcium silicate)

rhodonite: *metamorphic* (manganese iron magnesium calcium silicate)

sunstone: *magmatic, plutonite* (sodium calcium aluminum silicate)

turquoise: *sedimentary* (hydrated copper aluminum phosphate containing iron)

amazonite   kyanite   labradorite

larimar   rhodonite   sunstone

turquoise

Iron is the predominant element in the chemical composition of almost all triclinic stones.

Iron

Iron helps stimulate initiative and develop willpower among triclinic individuals, who feel weak and lost when confronted with life's challenges. Iron is a malleable, magnetic metal strongly influenced by the planet Mars. It encourages action rather than reaction, awakening the inner warrior in each of us. It promotes the inner calm necessary for understanding and integrating the lessons learned during difficult periods. The events experienced are thus transformed into challenges that themselves confer the strength needed to overcome them.

Physically, iron contributes to the formation of hemoglobin and red blood cells. It helps transport oxygen to the body, stimulates vitality and energy levels, and revitalizes and strengthens the immune system. A lack of iron can cause anemia, which leads to weakness and exhaustion.

The Mediator, Counselor-Therapist (Realism) Filiation

TRIGONAL ALLIANCE

Minimum Effort, Maximum Results

Keyword: simplicity.

Strengths: calm, candid, clear-minded, faith in life, genuine, loyal, nonjudgmental, realistic, reliable, sensible, simple, stable, tolerant, well-balanced.

Weaknesses: avoids conflict, indifferent, lacks empathy, lazy, lethargic, negligent, self-destructive, superficial.

Stones, minerals, and metals: agate, "blue lace" agate, fire agate, moss agate, ametrine, aventurine, calcite, carnelian, chalcedony, chrysoprase, dioptase, hematite, jasper, magnesite, onyx, petrified wood, phenacite, pietersite, rhodochrosite, ruby, sapphire, sardonyx, smithsonite, tourmaline; all quartz, including angel aura quartz, amethyst, aqua aura quartz, citrine, faden quartz, Herkimer diamond, rose quartz, rutilated quartz, and smoky quartz; all the "eyes," including bull's eye, hawk eye, tiger eye, and tiger iron (tigerite).

Focus: mental.

Professions and trades: carpenter, computer specialist, couples therapist, diplomat, entrepreneur, financial adviser, mediator/arbitrator, psychologist.

Polarity: masculine.

Ailments: corpulence, high blood pressure or other problems stemming from an unhealthy lifestyle (lack of exercise and poor diet) or long-standing bad habits (alcohol and tobacco).

Dress: comfortable, as low-maintenance as possible.

Well-known personalities: Garfield, Homer Simpson, Lucky Luke.

This chapter explores the trigonal or rhombohedral alliance. As its name indicates, the geometric shape underlying the trigonal alliance is the triangle, which, having the fewest sides, is the simplest geometric form. The triangle is said to represent the number three, a number also associated with the principle of creation and the achievement of perfect balance.

When in a negative mindset, the trigonals see themselves and life as follows:

- I'm powerless in the face of chaos and conflict.

- Life and others are chaotic and complicated.

- I therefore become indifferent, withdraw, or retreat into my shell.

Why make things complicated?

People living the trigonal lifestyle usually avoid complications, leading quiet, predictable lives. Simplicity and comfort play a major role in their well-being. A complicated situation or one that requires them to make an effort to resolve puts them in an intolerable position. To make it bearable, they develop a defense mechanism in the form of physical and emotional withdrawal. When their personal universe is threatened by conditions beyond their control, they retreat into their shell or back away before the situation gets out of hand.

Roger and Julie Goodall decide to invite a few friends over for a barbecue. Roger assumes that all he needs are a few steaks, some potatoes, and a good bottle of wine. Julie agrees to these simple plans and decides to add a cold soup, a seafood cocktail, a green salad, and some grilled vegetables. And then, of course, there's the chocolate rum soufflé for dessert. When the evening arrives, Julie is running late and has even managed to ruin the soufflé. Realizing that the preparations are becoming increasingly complicated, Roger leaves the kitchen without saying a word to his wife. He greets his guests, offers them a drink, and then sits down to enjoy their company, leaving Julie to cope with everything else on her own and forgetting to put the steaks on the barbecue.

A **tiger's eye** could be a great help to Roger since it would shield him from external stress, encourage him to take action, and be of valuable assistance in resolving confusion and complications. Tiger's eye provides support in troubled times, conferring the courage to face adversity.

> *Care enough to be simple, and to keep it simple,*
> *even if you are intelligently complex ...*[1]
>
> D.D.D.

No secrets, no surprises

With their stable energy and love of familiarity, trigonal personalities develop life habits that they'll maintain for years or throughout their entire lives. Once they've found what they think is a winning formula that they're happy with, they don't see any need for changes or schemes to make their life more interesting or varied. The more ingrained their habits and comfort become, the harder it will be for them to take action and change. This attitude can lead to health problems or conflicts in their relationship with their life partner.

In the evenings, Julie takes piano and tennis lessons and attends aerobics classes. While she's gone, Roger is more than happy to stay at home alone, comfortably ensconced in his favorite armchair, surfing from one channel to another while he waits for his wife. From time to time, he thinks about taking up a sport or getting a little exercise. But as the days, weeks, and even months go by, his good intentions gradually fade away. Roger remains in his armchair, enjoying the simple comfort of home. What's more, because he doesn't have any really close neighbors and he works nearby, he can sleep as late as possible and wastes little time commuting.

Calcite, a soothing, gentle stone, would be very good for Roger. It has a refreshing and revitalizing energy that promotes new ways of perceiving the world. It can eliminate various blockages and enable us to leave old habits and behaviors behind. Clear calcite, for example, has the power to transform thought into action, which would inspire Roger to get some exercise.

Minimum effort, maximum results

Although the triangle's basically simple form could suggest it has a limited capability, it is nonetheless an extremely powerful structure.

---

[1] D.D.D., *Knots of Eternity.*

130

Reflecting this characteristic, trigonal personalities are able to produce maximum results with minimum effort. Their ability to attain their objectives so effortlessly can be frustrating for those around them. While their coworkers are rushed off their feet trying to get everything done, trigonals comfortably jog along at their own pace. First of all, they carefully work out all the details of their plan of action in their heads. Then, once the scenario is complete, they translate it into written or oral form, revealing the results of their mental gymnastics in the blink of an eye. They're always relaxed because they know that they'll meet their deadline, an attitude that can be pretty annoying or stressful for their peers. Even though they seem to cross the finish line at the very last minute, trigonal personalities still manage to come up smelling like roses, to everyone's great surprise.

However, to expend the least energy possible, they can procrastinate for hours, wasting an incredible amount of time. They let their laziness take over instead of getting the very most out of the time available and their own abilities.

Take the example of Justin, a university student who constantly seems to cheat time. He always starts his assignments the evening before they're due. First of all, he has a good meal, then chats on the phone with his girlfriend for an hour, plays a few video games, and later sits out on the patio for a while. Around eleven o'clock, he's ready to get to work on his twenty-page essay. But before getting started, he makes himself a large thermos of strong coffee and exchanges a few words with his roommates before they go to bed. At about 12:30, when it's quiet, he finally sits down to write. He leisurely types his ideas on his computer as the hours tick away. Around seven in the morning, when everyone else is getting up, he's a bit worried because he's only on page fourteen and has just three hours left to meet his deadline. But he pulls himself together, keeps calm, and tells himself that he'll be able to make it. Justin finally finishes some twenty pages, and at 9:49 he strolls over to the campus to hand in his assignment—just in time.

Chrysoprase is a stone that imparts wisdom and creates openness to new situations. It stimulates our spiritual side without conflicting with logical and rational considerations. Chrysoprase would strengthen Justin's faith in life and also help him understand himself, his behavior, and the habits underlying his laziness and procrastination. This stone can reveal selfish motives that affect our development, which could be of great benefit to Justin.

> *If you take care of time,*
> *then each ticking second will take care of you.*
> D.D.D.

Avoiding conflict at any cost

Because they think facts are more important than feelings, trigonal personalities maintain that only what can be seen and touched, what is logical and concrete, is real and true. Focusing solely on their objective view of the world, they sometimes forget to pay attention to the subjective reality and feelings of those close to them. When a relationship becomes tense, trigonal personalities take refuge in indifference rather than considering the other person's point of view. Since their intuition usually tells them what they consider to be the truth, they rely on it unequivocally in an argument. This attitude, together with their strong desire to live a peaceful, uncomplicated life, increases their indifference, making them flee conflict, distance themselves from discord, isolate themselves, and turn inward. For them, feelings are just an added complication that serves no useful purpose.

Rhodochrosite can help people belonging to this alliance develop unconditional love for others. It also enables them to spontaneously express their feelings, encourages a positive and enthusiastic attitude toward life, and creates joy and lightheartedness.

> *Dare to take the next step even if your feet are bound in cement.*[1]
> D.D.D.

---

[1] D.D.D., *Knots of Eternity.*

Why take risks?

Trigonal personalities know how to make decisions and act effectively. However, their fear of conflict, dissension, and the danger of the unexpected means that they take very few risks. As long as they haven't learned to disengage themselves from extremes—negative/positive, easygoing/aggressive, pleasure/pain—it will be hard for them to maintain their balance and calmly face reality with strength and courage. Until then, their vision will be limited, obscuring the true patterns and deeper meaning of the events of their lives. They'll see only what's on the surface and fail to appreciate the treasures hidden beneath their experiences, missing out on the wealth of learning that their day-to-day lives offer. They don't take the time they should to learn the lessons that life is trying to teach them. But once they remove their blinders and expand their vision, they can quietly grow and understand that they share a purpose that is far greater than can be perceived through their senses, and one in which they can ultimately believe.

When people living this lifestyle lack balance, they are passive and ineffective. **Carnelian** is a stone that awakens vital energy, creativity, and passion and encourages risk taking, which in turn promotes growth. It stimulates action, suppresses the fear of making a mistake, and helps welcome change and transformation. Spiritually, carnelian assists us in making decisions and taking action that will lead to a greater purpose.

Throw yourself into the Grand Canyon of Life
and learn all about the gift of Wings.
D.D.D.

When in a positive mindset, the trigonals see themselves and life as follows:

- I'm armed with peace and anchored in light.

- The world needs quiet understanding and peaceful resolution.

- From now on, I must bravely shine this light where it is needed.

A balanced trigonal personality

If I make the necessary effort, life will carry me forward

When they're in their positive mode, trigonal personalities trust the energy and rhythm of their geometric alliance, which enables them to do what needs to be done and quietly flourish in a stable, uncomplicated way. If they are impatient and try to force their life into a different path or stubbornly advance to the rhythm of their own ego, their creative flow will drain away. They will temporarily lose this precious ability to move in harmony with the current of life and become apathetic, lazy, negligent, and indifferent.

By affirming that life is progressing as it should and reestablishing their faith in it and its wisdom, trigonal individuals can regain their balance. Along with this attitude, they must learn to supply the effort to effectively sustain what life offers them.

The gift of simplicity

The isosceles triangle is a stable and sturdy figure. Whichever side it is placed on, its base remains solid. It can therefore be a very reliable tool. The same may be said for trigonal personalities who have found their balance. They become trustworthy, loyal, and always open to others. No matter how we meet someone influenced by this alliance, there is always something familiar about them. There are never any unpleasant surprises in store. Since they reflect their inner values, we're always happy to have them as friends.

Because trigonal personalities have mastered the art of simplifying complicated situations, they make excellent advisers. Firmly grounded and clear-minded, they can explain a situation in a way that the right solutions immediately spring to mind. They are realistic and nonjudgmental, attentive to those seeking advice, and always unbiased. Thanks to their impartiality, they are exceptionally tolerant of everyone around them.

AFFIRMATION[1]

"Rig me with Light in the nescience of nite.
Arm me with Peace in the storm of siege."

STRENGTHS TO CULTIVATE[2]

May I empower myself with:

Perfect peace (equal mind)
« *Samathwastithi* »   OM AH HUM   JAH HUM BAH HOH   « *Samathwastithi* »

Effort
« *Srama* »   OM AH HUM   JAH HUM BAH HOH   « *Srama* »

Service
« *Seva* »   OM AH HUM   JAH HUM BAH HOH   « *Seva* »

See "The Forty-five Great Empowerments of the Soul," page 173

MÉDITATION

See "The Eye of the Hurricane," page 164

---

[1] Karta, "Seven Studies."

[2] Sri Adi Dadi, *Spiritual Science of Essential Yoga*, Volume II.

INVOCATION[1]

"S. S. S." SEVENTEEN
UPON RAY III

"The Self and the Lotus Illuminator"

I place my-Self,
In the Lord's Investigative Light
Under the Manifesting Evolution
Of the Lotus Illuminator.

"F. F." 17 "I Am the Lighted Purpose of Activity Itself and as I am here now
One, in Spirit and matter—I am healed!"

E.K.

---

[1] Karta, "Seven Studies."

Trigonal stones

Best-known stones

agate: *magmatic* (silicon dioxide)

ametrine: *magmatic* (silicon dioxide, iron and manganese)

aventurine: *magmatic, metamorphic, sedimentary* (silicon dioxide)

bull's eye: *sedimentary* (silicon dioxide)

calcite: *magmatic, sedimentary* (calcium carbonate)

carnelian: *magmatic* (silicon dioxide, iron)

chalcedony: *magmatic, sedimentary* (silicon dioxide)

chrysoprase: *sedimentary* (silicon dioxide)

dioptase: *sedimentary* (hydrated copper silicate)

hawk eye: *magmatic* (silicon dioxide)

hematite: *magmatic, metamorphic* (iron oxide)

jasper: *sedimentary* (silicon dioxide)

agate

ametrine

aventurine

bull's eye

calcite

carnelian

chalcedony

chrysoprase

dioptase

hawk eye

hematite

jasper

magnesite: *sedimentary, rarely magmatic* (magnesium carbonate)

onyx: *magmatic* (silicon dioxide)

petrified wood: *sedimentary* (silicon dioxide);

phenacite: *magmatic* (beryllium silicate)

pietersite: *sedimentary* (silicon dioxide)

rhodochrosite: *sedimentary* (manganese carbonate)

ruby: *magmatic, metamorphic* (aluminum oxide and chrome)

sapphire: *magmatic, metamorphic* (aluminum oxide, titanium, and iron)

sardonyx: *magmatic* (silicon dioxide and iron)

smithsonite: *sedimentary* (zinc carbonate)

tiger eye: *sedimentary* (silicon dioxide)

tiger iron (tigerite): *metamorphic* (silicon dioxide and iron)

tourmaline: *magmatic* (complex silicate of boron, sodium, aluminum, iron, magnesium, calcium; varies according to color)

magnesite

onyx

petrified wood

phenacite

pietersite

rhodochrosite

ruby

sapphire

sardonyx

smithsonite

tiger eye

tiger iron (tigerite)

tourmaline

ALL QUARTZ, INCLUDING

angel aura quartz: *magmatic* (silicon dioxide artificially bonded with silver and platinum)

amethyst: *magmatic* (silicon dioxide, iron, manganese)

aqua aura quartz: *magmatic* (silicon dioxide artificially bonded with gold)

citrine: *magmatic* (silicon dioxide)

faden quartz: *magmatic* (silicon dioxide)

Herkimer diamond: *magmatic* (silicon dioxide)

rose quartz: *magmatic* (silicon dioxide and manganese)

rutilated quartz: *magmatic* (silicon dioxide with titanium oxide)

smoky quartz: *magmatic* (silicon dioxide)

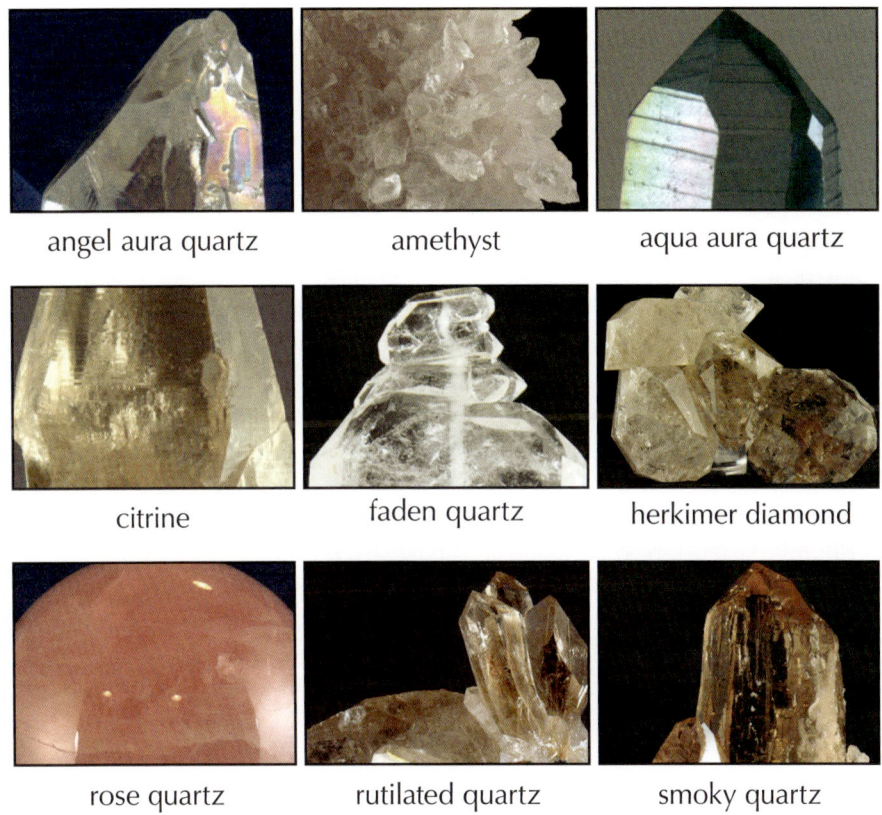

angel aura quartz

amethyst

aqua aura quartz

citrine

faden quartz

herkimer diamond

rose quartz

rutilated quartz

smoky quartz

Trigonal stones are generally endowed with great power. All varieties of quartz belong to this geometric alliance. As the most powerful electromagnetic mineral, quartz forms the basis of piezoelectricity. Used wisely, quartz can have a strong impact on the environment and on people. It is one of the rare minerals capable of both emitting vibrations and storing information and energy. That is why it is able to reenergize other stones.

Silicon

Silicon, the main element in the composition of trigonal stones, can significantly contribute to stabilizing people belonging to this system.

Silicon promotes bone remineralization for fractures and osteoarthritis through stimulating the metabolism of calcium. It relieves cartilage and joint problems and fortifies the skin, hair, and nails. It also strengthens immune reactions in the blood and lymph. In addition, it acts as a diuretic in cases of edema and cellulite. It also stimulates the lymph nodes, spleen, and lungs. Silicon can also help prevent aging because it stimulates the metabolism and cell division, improves the elasticity of blood vessels, and can lower high blood pressure.

Silicon promotes inner well-being, congeniality, and self-confidence, reducing dependency on external pleasures. It helps counter fear, excess sensitivity, and exhaustion, and it keeps us alert in all situations. By alleviating our fears, it helps dissolve fixed ideas and habits, enabling us to be more accepting of new ideas and inspiration.

Furthermore, silicon increases our receptiveness and brings us into harmony with universal physical and spiritual laws, allowing us to remain creatively attuned to the rhythm of life.

THE HERE-NOW, SPONTANEOUS, CREATIVE,
NONCONVENTIONAL,FREEDOM-LOVING, REBELLIOUS
(BUT STILL, OF THE MIDDLE WAY) FILIATION

BUDDHIC ALLIANCE

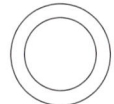

HERE AND NOW

Keyword: spontaneity.

Strengths: active, creative, detests routine, direct, fearless, gives one hundred percent, intuitive, lives in the present, optimistic and upbeat about the future, quick-witted, spontaneous, unconventional, versatile.

Weaknesses: aggressive, apathetic, avoids commitment, depressed, destructive, feels misunderstood and victimized by others and circumstances, solitary when in need of space, superficial, unstable, unstructured.

Stones and minerals: amber, jet, moldavite, obsidian, opal, petrified wood, tektite.

Focus: mental.

Professions and trades: artist (actor, writer, illustrator, designer, painter), explorer, inventor, psychologist, salesperson.

Polarity: feminine.

Ailments: allergies, arthritis, depression, bipolar disorders, lung and heart problems.

Dress: according to the mood of the moment since their dress reflects their inner state.

Well-known personalities: Ludwig van Beethoven, Jim Carrey, Albert Einstein, John Lennon, Mozart, Winnie the Pooh, Pablo Picasso, Elvis Presley, Robin Williams.

The buddhic alliance is characterized by a lack of inner crystal structure. Because these rocks were formed almost instantaneously, their component minerals were forced to bond together without having the opportunity to form a specific geometric shape.

Moldavite, a magnificent green stone formed about 15 million years ago when a meteorite collided with the Earth's crust, is a good example of this system. Rocks that were melted by the heat of the impact were projected into the air and solidified before falling to Earth about 250 miles away. The result was this extraordinary glass-like stone that has no definite inner geometric structure.

The same is true for its sister stone, obsidian, which is similar in origin, formed by rapidly cooling molten lava. In contrast, amber and opal, two other stones belonging to this alliance, were produced by the bonding of various substances, which explains why a piece of amber may contain an insect or a leaf, inclusions that are uncharacteristic of geometric alliances.

Buddhic personalities are often perceived as extravagant, atypical, unpredictable, dynamic, creative, and intuitive. They are born creators, motivators, and inventors. Being obsessed with the here and now, the present moment is always most important to them because that's when anything can be achieved and anything can happen.

When in a negative mindset, the buddhics see themselves and life as follows:

- I'm unpredictable.

- I avoid routine like the plague.

- Give me space.

Here and now

People influenced by this alliance often have an exceptional power of concentration that locks them into a world where anything can happen and the possibilities of creation are limitless. They unconsciously enclose themselves in a bubble where nothing can penetrate except the energy of the present moment. They hear and see nothing but what they're doing. They're caught up in the moment, which keeps them prisoner until another "moment" captures their attention.

Mary, a married woman in her forties, experiences these "moments" every day when she makes breakfast for her family. She starts by picking up the coffee pot and opening the fridge to get water out of the pitcher, but then she sees her vitamins and the yogurt her daughter likes to eat in the morning. She puts the pot on the counter, forgets it momentarily, picks up the vitamins, and then places them beside the pot. She then picks up the yogurt, forgetting the water and the vitamins. Placing the yogurt on the counter near the window, she takes a bowl out of the cupboard, notices that the coffee cups are empty, and then realizes that she forgot to make the coffee. She leaves the empty bowl and goes back to the fridge for the water, fills the coffee pot, and then pours the water into the coffee machine. Then her daughter asks for her yogurt, so Mary leaves the coffee and goes back to where she placed the yogurt on the counter.

I have to do everything right away so I won't forget

Mary does several things at the same time, trying hard not to forget the fleeting here and now. She hates keeping a day planner, often forgetting to look at it anyway as she's too busy doing something else that's more important at that "moment."

Laura, who owns a casting agency, claims the more work she has, the more empty spaces there are in her day planner because she doesn't take the time to write down her appointments and meetings. Like Mary, she often forgets to look at it because she's too busy with the present.

Jet, a stone that connects to earth energy, would be very appropriate for Mary and Laura to help them understand that they are in the right place at the right time. They would be less preoccupied and able to overcome their fear of forgetting things.

Every moment is new and unique

It goes without saying that buddhic personalities would never choose a life of routine. They love change and aren't interested in fixed points that represent an end, or in monotony and loss of the present moment, when anything is possible. Life isn't simply to be endured but to be joyously lived to the fullest. But this doesn't mean that those who live this lifestyle are in perpetual motion. They enjoy a rest as much as they like being active because they know how to be attuned to the needs of the moment. They can flutter around like a butterfly, but they can also take the time to laze in the sun like a lizard.

A buddhic lifestyle isn't a conventional one. Buddhic personalities tend to be rebellious, preferring to take off rather than be caught in a situation where all the rules are set out in advance. They have no trouble conforming to certain rules and regulations if they think they're valid. However, if they disagree, they give in ungraciously and can barely contain their anger.

Donna, a nurse in a trauma center, has a phobia about marriage. She has a pathological fear of becoming a "possession" and losing her freedom. One evening, when they're out for dinner with friends, her boyfriend surprises her with a marriage proposal and suggests they get married the following week. Donna is so dumbfounded that she doesn't know what to say. The "moment" is precious and ripe with possibilities. She appreciates this unique moment and spontaneously accepts his unexpected proposal. Five days later they take off for Las Vegas and tie the knot in a quiet spot in the desert. Everything has happened so fast that Donna scarcely realizes she's married. It was an extraordinary day, unconventional and full of surprises.

Amber, a stone that confers flexibility and joy, would help Donna feel free even when she's embarking on a conventional path. It would be useful to her to wear this stone on certain occasions, such as dull family get-togethers where she feels trapped.

Give me space

There's nothing more painful for buddhic personalities than suffocating in a relationship that leaves them no inner space. They are deeply unhappy around people who are possessive or try to control them.

Elizabeth has been married for ten years. She just loves being on her own in her little suburban condominium, where she sometimes stays during the week to save herself the hour-long trip to the home she shares in the country with her husband. Staying here gives her a much-needed break and time to enjoy her own space before heading back to another day at the hospital where she works as a doctor. Elizabeth readily admits that this "space" is absolutely essential for her. She can let go and relax, "do her own thing" and recharge her batteries in peace. Of course she misses her husband, but she also loves the times when they get together again, which unfailingly breathe new life into their relationship.

Since **jet** helps restore energy and create a restful atmosphere, it would help Elizabeth leave the tensions of her day behind.

When people associated with the buddhic alliance feel they're being held captive by a particular situation or person, they become bitter and disheartened. They lose their creativity, become depressed, and can't see the light at the end of the tunnel. They may find it hard to overcome these feelings as long as the obstacle or "jailor" remains, but as soon as they're offered a breath of fresh air, everything returns to normal.

I need air

All buddhic stones contain an oxide that is a mix of oxygen and another substance. And this characteristic is clearly reflected in the attitude of those living the buddhic lifestyle. Air, or the oxygen it contains, is absolutely essential to them.

Life on Earth would be impossible without oxygen. Similarly, life without their own space would be unbearable for buddhic personalities. Like the air signs in astrology, they have an overwhelming need of breathing space since it represents the fuel that enables them to function. Without it, they would suffocate and die a symbolic inner death, deprived of the source that allows them to open up and live.

Buddhic personalities that are destabilized by a lack of breathing space tend to have respiratory problems, are susceptible to flu and allergies, and are prime candidates for asthma.

Moderation is always in good taste

Yet too much space, just like too much air, can sometimes be harmful for these personalities, who need to be loved and appreciated. Like fire, a little air fans the flames; too much puts them out.

Individuals influenced by this alliance need to be supported, not smothered. Ideally, their friends and families are a source of inspiration, a driving force for their creativity. Remove this source, and they plunge into the darkest depths of nonbeing, losing all motivation and inspiration.

The more mature buddhic personalities become, the more this maturity is reflected in their relationships. They cultivate and preserve the precious ties they have forged with those around them. However, the less mature they are, the greater their need for change, even in their love life. They flee meaningful relationships, preferring to keep things on a superficial level for fear of being trapped. This is why Picasso had a string of muses and John Lennon had just one.

I'm not usually afraid of anything

Life is a game where anything is possible. Buddhic personalities aren't afraid of anything as long as they are active, creative, and spontaneous. They always have a solution to any problem and view obstacles as mere challenges. They enthusiastically embrace life knowing that nothing ever stays the same and anything can happen. They have faith in their life's potential as long as they can express themselves. But if something occurs that triggers their fear of being shut in, they'll be afraid of lacking the oxygen they so desperately need.

For Ron, a young fifty-something, life just couldn't be better. In his view, there's always a solution to any problem. He loves taking a different route to work every day simply to break the routine. He's capable of belting out an aria at a birthday dinner or sharing an astronomically expensive bottle of wine to celebrate his first gray hair. In short, he's always smiling, happy, and optimistic. His infectious laugh is the one you hear most when he's out with his friends.

However, the purchase of a new house almost dampens his spirit for a time as he considers having to limit his spending. For buddhic personalities, counting each and every cent and sticking to a budget is a real constraint that could momentarily clip their wings. As long as Ron feels trapped by the situation and isn't able to breathe freely, he'll be preoccupied and uncommunicative. His good nature will resurface when he realizes that the situation isn't smothering him and he still has the space to express who he really is: a happy, unpretentious person who celebrates life each day by giving his very best at work and at play.

Moldavite is an ideal stone for Ron as it has a liberating effect. It could help him forget his money problems and restore his faith in life. What's more, it is useful in resolving problems that may at first seem insurmountable.

I think therefore I create

Buddhic personalities are sharp and quick-witted. Their heads are full of a thousand ideas that they scatter to the wind. They serve as catalysts that spur their coworkers on to greater efficiency. Each minute contains countless opportunities that could change a project's direction or importance.

> *All transformation happens at the right time ... not before!*
> D.D.D.

Laura's coworkers know that every time she schedules a meeting, she'll introduce a ton of new ideas to benefit the company. She lays out her plans, starts up new projects, remembers details that have been forgotten, and listens to everyone's suggestions to make sure everything's on target. Laura loves to see her team members working well together and encourages them to do so. When she speaks, she's eloquent, clear, and comprehensive; when her ideas flow faster than her words, she impatiently waves her hands. Laura sees these meetings as a chance to improve the company and expand its growth. Her coworkers see them as motivational sessions to which everyone has to contribute.

Amber would be an excellent stone for Laura. In addition to encouraging spontaneity, it can facilitate openness to suggestions from others, increase the creativity of team members, and spur them to action. Worn with amber, **moldavite** inspires spontaneous, creative ideas and helps solve unexpected problems.

Buddhic personalities' minds are always racing; they never stop. Fortunately, there are a few occasions when they're able to relax mentally, for instance when they're watching a good movie or reading an interesting book. Then peace and tranquility momentarily take over and they can recharge their batteries. They can daydream, thinking about enjoying a good bottle of wine or buying a new outfit for Christmas. No longer slaves to their thoughts, they let themselves be carried away. But this period of respite is often very brief. One thought inevitably leads to another that may seem to have no connection to what prompted them to relax in the first place. Everything is a source of inspiration, and rest is an illusion.

When in a positive mindset, the buddhics see themselves and life as follows:

- I'm spontaneous.

- Life is too wonderful to waste time being bored. Forget routine.

- I respect my own and others' space.

A BALANCED BUDDHIC PERSONALITY

One idea attracts another

People influenced by this alliance have limitless creative faculties. They are leaders who lead well and effectively, and visionaries who see everything. Tireless, they have no room for doubt because one idea follows another at lightning speed. Buddhic personalities are the ultimate catalysts who give momentum to a project. They surprise and energize everyone around them and create a climate where there's room for creativity to emerge.

Life offers us the present moment

Those living this lifestyle are comfortable with themselves and are friendly and at ease with people of all ages. As life companions, they don't take themselves too seriously and can always be counted on to surprise their partners. Once they're no longer afraid of commitment, they become loving, sparkle with life, and are loyal friends who understand others' needs.

AFFIRMATION[1]

"The harmonious hue of all that is Holy
hones me to simply Be, in Beauty."

STRENGTHS TO CULTIVATE[2]

May I empower myself with:

The creative consciousness
« *Mayamayi* »   OM AH HUM   JAH HUM BAH HOH   « *Mayamayi* »

Freedom from egoism or self-will
« *Nirahamkara* » OM AH HUM   AH HUM BAH HOH   « *Nirahamkara* »

Patience
« *Dama* »   OM AH HUM   JAH HUM BAH HOH   « *Dama* »

See "The Forty-five Great Empowerments of the Soul," page 173

MEDITATION

See "Circulation of the Light," page 163

---

[1] Karta, "Seven Studies."

[2] Sri Adi Dadi, *Spiritual Science of Essential Yoga,* Volume II.

INVOCATION[1]

So Be the Light in Our Life

From the Light of being in God
And the Light of being near God

To the Light of being of God
And the Light of being just God

And from the Light of always travelling
From God going to God within God

Do we stand as the Light,
Surrounded by the Light.

Do we stand as more Light
And more Light, and still, as more Light.

And blessed and protected
Are we by that Light,

As we give of the Light
With all of our might,

As we give of the Light
To all in our sight,

As we give of the Light
With all of God's right,

As we are in the Light
In God all a-Bright,

As we ask for the Light
And the Light and the Light,

And so be the Light in our Life.

D.D.D.

Buddhic stones

Best-known stones

amber: *sedimentary* (carbon-based fossil resin)

jet: *sedimentary* (silicon dioxide)

moldavite (tektite family): *metamorphic* (silicon dioxide and aluminum oxide)

obsidian: *magmatic* (volcanic rock containing silica)

opal: *sedimentary* (hydrated silicon dioxide)

fire opal: *magmatic* (hydrated silicon dioxide)

petrified wood: *sedimentary* (silicon dioxide)

tektite: *metamorphic* (silicon dioxide)

A number of buddhic stones contain silicon.

Silicon

Silicon generates well-being and inner warmth. It can be valuable in calming the emotions and providing the inner stability necessary for decision making. It can also make us more flexible and open-minded. Physically, it enhances collagen production and plays an important role in bone metabolism. It can help slow aging, regulate the nervous system, and even lower cholesterol.

amber

jet

moldavite

obsidian

opal

fire opal

petrified wood

tektite

Precious Companions to Sustain the Geometric Alliances

Stones, crystals, meditation, and visualization

Stones and crystals have been used in meditation throughout the ages to enhance the purification and internalization processes that constitute the first steps toward any expansion of consciousness. For example, placing a purple stone like amethyst or a blue stone like kyanite on the third eye promotes inner peace, quiets distracting thoughts, and calms the mind. Placing a pink stone like rose quartz or a green stone like aventurine on the heart chakra encourages unconditional love and helps heal emotional trauma.

If you aren't sure exactly where on your body or on which chakra you should place the stone or crystal you'll be using to meditate, you can simply hold it in your hands and let the energy clear a path to the parts of your being that need help and support. Stones and crystals can become true friends that can support us in our daily meditation. The secret lies in sincere, sustained effort.

The following pages describe a number of guided meditations that can be useful for specific geometric alliances. Stones associated with these alliances can be used as complementary tools to increase the efficacy of the meditation.

Stones and the asanas-mudras

The *asanas-mudras* are sacred gestures that allow the divine to enter our being. Each gesture brings powerful sustaining energy to both body and spirit, enabling us to overcome obstacles that prevent us from following our true path. Certain dynamic *asanas* (postures) *mudras* (gestures made with the hands that symbolize the power of a divinity within our subjective consciousness) can be considered active meditation.

Stones and crystals can be used to supplement the three asanas-mudras presented in this section to heighten the effectiveness of a meditative technique that is becoming increasingly popular in the Western world.

If possible, hold the stone or crystal in your hands. If not, it should be worn or placed near enough for its energy to penetrate your aura.

STONES AND THE RECITATION OF MANTRAS

Reciting a mantra, a sacred word or phrase that embodies divine energy, enables us to concentrate on a powerful word, a name of God. It can gradually calm our usually racing thoughts, creating inner silence. While most mantras come from Sanskrit, a language with a high power of vibration, they also exist in other languages such as Latin, Tibetan, Arabic (*dhikr* or prayer), and Japanese.

Here again, using a stone or a crystal helps refine our concentration so that we can more easily attain a state of peace and tranquility. Once we reach this state, where we are able to focus all our attention on the rhythmic energy of a name of God or a set of syllables invoking divine power, the mantra frees us from its grasp and leads us on a path of no return toward the awakening of consciousness. The mantra carries us forward, clearing a path in our energetic body, starting from our lips, passing through the heart and throat chakras, and ending up in the crown chakra.

Each chapter devoted to a specific geometric alliance sets out three strengths to be cultivated and indicates the mantras that can be used to help us develop the positive qualities associated with that alliance.

STONES, CRYSTALS, AND THE NEW SCIENCE OF INVOCATION

The power of invocation, this form of prayer accompanying the Age of Aquarius, resides in the ability of anyone who meditates, anywhere on the planet, to unite his or her consciousness with that of others. An altruistic group consciousness can then emerge, striving toward the common goals of love, compassion, and goodwill for all of humanity.

Through its conscious, purposeful syntax, the invocation calls on higher energies and other dimensions. It acts as a magnet that draws the light toward those reciting it, who then serves as "transmitters," diffusing these energies throughout their environment. Each practitioner can thus work creatively in the physical world by accepting the responsibility of becoming a Bearer of Light. It is therefore extremely important to free the consciousness from negative thoughts and criticism, to have an open heart, and to seek to create a sacred inner space where divine energies can enter and be preciously preserved.

An entire invocation may be said out loud or recited silently a number of times a day. It can also be broken down into key stanzas that we can focus on during the day and can accompany us anywhere we go. When the invocation is used properly, it will be possible to actively work toward the emergence of Light on Earth.

Note: Although specific invocations are suggested for each geometric alliance, they do not "belong" to a particular alliance, and readers are free to use them as they wish.

Meditations and Visualizations

Circulation of the Light

Purpose: To identify less and less with the weaknesses and dark side of our personality in order to be able to recognize and then transform them.

· Breathe very slowly and deeply.

· Feel the interdependence between your heartbeat and the rhythm of your breath.

· Focus your attention on a golden point in the center of your chest.

· Place the stone you have chosen at the level of the heart chakra or simply hold in your hands.

· Feel your heartbeats synchronize with the energy of the golden light circulating and expanding within you.

· Let the light spread throughout your body while remaining in harmony with the beating of your heart.

· When you feel the light everywhere within you, let it expand outside your body to fill the room, the building, the city, the country, the planet and the entire universe.

· You are now one with the universe; your heart is beating to the same rhythm.

· This light can release and reveal the hidden, and even the darkest, facets of your being.

· Observe these facets that are not "you."

· Let them dissolve in the brilliant golden light.

· You may continue to meditate with your stone or simply open your eyes.

The eye of the hurricane

Part 1

Purpose: To remain grounded in the Higher Self despite the many trials and tribulations of our lives.

This meditation can be performed while lying down.

- Place a blue stone at the level of the third eye.

- Connect to its stabilizing and soothing energy.

- Take a few minutes to center yourself and calm your thoughts.

- Now place the stone at the level of your heart and breathe deeply.

- Imagine a brilliant blue light in the center of your chest.

- Regulate your breathing through the abdomen and anchor yourself in the center of your chest.

- Imagine this center becoming brighter and stronger with each breath.

- Feel it gradually expand until it fills your body with a radiant blue light.

- Anchor yourself there in the light and become this light.

The eye of the hurricane

Part 2

· Now imagine that all your stress and problems have become a hurricane raging around you.

· Become the eye of this hurricane, strong, stable, and immobile in the center, surrounded and deeply penetrated by the blue light of your stone.

· You are the eye of the hurricane.

· You are surrounded by a whirlwind, but you remain immobile, centered, intact, alert, and aware.

· Hold this position for a few minutes; realize that you are not the hurricane and that this space within you remains accessible at all times.

· You may continue to meditate with your stone or simply open your eyes.

GREEN TARA

Purpose: To awaken our inner strength through the principle of the divine feminine within each of us.

- · Select a green stone and place it on the heart chakra or hold it in your hands.

- · Relax your body and clear your mind.

- · Breathe slowly and deeply.

- · Visualize the image of Green Tara and repeat the mantra:
  OM TARE TUTTARE TURE SVAHA.

- · Imagine a brilliant green light coming from Tara's heart.

- · Like magnificent incandescent ribbons, this light flows into your heart.

- · Let your being be filled with light and feel its healing protection all around you.

Who is Tara?

Tara is a very well-known goddess who is primarily worshiped in Asia; in the Tibetan form of Buddhism, she is called Drolma. Recognized as the "mother of all the Buddhas," she embodies wisdom and compassion. She has many aspects and many forms. The most common, White Tara and Green Tara, are briefly described below:

> **White Tara** represents purity, wisdom, and truth. She brings longevity, healing, health, strength, clarity, and understanding. White Tara has seven eyes; as well as the usual two, she has a third eye on her forehead and one on each hand and foot. Through these eyes she sees and feels the suffering and tears of those who ask for her help.

> **Green Tara** is believed to be a king's daughter who made a vow to continually be reincarnated in a woman's body. She achieved enlightenment and is now considered a female Buddha. Green Tara represents youth, beauty, and luminosity and offers protection against the eight great fears (attachment, avarice, anger, doubt, ignorance, wrong views, jealousy, and pride). She is known for her great compassion and power to heal all sensitive beings. Men, women, and children all ask for her protection and guidance.

MEDITATIONS AND ASANAS-MUDRAS[1]

Each of the following meditations and asanas-mudras may be applied to all the geometric alliances.

SPIRITUAL CURE FOR THE AURA

Purpose: To create a protective magnetic field within the aura, which will help balance the various external energies that may assail us, as well as give us strength and courage in the face of adversity. By increasing the circulation within the *ida* and *pingala*[2] channels, we lose less energy from our etheric field, and obsessive desires from our consciousness disappear.

Body position

Seated with your back straight, bend your left leg, and with your left hand press your knee against your chest, and put your right hand over your left; place your right ankle in front of your left, resting it atop your left foot.

MANTRA: "OM TAT SAT OM"

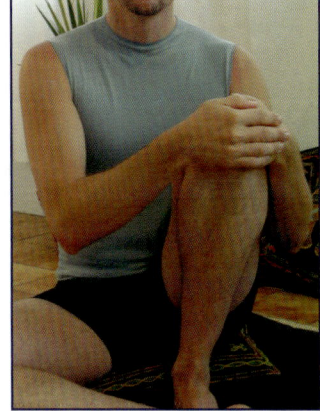

---

[1] Sri Adi Dadi, *The Spiritual Science of Essential Yoga: Techniques of Meditation, Mantrams and Invocations*, Volume I (Montreal: Paume de Saint-Germain Publishing, 2004).

[2] Ida and pingala, two key energy channels that carry the life principle (prana) to all the various parts of the body. Ida absorbs prana through the left nostril, pingala through the right. They correspond to the parasympathetic nervous system.

Procedure

- Take a moment to internalize by taking a deep breath.

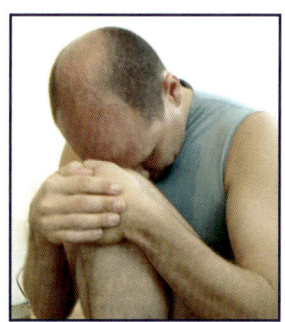

- Inhale and silently repeat the mantra "OM TAT SAT OM" in four counts, while slightly lowering your head until your forehead rests on your knee.

- Hold your breath for seven counts while silently repeating "OM TAT SAT OM TAT SAT OM."

- While in the same position, exhale and silently repeat "OM TAT SAT OM" in four counts, propelling the energy to the third eye. The head remains resting on the knee.

- Slowly raise your head while inhaling and exhaling once.

Repeat steps 1 to 5 eleven times, then change legs. In other words, bend the right leg, and place the left ankle in front of the right one, on top of the right foot. In this new position, repeat steps 1 to 5 eleven times. Eventually, this exercise could be repeated twenty-two or thirty-three times.

This exercise is very effective when it is done at sunset. If at times you experience a slight trembling in the hands or in one of your arms, move the opposite arm in a repetitive motion, as if you were hitting a ball with a tennis racquet. These movements can rebalance the energies. Crawling on all fours can also be a useful technique for regulating this mild discomfort.

"HAMSA" HEART MEDITATION—LOTUS MEDITATION

Purpose: To activate the heart chakra, which will awaken humility, compassion, and tenderness within.

Body position

Seated with your back straight, form a chalice or a lotus flower by joining your little fingers, thumbs, and wrists. The other fingers remain wide open. This hand formation should be placed about four inches from the heart region in front of the chest.

MANTRAS:
"HAM SA" or "OM MANI PADME HUM"

Procedure

· With your eyes open, fix your gaze on this hand position.

· Inhale and inwardly repeat, "HAM" or "OM MANI" while maintaining your gaze on your two thumbs.

· Exhale while inwardly repeating "SA" or "PADME HUM." Your attention is then focused on your thumbs as well as on the form of the chalice or lotus that you have created with your hands. You may feel a tingling sensation in your hands, which merely signifies that the energy is circulating well.

· The inhalations and exhalations should be long and profound.

· Allot as much time as you wish to this exercise.

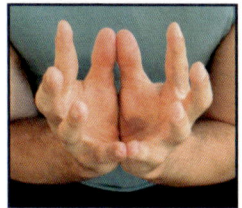

MEDITATION FOR CHANGE

Purpose: To teach us detachment from the desires of the ego, and how to yield to the Higher Self. By improving our inner communication and by analyzing ourselves, we view life and our patterns more objectively, which in turn diminishes doubt and resistance to change.

Body position

Seated with your back straight, close your fists, keeping the thumbs on the outside. Join the thumbs at the tips, and join the two middle fingers at the second joints. Point the thumbs toward the heart and press them against the chest. Place all of your attention on this point, keeping your eyes closed.

Procedure

· Simply inhale and exhale without a mantra. Be aware of your breathing and the point where your thumbs press against your chest.

· This exercise should be done for thirty-one minutes.

· Relax for five minutes.

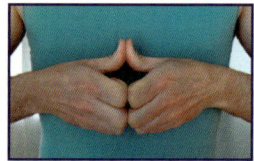

THE FORTY-FIVE GREAT EMPOWERMENTS OF THE SOUL[1]

Tibetan master Djwal Khul has said that the greatest gift we can bestow on humanity, and consequently promote its evolution, is mastery over our emotions. All serious spiritual teachings should therefore emphasize the purification of emotions, which are major obstacles to our progress on the Path and to the acquisition of the qualities inherent in the power of the soul.

This exercise is intended to complement the "Purification of the 31 Negative Qualities" presented in Volume I of Sri Adi Dadi's *The Spiritual Science of Essential Yoga*, designed to help liberate us from the gross negative vibrations that surround our being and prevent them from polluting our consciousness.

It is also inspired by Tibetan and Hindu teachings and will allow us to empower ourselves with inner strength and the powerful qualities of the soul. By using specific mantras, we can generate the energy associated with the quality invoked and then absorb it into our being.

In this exercise, the mantras should not be repeated automatically: all these mantric formulas release a powerful energy when they are used with a sincere and profound understanding. It is through the judicious combination of these powerful words, pronounced in a purposeful rhythm and order, that we can raise our consciousness by acquiring the powerful energy offered by the qualities of the soul.

---

[1] Sri Adi Dadi, *Spiritual Science of Essential Yoga*, Volume II.

Procedure

The exercise consists of three main steps:

Step I

With the first step, we identify the quality among the forty-five listed below with which we wish to be empowered.

Examples :

May I empower myself with courage: *DHAIRYA*
May I empower myself with strength: *BALA*
May I empower myself with fortitude: *SAHANA*

Step II

The purpose of this step is to empower us with the quality we have chosen through the use of a Sanskrit mantra that cleanses, increases, and kindles the quality or energy invoked.

Example :

OM AH HUM
(I) cleanse, increase, and kindle the quality or energy of courage.

Step III

With this third step, we use a mantra to assimilate the energy of the quality invoked and to help us summon, absorb, bind, and dissolve its power within our being.

Example :

JAH HUM BAH HOH *DHAIRYA*
(I) summon, absorb, bind and dissolve courage within me.

Note: Depending on your intention or your needs, you can select one quality a day and repeat the corresponding mantra throughout the day. You can also select a series of seven qualities and repeat the corresponding mantras every day for one week; you can then follow this with another series of seven the following week, until the assimilation of all the forty-five qualities has been invoked. As well, you can work on just one quality over a period of twenty-one consecutive days, the time necessary for a transformation to occur. It is up to you to decide on a suitable rhythm and adapt the exercise to your needs.

Summary of the above steps:

May I empower myself with courage (DHAIRYA):

OM AH HUM
(I) cleanse, increase and kindle its energy.

JAH HUM BAH HOH DHAIRYA
(I) summon, absorb, bind and dissolve courage within me.

The Forty-five Great Empowerments of the Soul

Invocation and quality to be invoked	Sanskrit term	The Empowerment Mantra			The Dissolving-within Mantra				
		Cleansing-increasing-kindling the quality or energy invoked			*I summon*	*absorb*	*bind*	*dissolve*	*within me:*
1. *May I empower myself with:* Courage Strength Fortitude	Dhairya Bala Sahana	OM OM OM	AH AH AH	HUM HUM HUM	JAH JAH JAH	HUM HUM HUM	BAH BAH BAH	HOH HOH HOH	Dhairya Bala Sahana
2. *May I empower myself with:* Sincerity Humility	Rjuthwam Amanithwam	OM OM	AH AH	HUM HUM	JAH JAH	HUM HUM	BAH BAH	HOH HOH	Rjuthwam Amanithwam
3. *May I empower myself with:* Purity Joy	Soucha Santosha	OM OM	AH AH	HUM HUM	JAH JAH	HUM HUM	BAH BAH	HOH HOH	Soucha Santosha
4. *May I empower myself with:* Truth Justice Goodness Beauty	Satyam Nayam Sivam Sundaram	OM OM OM OM	AH AH AH AH	HUM HUM HUM HUM	JAH JAH JAH JAH	HUM HUM HUM HUM	BAH BAH BAH BAH	HOH HOH HOH HOH	Satyam Nayam Sivam Sundaram
5. *May I empower myself with:* Patience Serenity Service Charity	Dama Sama Seva Dana	OM OM OM OM	AH AH AH AH	HUM HUM HUM HUM	JAH JAH JAH JAH	HUM HUM HUM HUM	BAH BAH BAH BAH	HOH HOH HOH HOH	Dama Sama Seva Dana
6. *May I empower myself with:* Virtue Righteous living	Sath-Seela Dharma	OM OM	AH AH	HUM HUM	JAH JAH	HUM HUM	BAH BAH	HOH HOH	Sath-Seela Dharma
7. *May I empower myself with:* Discrimination Detachment	Viveka Vairagya	OM OM	AH AH	HUM HUM	JAH JAH	HUM HUM	BAH BAH	HOH HOH	Viveka Vairagya
8. *May I empower myself with:* Effort Discipline (spiritual)	Srama Sadhana	OM OM	AH AH	HUM HUM	JAH JAH	HUM HUM	BAH BAH	HOH HOH	Srama Sadhana
9. *May I empower myself with:* Love Compassion Forgiveness	Prema Karuna Kshama	OM OM OM	AH AH AH	HUM HUM HUM	JAH JAH JAH	HUM HUM HUM	BAH BAH BAH	HOH HOH HOH	Prema Karuna Kshama

Invocation and quality to be invoked	Sanskrit term	The Empowerment Mantra			The Dissolving-within Mantra				
		Cleansing-increasing-kindling the quality or energy invoked			*I summon*	*absorb*	*bind*	*dissolve*	*within me:*
10. *May I empower myself with:* Single-mindedness	Dharana	OM	AH	HUM	JAH	HUM	BAH	HOH	Dharana
One-pointedness (in God)	Ekagrata	OM	AH	HUM	JAH	HUM	BAH	HOH	Ekagrata
11. *May I empower myself with:* Faith	Sraddha	OM	AH	HUM	JAH	HUM	BAH	HOH	Sraddha
Steadfastness	Tithiksha	OM	AH	HUM	JAH	HUM	BAH	HOH	Tithiksha
12. *May I empower myself with:* Sweet and gentle talk	Madhura Swara	OM	AH	HUM	JAH	HUM	BAH	HOH	Madhura Swara
Pleasant speech	Priya Vada	OM	AH	HUM	JAH	HUM	BAH	HOH	Priya Vada
Inspired speech	Vangmayi	OM	AH	HUM	JAH	HUM	BAH	HOH	Vangmayi
13. *May I empower myself with:* Repentance	Pascatha	OM	AH	HUM	JAH	HUM	BAH	HOH	Pascatha
Penance (discipline that purifies)	Thapa	OM	AH	HUM	JAH	HUM	BAH	HOH	Thapa
Renunciation (inner)	Sanyasa	OM	AH	HUM	JAH	HUM	BAH	HOH	Sanyasa
Sacrifice	Thyaga	OM	AH	HUM	JAH	HUM	BAH	HOH	Thyaga
14. *May I empower myself with:* The Witness	Atma Chaitanyam	OM	AH	HUM	JAH	HUM	BAH	HOH	Atma Chaitanyam
15. *May I empower myself with:* Auspiciousness	Srimayi	OM	AH	HUM	JAH	HUM	BAH	HOH	Srimayi
No worry	Chintama-nisiddhi	OM	AH	HUM	JAH	HUM	BAH	HOH	Chintama-nisiddhi
16. *May I empower myself with:* The killing of "I"	Hana ahamkara	OM	AH	HUM	JAH	HUM	BAH	HOH	Hana ahamkara
17. *May I empower myself with:* The equal breath	Prana-Apana-Samykta	OM	AH	HUM	JAH	HUM	BAH	HOH	Prana-Apana-Samykta
18. *May I empower myself with:* God's grace	Anugraha	OM	AH	HUM	JAH	HUM	BAH	HOH	Anugraha
Emptiness	Shunyata	OM	AH	HUM	JAH	HUM	BAH	HOH	Shunyata
19. *May I empower myself with:* Cheerfulness	Prasada	OM	AH	HUM	JAH	HUM	BAH	HOH	Prasada
Contentment	Tushti	OM	AH	HUM	JAH	HUM	BAH	HOH	Tushti

Invocation and quality to be invoked	Sanskrit term	The Empowerment Mantra			The Dissolving-within Mantra				
		Cleansing-increasing-kindling the quality or energy invoked			*I summon*	*absorb*	*bind*	*dissolve*	*within me:*
20. *May I empower myself with:* Physical nonviolence	Sharirik Ahimsa	OM	AH	HUM	JAH	HUM	BAH	HOH	Sharirik Ahimsa
Verbal nonviolence	Vacheka Ahimsa	OM	AH	HUM	JAH	HUM	BAH	HOH	Vacheka Ahimsa
Mental nonviolence	Manasika Ahimsa	OM	AH	HUM	JAH	HUM	BAH	HOH	Manasika Ahimsa
21. *May I empower myself with:* The gesture of humility	Namaste Mudra	OM	AH	HUM	JAH	HUM	BAH	HOH	Namaste Mudra
22. *May I empower myself with:* The power of spiritual action	Kriya-Sakti	OM	AH	HUM	JAH	HUM	BAH	HOH	Kriya-Sakti
The power of cocreation	Shiva-Shakti	OM	AH	HUM	JAH	HUM	BAH	HOH	Shiva-Shakti
23. *May I empower myself with:* Contemplation	Manana	OM	AH	HUM	JAH	HUM	BAH	HOH	Manana
Meditation	Dhyana	OM	AH	HUM	JAH	HUM	BAH	HOH	Dhyana
Concentration (intense upon the Lord)	Samdhya	OM	AH	HUM	JAH	HUM	BAH	HOH	Samdhya
24. *May I empower myself with:* Spiritual inquiry	Vichara	OM	AH	HUM	JAH	HUM	BAH	HOH	Vichara
Soul inquiry (the nature of the Self)	Atma Vichara	OM	AH	HUM	JAH	HUM	BAH	HOH	Atma Vichara
25. *May I empower myself with:* Inner silence	Mooka (Mouna)	OM	AH	HUM	JAH	HUM	BAH	HOH	Mooka (Mouna)
Inner solitude	Ekanthavasam	OM	AH	HUM	JAH	HUM	BAH	HOH	Ekanthavasam
26. *May I empower myself with:* Equanimity	Samatvam	OM	AH	HUM	JAH	HUM	BAH	HOH	Samatvam
Peace	Shanti	OM	AH	HUM	JAH	HUM	BAH	HOH	Shanti
Perfect peace (equal mind)	Samathwastithi	OM	AH	HUM	JAH	HUM	BAH	HOH	Samathwastithi
27. *May I empower myself with:* The inner light	Anta Jyothi	OM	AH	HUM	JAH	HUM	BAH	HOH	Anta Jyothi
The soul's light	Jivam [Atma]	OM	AH	HUM	JAH	HUM	BAH	HOH	Jivam [Atma]
The monad's light	Jyothi Svayamjyothi	OM	AH	HUM	JAH	HUM	BAH	HOH	Jyothi Svayamjyothi
28. *May I empower myself with:* The sun-self	Atma Surya	OM	AH	HUM	JAH	HUM	BAH	HOH	Atma Surya
Pure, eternal consciousness	Suddha Buddha	OM	AH	HUM	JAH	HUM	BAH	HOH	Suddha Buddha

Invocation and quality to be invoked	Sanskrit term	The Empowerment Mantra				The Dissolving-within Mantra				
		Cleansing-increasing-kindling the quality or energy invoked				*I summon*	*absorb*	*bind*	*dissolve*	*within me:*
29. *May I empower myself with:* The divine nature	Daivi Sampath	OM	AH	HUM		JAH	HUM	BAH	HOH	Daivi Sampath
The life of the soul	Atmadharma	OM	AH	HUM		JAH	HUM	BAH	HOH	Atmadharma
30. *May I empower myself with:* Desirelessness (for the joys of this and other worlds)	Ihautraphal-abhoga Vairaga	OM	AH	HUM		JAH	HUM	BAH	HOH	Ihautraphal-abhoga Vairaga
31. *May I empower myself with:* Desire for liberation (salvation)	Mumukshatva	OM	AH	HUM		JAH	HUM	BAH	HOH	Mumukshatva
32. *May I empower myself with:* -Remembering the name	Smarana	OM	AH	HUM		JAH	HUM	BAH	HOH	Smarana
-Repeating the name	Japam	OM	AH	HUM		JAH	HUM	BAH	HOH	Japam
-Fully aware, vigilant, alert—intense, mental recitation of the name	Manovaak-kaaya	OM	AH	HUM		JAH	HUM	BAH	HOH	Manovaak-kaaya
-Potent formulas (relating to God's spirit)	Mantram	OM	AH	HUM		JAH	HUM	BAH	HOH	Mantram
-Repeated concentration (in the heart) of the name and the form (of the Lord)	Namasmaran	OM	AH	HUM		JAH	HUM	BAH	HOH	Namasmaran
-The constant recollection (of the name) of Ram(a)	Ramanam	OM	AH	HUM		JAH	HUM	BAH	HOH	Ramanam
33. *May I empower myself with:* Spiritual listening	Sravana	OM	AH	HUM		JAH	HUM	BAH	HOH	Sravana
Spiritual pondering (deep thinking and reflection)	Manana	OM	AH	HUM		JAH	HUM	BAH	HOH	Manana
Spiritual practice (absorption and assimilation)	Nididhyasam	OM	AH	HUM		JAH	HUM	BAH	HOH	Nididhyasam
The whole of the above as one continuous process	Amnaya	OM	AH	HUM		JAH	HUM	BAH	HOH	Amnaya
34. *May I empower myself with:* Immorality (the nectar of)	Amritha	OM	AH	HUM		JAH	HUM	BAH	HOH	Amritha
Eternal delight	Nythyanan-damayi	OM	AH	HUM		JAH	HUM	BAH	HOH	Ithyanan-damayi
The bliss of being One, alone, without a second	Adwait-hananda	OM	AH	HUM		AH	HUM	BAH	HOH	Adwait-hananda

Invocation and quality to be invoked	Sanskrit term	The Empowerment Mantra				The Dissolving-within Mantra				
		Cleansing-increasing-kindling the quality or energy invoked				*I summon*	*absorb*	*bind*	*dissolve*	*within me:*
35. *May I empower myself with:* The experience of unity Direct realization (perception, knowing)	Ekathwam Sakshatkara	OM OM	AH AH		HUM HUM	JAH JAH	HUM HUM	BAH BAH	HOH HOH	Ekathwam Sakshatkara
36. *May I empower myself with:* The ceaseless sound current, music of God The very sound of God Itself The primal Om (everywhere present)	Anhad Bani Shabda Brahma Pravana and Omkar	OM OM OM	AH AH AH		HUM HUM HUM	JAH JAH JAH	HUM HUM HUM	BAH BAH BAH	HOH HOH HOH	Anhad Bani Shabda Brahma Pravana and Omkar
37. *May I empower myself with:* The soundless	Asabda	OM	AH		HUM	JAH	HUM	BAH	HOH	Asabda
38. *May I empower myself with:* Actionless action (effortless effort) (non-karmic deeds) Complete unending joy	Naishkarma Hrishikeya	OM OM	AH AH		HUM HUM	JAH JAH	HUM HUM	BAH BAH	HOH HOH	Naishkarma Hrishikeya
39. *May I empower myself with:* The nature of God (His essence) His splendor His sweetness His beauty His boundless mercy His infinite compassion	Swabhava Shoba Maadhurya Saundarya Mahadayal Mahakaruna	OM OM OM OM OM OM	AH AH AH AH AH AH		HUM HUM HUM HUM HUM HUM	JAH JAH JAH JAH JAH JAH	HUM HUM HUM HUM HUM HUM	BAH BAH BAH BAH BAH BAH	HOH HOH HOH HOH HOH HOH	Swabhava Shoba Maadhurya Saundarya Mahadayal Mahakaruna
40. *May I empower myself with:* Continuous wisdom Illumination	Sthitaprajana Thejas	OM OM	AH AH		HUM HUM	JAH JAH	HUM HUM	BAH BAH	HOH HOH	Sthitaprajana Thejas
41. *May I empower myself with:* Surrender to the Lord	Easwara-pranidhaana	OM	AH		HUM	JAH	HUM	BAH	HOH	Easwara-pranidhaana
42. *May I empower myself with:* Steady reverence (and worship) The voice of the teacher	Upasana Upadesh	OM OM	AH AH		HUM HUM	JAH JAH	HUM HUM	BAH BAH	HOH HOH	Upasana Upadesh

Invocation and quality to be invoked	Sanskrit term	The Empowerment Mantra			The Dissolving-within Mantra				
		Cleansing-increasing-kindling the quality or energy invoked			*I summon*	*absorb*	*bind*	*dissolve*	*within me:*
43. *May I empower myself with:*									
Freedom from jealousy	Anasya	OM	AH	HUM	JAH	HUM	BAH	HOH	Anasya
Effortless repetition of the holy name	Ajapajapam	OM	AH	HUM	JAH	HUM	BAH	HOH	Ajapajapam
That state beyond duality	Dwand-watitham	OM	AH	HUM	JAH	HUM	BAH	HOH	Dwand-watitham
44. *May I empower myself with:*									
An absence of desire (from objects)	Asakthi-Anaasakthi	OM	AH	HUM	JAH	HUM	BAH	HOH	Asakthi-Anaasakthi
The Lord as remover of obstacles and difficulties	Ganesha	OM	AH	HUM	JAH	HUM	BAH	HOH	Ganesha
The supreme consciousness	Swayamjyothi	OM	AH	HUM	JAH	HUM	BAH	HOH	Swayamjyothi
The Creative Consciousness	Mayamayi	OM	AH	HUM	JAH	HUM	BAH	HOH	Mayamayi
45. *May I empower myself with:*									
Freedom from egoism (or self-will)	Nirahamkara	OM	AH	HUM	AH	HUM	BAH	HOH	Nirahamkara
Being the eternal witness	Saakshib-hootam	OM	AH	HUM	JAH	HUM	BAH	HOH	Saakshib-hootam
A personal picture of God in my heart	Bhaavachitram	OM	AH	HUM	JAH	HUM	BAH	HOH	Bhaavachitram
Service to the spiritual teacher	Aachary-opasana	OM	AH	HUM	JAH	HUM	BAH	HOH	Aachary-opasana
Service to the Lord	Seva Sarveswara	OM	AH	HUM	JAH	HUM	BAH	HOH	Seva Sarveswara

Stone	Formation Process	Geometric Alliance	Classification	Composition
Agate	magmatic	trigonal (rhomboedric)	oxides (quartz group)	silicon dioxide
Alexandrite *(Variety of Chrysoberyl)*	metamorphic	rhombic (orthorhombic)	oxides (chrysoberyl family)	beryllium aluminum oxide
Amazonite	magmatic, metamorphic, sedimentary	triclinic	tectosilicates (feldspar family)	potassium aluminum silicate
Amber	sedimentary	buddhic	organic gems	carbon-based fossil resin
Amethyst	magmatic	trigonal (rhomboedric)	oxides (quartz group)	silicon dioxide, iron, manganese
Ametrine	magmatic	trigonal (rhomboedric)	oxides (quartz group)	silicon dioxide, iron, manganese
Andalusite	magmatic, metamorphic	rhombic (orthorhombic)	neosilicates (andalusite family)	aluminum silicate
Angel Aura Quartz	magmatic	trigonal (rhomboedric)	oxides (quartz group)	silicon dioxide artificially bonded with silver and platinum
Apatite	magmatic, metamorphic, sedimentary	hexagonal	phosphates	calcium phosphate with fluorine and chlorine
Apophyllite	magmatic	quadratic (tetragonal)	phyllosilicates	complex hydrous calcium potassium silicate containing fluorine
Aqua Aura Quartz	magmatic	trigonal (rhomboedric)	oxides (quartz group)	silicon dioxide artificially bonded with gold
Aquamarine	magmatic	hexagonal	cyclosilicates (beryl family)	beryllium aluminum silicate
Aragonite	magmatic, sedimentary	rhombic (orthorhombic)	carbonates	calcium carbonate
Aventurine	magmatic, metamorphic, sedimentary	trigonal (rhomboedric)	oxides (quartz group)	silicon dioxide
Azurite	sedimentary	monoclinic	carbonates	basic copper carbonate
Azurite-Malachite	sedimentary	monoclinic	carbonates	basic copper carbonate

Hardness	Chakra	Color	Purification, *Recharging*
6.5 to 7	according to color	blue, brown, yellow, red, green	cold water, saltwater, incense, earth *quartz cluster, sunlight*
8.5	solar plexus, heart, third eye, crown	violet in artificial light with emerald green reflections in sunlight	saltwater in low light, rinse in cold water, sunlight *quartz cluster, sunlight*
6 to 6.5	all, but mainly heart, throat, and third eye	blue green	cold water, incense, sunlight, earth *quartz cluster, sunlight (rapidly discharges)*
2 to 2.5	throat, solar plexus	milky white, light yellow to brown, black, red, green tones, and rarely blue	quartz cluster, incense, earth *quartz cluster*
7	crown, third eye	deep violet to pale lavender, almost to the point of being clear (crystals)	saltwater, cold water, incense, earth *quartz cluster, sunlight (for short periods only or it may lose its luster)*
7	solar plexus, third eye	yellow, violet	cold water, saltwater, incense, sunlight, earth *quartz cluster, sunlight*
7.5	heart, root, solar plexus	brown, gray, from green yellowish shades to green brown, red brown	cold water, saltwater, incense, sunlight, earth (rarely necessary) *quartz cluster, sunlight*
7	crown, chakras above the crown	pink, yellow, and blue iridescent reflections in clear base	cold water, saltwater, incense, sunlight, earth *quartz cluster, sunlight*
5	heart, throat, third eye	white, blue, brown, gray, yellow, purple, dark red, green, violet	cold water, incense, sunlight, earth *quartz cluster, sunlight*
4.5 to 5	heart, third eye, crown	white, yellowish, clear, blue green	cold water, incense, sunlight, earth *quartz cluster, sunlight*
7	throat, third eye	blue, from pale to dark	cold water, saltwater, incense, sunlight, earth *quartz cluster, sunlight*
7.5 to 8	crown, throat, third eye	green to clear blue	cold water, saltwater, incense, sunlight, earth *quartz cluster, sunlight*
3.5 to 4	according to color	white, blue, yellow, golden, yellow, brownish red, green, greenish brown	cold water, incense, abundant sunlight, earth *quartz cluster, sunlight*
7	heart	iridescent green	cold water, saltwater, incense, sunlight, earth *quartz cluster, sunlight*
3.5 to 4	throat, third eye	deep blue	cold water, incense, moonlight, earth *quartz cluster, moonlight, limited sunlight*
3.5 to 4	throat	deep blue, green, black	cold water, incense, earth *quartz cluster, limited sunlight*

Stone	Formation Process	Geometric Alliance	Classification	Composition
Barite *Barytine*	magmatic, sedimentary	rhombic (orthorhombic)	sulfates	barium sulfate
Beryl	magmatic	hexagonal	cyclosilicates (beryl family)	beryllium aluminum silicate
Boji	sedimentary	cubic	sulfides	iron sulfide
Bull's eye	sedimentary	trigonal (rhomboedric)	oxides	silicon dioxide
Calcite	magmatic, sedimentary	trigonal (rhomboedric)	carbonates	calcium carbonate
Carnelian	magmatic	trigonal (rhomboedric)	oxides (quartz group)	silicon dioxide, iron
Cat's Eye *Cymophane*	magmatic, metamorphic	rhombic (orthorhombic)	oxides (chrysoberyl family)	beryllium aluminate
Celestite	sedimentary	rhombic (orthorhombic)	sulfates	strontium sulfate
Chalcedony	magmatic, sedimentary	trigonal (rhomboedric)	oxides (quartz group)	silicon dioxide
Chalcopyrite	magmatic, metamorphic, sedimentary	quadratic (tetragonal)	sulfides	copper iron sulfide
Charoite	metamorphic	monoclinic	phyllosilicates	hydrated potassium sodium calcium silicate
Chiastolite	metamorphic	rhombic (orthorhombic)	neosilicates	aluminum silicate with carbon inclusions
Chrysoberyl	magmatic, metamorphic	rhombic (orthorhombic)	oxides	beryllium aluminum oxide
Chrysocolla	sedimentary	rmonoclinic	cyclosilicates	hydrated copper silicate
Chrysoprase	sedimentary	trigonal (rhomboedric)	oxides	silicon dioxide
Citrine	magmatic	trigonal (rhomboedric)	oxides (quartz group)	silicon dioxide
Danburite	magmatic	rhombic (orthorhombic)	tectosilicates	calcium boron silicate

Hardness	Chakra	Color	Purification, *Recharging*
3 to 3.5	crown	colorless, white, pale yellow	incense, sunlight, avoid water *quartz cluster, abundant sunlight*
7.5 to 8	from the root to the crown according to colors	gold (heliodor), green, pink (morganite), red (bixbite), transparent (goshenite), yellow	cold water, saltwater, incense, sunlight, earth (rarely necessary) *quartz cluster, regular sunlight*
7.5	throat, third eye	brown to black	incense, earth *quartz cluster, limited sunlight*
7	solar plexus, root	shimmering nuances of red and reddish brown	quartz cluster, cold water, saltwater, incense, sunlight, earth *quartz cluster, sunlight*
3	according to color	almost all colors	cold water, incense, sunlight, earth *quartz cluster, sunlight*
6.5 to 7	hara, root	brownish orange, brownish red, orange, red	cold water, saltwater, incense, sunlight, earth *quartz cluster, abundant sunlight*
8.5	heart, solar plexus	brownish green to yellow with a light iridescent stripe on the surface that moves according to the direction of light	cold water, saltwater, incense, moonlight, sunlight, earth *quartz cluster, moonlight, sunlight*
3 to 3.5	heart, throat	white, blue, yellow, red, reddish brown	cold water, incense, earth *quartz cluster*
6.5 to 7	according to color	great variety of colors	cold water and saltwater in moderation (chalcedony is a porous stone), incense, sunlight, earth *quartz cluster, sunlight*
3.5 to 4	crown, third eye	golden metallic sheen, sometimes with orange nuances and multicolored iridescence on the surface	cold water, incense, sunlight, earth *quartz cluster, abundant sunlight*
5 to 6	third eye	violet purple scattered with white and deep violet	cold water, incense, moonlight, earth *quartz cluster, moonlight*
6.5 to 7.5	heart, solar plexus, root	brown, gray, yellowish green, pink with black cruciform inclusions	saltwater, incense *quartz cluster, sunlight*
8.5	solar plexus	yellow to brownish green	saltwater, cold water, incense, earth, sunlight *quartz cluster, abundant sunlight*
2.5	heart, throat, hara, solar plexus, third eye	blue turquoise, green	cold water, incense, sunlight, earth *quartz cluster, sunlight*
6.5 to 7	heart, solar plexus	lemon, clear green to deep green, apple green	cold water, saltwater, incense, abundant sunlight, earth *quartz cluster, sunlight*
7	solar plexus	yellow	cold water, saltwater, incense, sunlight, earth *quartz cluster, sunlight*
7 to 7.5	heart, crown	light blue, translucent gold, colorless, pale pink	cold water, incense, early morning sunlight, earth *quartz cluster, early morning sunlight*

Stone	Formation Process	Geometric Alliance	Classification	Composition
Diamond	metamorphic	cubic	native elements	carbon
Dioptase	sedimentary	trigonal (rhomboedric)	neosilicates	hydrated copper silicate
Emerald	magmatic, metamorphic	hexagonal	cyclosilicates (beryl family)	beryllium aluminum silicate
Epidote	magmatic, metamorphic	monoclinic	sorosilicates	structurally complex calcium aluminum iron silicate hydroxide
Faden Quartz	magmatic	trigonal (rhomboedric)	oxides (quartz group)	silicon dioxide
Fire Opal	magmatic	buddhic	oxides	hydrated silicon dioxide
Fluorite Fluorine	magmatic	cubic	halides	calcium fluoride
Garnet	metamorphic	cubic	neosilicates	aluminum, calcium iron silicate
Gem Silica	sedimentary	monoclinic	cyclosilicates	hydrated copper silicate and silicium oxide
Graphite	metamorphic	hexagonal	native elements	carbon
Halite	sedimentary	cubic	halides	sodium chloride
Hawk Eye	magmatic	trigonal (rhomboedric)	oxides	silicon dioxide
Hematite	magmatic metamorphic	trigonal (rhomboedric)	oxides	iron oxide
Herkimer Diamond	magmatic	trigonal (rhomboedric)	oxides	silicon dioxide
Howlite	sedimentary	monoclinic	neosilicates	calcium borosilicate hydroxide
Iolite	magmatic	rhombic (orthorhombic)	cyclosilicates	magnesium aluminum silicate

Hardness	Chakra	Color	Purification, *Recharging*
10	crown, third eye	light blue, colorless, from yellow to brown, black, light pink, rarely green	cold water, saltwater, incense, sunlight, earth *quartz cluster, sunlight*
5	heart	dark blue, emerald green	cold water, saltwater, incense, sunlight, earth (required before each treatment) *quartz cluster, sunlight*
7.5 to 8	heart	from yellowish green to blue green	cold water, incense, sunlight, earth (rarely needed as emerald absorbs very little negative energy) *sunlight*
6 to 7	heart, solar plexus	green	cold water, saltwater, incense, sunlight, earth *quartz cluster, sunlight*
7	all	clear with a fine white line running through it	cold water, saltwater, incense, sunlight, earth *quartz cluster, sunlight*
5.5 to 6.5	hara, root	yellow orange to fluorescent orange red	quartz cluster, abundant water, incense, moonlight, sunlight, earth, no salt *quartz cluster, water, moonlight, sunlight*
4	according to color	all the colors of the spectrum	cold water, incense, sunlight, earth. Fluorite should be cleansed after each use. *quartz cluster, sunlight*
6.5 to 7.5	according to color	brown, yellow, black, orange, pink, red, green, and sometimes purplish	cold water, saltwater, incense, sunlight, earth (recommended before or after each use) *quartz cluster, sunlight*
6 to 7	heart, throat, third eye	blue, turquoise, translucent green	cold water, incense, sunlight, earth *rarely required—incense and quartz cluster at the user's discretion (crystals)*
1.5 to 2	throat, root	metallic light gray to black	incense *quartz cluster, candle flame*
2 to 2.5	all (according to color)	white, blue, clear, gray, yellow, purple, black, pink, red violet	not required since halite does not absorb negative energies; contact with water must be avoided to prevent disintegration *sunlight*
7	throat, third eye	shimmering nuances of blue gray and green gray blue	cold water, saltwater, incense, moonlight, sunlight, earth *quartz cluster, moonlight, sunlight*
5 to 6	root	metallic gray	cold water, incense, sunlight, earth *quartz cluster, sunlight*
7	all	colorless, sometimes with inclusions of rutile, silicate, etc.	saltwater, rinse under running water, must be cleansed after each use that requires it to be reprogrammed *quartz cluster, abundance of morning sunlight*
3.5	third eye	white, blue, green	water, incense, earth *quartz cluster , limited sunlight*
7 to 7.5	third eye	blue, yellow, gray, violet	quartz cluster, cold water, saltwater, incense, abundant sunlight, earth *quartz cluster, abundant sunlight*

Stone	Formation Process	Geometric Alliance	Classification	Composition
Jade	metamorphic	monoclinic	inosilicates	basic calcium magnesium iron silicate
Jasper	sedimentary	trigonal (rhomboedric)	oxides (quartz group)	silicon dioxide
Jet	sedimentary	buddhic	organic gemstones	silicon dioxide
Kunzite	magmatic	monoclinic	inosilicates (spodumene family)	lithium aluminum silicate
Kyanite *Cyanite, Disthene*	metamorphic	triclinic	neosilicates	aluminum silicate
Labradorite *Spectrolite*	magmatic	triclinic	tectosilicates (feldspar family)	aluminum calcium silicate
Lapis Lazuli	metamorphic	cubic	tectosilicates	sodium aluminum silicate with sulfur and chlorine
Larimar *Pectolite, Dolphin Stone*	magmatic	triclinic	inosilicates	complex sodium calcium silicate
Lepidolite	magmatic	monoclinic	phyllosilicates (mica group)	potassium lithium aluminum silicate fluoride hydroxide
Magnesite	sedimentary, rarely magmatic	trigonal (rhomboedric)	carbonates	magnesium carbonate
Magnetite	magmatic, metamorphic	cubic	oxides	magnetic iron oxide
Malachite	sedimentary	monoclinic	carbonates	basic copper carbonate
Marcasite	magmatic, sedimentary	rhombic (orthorhombic)	sulfides	iron disulfide
Moldavite *Tektite Family*	metamorphic	buddhic	oxides	silicon dioxide and aluminum oxide
Moonstone	magmatic	monoclinic	tectosilicates (feldspar family)	potassium aluminum silicate
Obsidian	magmatic	buddhic	oxides	volcanic rock containing silica

Hardness	Chakra	Color	Purification, *Recharging*
6.5 to 7	heart	white, beige brown, red brown, green, purple blue, black	cold water, saltwater, incense, sunlight, earth *quartz cluster, sunlight*
6.5 to 7	according to color	brown, yellow, black, red, green.	cold water, saltwater, incense, sunlight, earth *quartz cluster, sunlight*
2.5 to 4	root	black	quartz cluster, cold water, incense, moonlight, earth *quartz cluster, moonlight*
6 to 7	heart, throat, third eye	clear, gray, green, pink violet, purple, yellow	cold water, saltwater, incense (requires little purification) *quartz cluster, no sunlight*
4 to 5 in length; 7 in width	throat, third eye	blue and white, gray, yellow, black, pink, green	cold water, incense, moonlight, earth *quartz cluster, moonlight*
6 to 6.5	all	grayish to black, with slight blue, green, red, and yellow reflections	cold water, saltwater, incense, early morning sunlight, earth *quartz cluster, abundant sunlight, early morning sunlight*
5 to 6	throat, third eye	blue stippled with white, with pyrite inclusions	cold water, incense, moonlight, sunlight, earth *quartz cluster, moonlight, sunlight*
4.5 to 5	heart, crown, throat, third eye	blue, gray, or red with white, green blue	cold water, incense, sunlight, earth *quartz cluster, sunlight*
2.5 to 3	heart, third eye	pink to violet pink, with pearly and translucent luster	cold water, saltwater, incense, minimal sunlight, earth; should be purified after each use *quartz cluster, limited amount of sunlight*
4 to 4.5	heart, third eye, crown	creamy white	cold water, saltwater, sunlight, earth *quartz cluster, sunlight*
5.5	root	black metallic, matte	cold water (avoid salt), sunlight, earth *quartz cluster, sunlight*
4	heart, solar plexus	green with black	cold water, incense, sunlight, earth; avoid using salt, which could damage the stone's surface *quartz cluster, sunlight, olive oil (very absorbent, must be cleansed after each use)*
6 to 6.5	solar plexus	pale greenish yellow	cold water, incense, earth, sunlight *quartz cluster, sunlight*
5.5	heart, crown, throat, third eye	green	quartz cluster, cold water, incense, moonlight, sunlight, earth *quartz cluster, moonlight, sunlight*
6 to 6.5	crown, third eye	of the rainbow, gray, peach, white	cold water, saltwater, incense, moonlight, sunlight, earth *quartz cluster, abundant sunlight and moonlight*
5 to 5.5	root	brown, black, glints of silver, gold, or multicolored	quartz cluster, cold water, incense, moonlight, sunlight, earth *quartz cluster, moonlight, sunlight*

Stone	Formation Process	Geometric Alliance	Classification	Composition
Onyx	magmatic	trigonal (rhomboedric)	oxides	silicon dioxide
Opal	sedimentary	buddhic	oxides	hydrated silicon dioxide
Peridot *Olivine, Chrysolite*	magmatic	rhombic (orthorhombic)	neosilicates	iron magnesium silicate
Petrified Wood *Xyloid*	sedimentary	trigonal (rhomboedric) or buddhic	oxides	silicon dioxide
Phenacite	magmatic	trigonal (rhomboedric)	neosilicates	beryllium silicate
Pietersite *Tempest Stone*	sedimentary	trigonal (rhomboedric)	oxides	silicon dioxide
Prehnite	magmatic	rhombic (orthorhombic)	sorosilicates	calcium aluminum silicate
Pyrite	magmatic, metamorphic, sedimentary	cubic	sulfides	iron disulfide
Rhodochrosite	sedimentary	trigonal (rhomboedric)	carbonates	manganese carbonate
Rhodonite	metamorphic	triclinic	inosilicates	manganese iron magnesium calcium silicate
Rose Quartz	magmatic	trigonal (rhomboedric)	oxides (quartz group)	silicon dioxide and manganese
Ruby	magmatic, metamorphic	trigonal (rhomboedric)	oxides (corundum family)	aluminum oxide and chrome
Rutilated Quartz *Venus Hair*	magmatic	trigonal (rhomboedric)	oxides (quartz group)	silicon dioxide with titanium oxide
Rutile	magmatic	quadratic (tetragonal)	oxides	titanium oxide
Sapphire	magmatic, metamorphic	trigonal (rhomboedric)	oxides (corundum family)	aluminum oxide, titanium, iron
Sardonyx	magmatic	trigonal (rhomboedric)	oxides (quartz group)	silicon dioxide and iron

Hardness	Chakra	Color	Purification, *Recharging*
6.5 to 7	root	black	cold water, saltwater, incense, sunlight, earth *quartz cluster, moonlight, sunlight*
5.5 to 6.5	according to type	according to type	quartz cluster, abundant water, no salt, incense, moonlight, sunlight, earth *quartz cluster, water, moonlight, sunlight, olive oil*
6.5 to 7	heart, solar plexus	from pale green to yellowish green to olive green	cold water, saltwater, incense, sunlight, earth (rarely necessary as peridot is very resistant to negative energies) *quartz cluster, sunlight*
7	solar plexus, root	brown, yellow, reddish	water, incense, sunlight, earth *quartz cluster, abundant sunlight*
7.5 to 8	heart, crown, solar plexus, third eye	colorless, very pale yellow, very pale pink	cold water, saltwater, incense, sunlight, earth *quartz cluster, sunlight*
7	heart, throat, solar plexus, third eye	golden brown to blue gray with black traces	cold water, distilled saltwater, incense, moonlight, sunlight, earth *quartz cluster, moonlight, sunlight*
6 to 6.5	heart, solar plexus, third eye	light green to yellowish green	cold water, incense, sunlight, earth *quartz cluster, sunlight*
6 to 6.5	third eye, solar plexus	golden yellow	cold water, incense, sunlight, earth *quartz cluster, sunlight*
4	heart, solar plexus	from pale to bright pink, in irregular layers, often with white or pale gray bands; may be orange or dark orange red if it is gem quality	cold water, incense, sunlight, earth; frequent purification is recommended. *quartz cluster, sunlight*
5.5 to 6.5	heart	pink, red with mottled black	cold water, saltwater, incense, sunlight, earth *quartz cluster, sunlight*
7	heart	pale pink to dark pink	cold water, saltwater, incense, sunlight, earth *quartz cluster, sunlight*
9	root	red	cold water, saltwater, incense, sunlight, earth *quartz cluster, abundant sunlight*
7	gold at the crown, copper or red at the root and the solar plexus	light with copper-red or gold fibers	cold water, saltwater, incense, sunlight, earth *quartz cluster, sunlight*
6 to 6.5	crown, root	dark gray with metallic shine, generally gilded and occasionally orange red	cold water, saltwater, incense, sunlight, earth *quartz cluster, abundant sunlight*
9	throat, third eye	blue, colorless, yellow, black	cold water, saltwater, incense, moonlight, earth *quartz cluster, moonlight*
6 to 7	root	light orange to dark orange	cold water, saltwater, incense, sunlight, earth *quartz cluster, sunlight*

Stone	Formation Process	Geometric Alliance	Classification	Composition
Selenite	sedimentary	monoclinic	sulfates	hydrated calcium sulfate
Seraphinite	metamorphic, sedimentary	monoclinic	neosilicates (aluminum silicate)	magnesium iron aluminum silicate hydroxide
Serpentine	metamorphic	monoclinic	phyllosilicates	basic magnesium silicate
Smithsonite *Bonamite*	sedimentary	trigonal (rhomboedric)	carbonates	zinc carbonate
Smoky Quartz	magmatic	trigonal (rhomboedric)	oxides (quartz group)	silicon dioxide
Sodalite	magmatic	cubic	tectosilicates	sodium aluminum silicate with chlorine
Stibnite	magmatic	rhombic (orthorhombic)	sulfides	antimony sulfide
Sugilite *Luvulite or Royal Azel*	magmatic	hexagonal	cyclosilicates	potassium sodium lithium iron manganese aluminum
Sulfur	magmatic, sedimentary	rhombic (orthorhombic)	native elements	pure sulfur
Sunstone	magmatic	triclinic	tectosilicates (feldspar family)	sodium calcium aluminum silicate
Tanzanite *Blue Zoisite*	metamorphic	rhombic (orthorhombic)	sorosilicates	calcium aluminum silicate with strontium
Tektite	metamorphic	buddhic	oxides	silicon dioxide
Tiger Eye	sedimentary	trigonal (rhomboedric)	oxides	silicon dioxide
Tiger Iron *Tigerite*	metamorphic	trigonal (rhomboedric)	oxides	silicon dioxide and iron
Topaz	magmatic	rhombic	neosilicates	aluminum silicate
Tourmaline	magmatic	trigonal (rhomboedric)	cyclosilicates	complex silicate of boron, sodium, aluminum, iron, magnesium, calcium—varies according to color

Hardness	Chakra	Color	Purification, *Recharging*
2	according to color	beige, brown white, pink, transparent (rare gem quality), greenish	incense, abundant sunlight, avoid water and salt *quartz cluster, abundant sunlight (frequently)*
4	all	green with a silver gleam, occasionally white, brown, yellow, red	quartz cluster, green clay, cold water, sunlight, earth *quartz cluster, sunlight*
2.5 to 4	heart, throat	pale green to yellowish green	cold water, incense, earth *quartz cluster, avoid sunlight*
5	according to color	white to gray, lavender, purple, pink, green to blue, brown, yellow	cold water, earth, no salt *moonlight*
7	root	brown to black	cold water, saltwater, incense, sunlight, earth *quartz cluster, sunlight*
5.5 to 6	throat, third eye	blue with black and white inclusions	cold water, incense, moonlight, earth *quartz cluster, moonlight*
2	root	metallic gray	incense *quartz cluster, moonlight*
6.5 to 7	all	black, violet, translucent	cold water, saltwater, incense, sunlight, earth *quartz cluster, sunlight*
1.5 to 2	solar plexus	bright yellow, sometimes slightly brownish or brownish green	incense, sunlight *quartz cluster, sunlight*
6 to 6.5	throat, hara, solar plexus, root	brown, yellow orange, peach, pink, red with shimmering inclusions of goethite or hematite	cold water, incense, sunlight, earth *quartz cluster, sunlight*
6.5 to 7	throat, third eye, crown	indigo, purplish blue, bluish violet	saltwater *quartz cluster, limited sunlight, abundant moonlight*
5 to 5.5	root	black, brown black	quartz cluster, cold water, incense, sunlight, earth *quartz cluster, sunlight*
7	hara, solar plexus, root	shimmering nuances of golden yellow and brown	cold water, saltwater, incense, sunlight, earth *quartz cluster, sunlight*
7	hara, solar plexus, root	layered aggregates of red jasper, black, and metallic gray iron oxides (magnetite, hematite) and golden brown tiger eye	quartz cluster, cold water, avoid salt unless the stone has been polluted by a highly negative energy, incense, moonlight, sunlight, earth *quartz cluster, moonlight, sunlight*
8	heart, crown, throat, third eye	blue, clear brown, golden yellow, reddish pink, green	cold water, saltwater, incense, sunlight, earth *quartz cluster, abundant sunlight*
7 to 7.5	according to color	blue, yellow, black, pink green	cold water, saltwater, incense, sunlight, earth *quartz cluster, sunlight*

Stone	Formation Process	Geometric Alliance	Classification	Composition
Turquoise	sedimentary	triclinic	phosphates	hydrated copper aluminum phosphate containing iron
Vanadinite	sedimentary	hexagonal	ph./vanadates	vanadium oxide and lead chloride
Variscite *Utahite*	sedimentary	rhombic (orthorhombic)	phosphates	hydrated aluminum phosphate with iron
Vesuvianite *Idocrase*	metamorphic	quadratic (tetragonal)	sorosilicates	complex calcium magnesium iron aluminum silicate
Wulfenite	sedimentary	quadratic (tetragonal)	sulfur/molybdate	lead molybdate
Zincite	metamorphic	hexagonal	oxides	zinc oxide
Zircon	magmatic	quadratic (tetragonal)	neosilicates	zirconium silicate
Zoizite	metamorphic	rhombic (orthorhombic)	sorosilicates	calcium aluminum silicate

Hardness	Chakra	Color	Purification, *Recharging*
5 to 6	all, although mainly the heart, throat, hara, solar plexus, and third eye	blue, turquoise, green	cold water, incense, earth *quartz cluster, limited amount of sunlight*
3	hara, solar plexus, root	reddish brown, orange brown, chestnut brown, light brown	incense *quartz cluster, avoid sunlight, moonlight*
4 to 5	heart, throat	colorless, green, gray	cold water, no salt *quartz cluster, sunlight*
6.5 to 7	hara, solar plexus	ocher olive green to orange brown	cold water, incense, sunlight, earth *quartz cluster, abundant sunlight*
3	hara, solar plexus	from honey yellow to orange yellow, vermilion red	cold water, incense, sunlight, earth *quartz cluster, abundant sunlight*
4	hara, solar plexus, root	red, reddish brown, orange yellow, green, translucent	distilled saltwater, cold water, saltwater, incense, moonlight, sunlight *quartz cluster, moonlight, sunlight*
7.5	hara, third eye	clear, blue, brown, yellow orange, red	cold water, saltwater, incense, sunlight, earth quartz cluster, sunlight
6.5 to 7	heart, root, third eye	green or brownish green with red (ruby)	cold water, incense, sunlight, earth *quartz cluster, sunlight*

CATEGORIES OF MINERALOGICAL CLASSIFICATIONS AND THEIR PROPERTIES

Mineralogical Classifications	Nonmetals	Properties
I. Native elements	Consists of a single element	Metals: gold, silver, copper; nonmetals: diamond, sulfur. These metals have the ability to resist any influence. They help us recognize what will help or harm us.
II. Sulfides	Sulfur	Opaque, metal, mirrorlike sheen. Sulfurs are merciless mirrors of what is hidden, shedding light on the darker aspects of our nature.
III. Halides	Fluorine, chlorine, bromine, iodine	Halos gene: salt-forming. When combined with hydrogen, they form hydrofluoric acid (HF) et hydrochloric acid (HCl), both particularly aggressive acids that form transparent minerals when they come in contact with metals. Halides have a dissolving effect and can help us break away from ties that bind us.
IV. Oxides	Oxygen	Oxys genes: acid-forming. They can occur wherever there is oxygen. Oxides transform and restore stability. They also help us with all the unfinished business in our lives.
V. Carbonates	Carbonic acid	Carbo: coal. Carbonic acid is an unstable compound of liquid and gas. Firmer and more stable compounds are only formed when carbonic acid reacts with metals. Carbonates are seldom stable and tend to be altered by new influences. Carbonates affect developmental processes, stabilizing us and guiding us toward permanent change.
VI. Sulfates	Sulfuric acid	Sulfur: sulfur. Sulfuric acid is a dense liquid that is a compound of water and sulfur trioxide. Its compounds are very stable and persistent. Sulfates can insulate us and shield us from outside influences. They can temporarily slow down the development process, allowing us a period of rest.
VII. Phosphates	Phosphoric acid	Phosphorus: light-bearing. Phosphorous carries energy in our bodies. It has a buffering action that can help neutralize acids and alkalis. Phosphates promote balance and mobilize energy reserves. They have a stabilizing effect on our health and mood.

Mineralogical Classifications	Nonmetals	Properties
VIII. Silicates	Silicic acid	1. **Neosilicates** are composed of individual silicate molecules. The way they are structured produces compact, high-density minerals. Neosilicates strengthen resistance. They reinforce individuality, stabilize our health, and help us remain true to our convictions in crises. 2. **Sorosilicates** are composed of silicate molecules usually bound together in pairs or groups of four. Sorosilicates stimulate regenerative faculties, assist in recovery after an illness, and enable us to rediscover our basic goals and intentions. They provide excellent support when we face a new beginning. 3. **Cyclosilicates** are ring silicates stacked to form columns. Depending on how they are arranged, they can also form sponge-like structures that result in opaque minerals. Cyclosilicates direct and conduct the flow of energy when levels are too high or too low. Those with a column-like structure have a stimulating effect. Those with a sponge-like structure have a calming effect and can relieve fevers or reduce heat and pain. 4. **Inosilicates** are composed of long chains of silicate. They stimulate energy flows and accelerate healing and developmental processes. They help balance energy in the organism, stabilizing the emotions and improving mental agility. 5. **Phyllosilicates** consist of sheets of silicate that may be easily separated but are hard to cut. Phyllosilicates shield us from outside energy forms and help us better define who we are. 6. **Tectosilicates** are made up of a three dimensional framework that usually includes other substances. They act as filters that have an absorbing effect. They also have a calming influence and can relieve fevers and reduce heat and pain. They also help us view the world from a new perspective and broaden our horizons.

STONE PROPERTIES
AND THEIR GEOMETRIC ALLIANCES

STONES OF THE CUBIC ALLIANCE

BOJI STONES

Geometric alliance: cubic
Colors: brown to black
Chakras: throat, third eye
Hardness: 7.5
Origin: United States
Formation Process: sedimentary
Purification: incense, earth
Recharging: quartz cluster, limited sunlight

Generalities

Boji stones can disintegrate if left on the ground or in the open air. Although they come as a pair, they should always be kept apart, as regular contact will also cause them to eventually disintegrate. The energy of the smooth stone is feminine while that of the rougher stone is masculine.

Lithotherapy

- Grounds and protects
- Supports people who feel uncomfortable in their present incarnation
- Favors a smooth return to the earth plane and within the body
- Helps to confront the darker side of the personality and instill a calm and inner harmony
- Helps to overcome obsessions and patterns by making them more evident
- Balances and harmonizes masculine and feminine energies
- Increases energy and aligns the chakras and subtle bodies
- Sharpens the vision and intellect and helps to see what is fair and natural
- Releases repressed emotions and heals painful memories
- Repairs auric holes and replenishes lost energy

- Stimulates and regularizes the circulation of energy throughout the meridians
- Relieves pain and favors tissue regeneration
- Increases physical energy as needed
- Has a preventive effect against disease in general
- Less suitable to relieve very acute pain

A pair of boji stones can be held in the hands for ten to thirty minutes. They can also be placed near the area on the body to be treated. One can be placed at the head and the other at the feet for a balancing, energizing, and grounding effect.

DIAMOND

Geometric alliance: cubic
Colors: black, colorless, from yellow to brown, light blue, light pink, rarely green
Chakras: crown, third eye
Hardness: 10
Origin: Australia, Brazil, Russia, South Africa
Formation Process: metamorphic
Purification: cold water, saltwater, incense, sunlight, earth
Recharging: quartz cluster, sunlight

Generalities

The name "diamond" comes from the Greek word *adamas*, which means "invincible." It symbolizes force, courage, and immunity. A particularly powerful stone, the diamond can accentuate our qualities as much as our faults. Hence this stone should be used with caution and with full awareness of its capacity. When using a diamond in lithotherapy, it is recommended to place a black tourmaline at the root chakra for grounding purposes.

Lithotherapy

- Contributes to inner transformation and unification
- Symbolizes wisdom, enlightenment, purity, and clarity
- Protects and acts as a powerful purifier
- Increases the power of other stones

200

- Encourages the fusion of personality and soul
- Amplifies thought forms
- Develops self-confidence and a desire for independence; combats jealousy
- Purifies the energy body and eliminates blockages
- Is an excellent tonic for combating stress and during convalescence or periods of exhaustion when left in a glass of water overnight and drunk the next morning
- Prevents the formation of kidney and gallstones
- Fortifies the bladder
- Favors the healing of wounds
- Reinforces the immune activity of the thymus
- Alleviates the impact of bone diseases
- Acts as a treatment for gout

FLUORITE FAMILY

Geometric alliance: cubic
Colors: all the colors of the spectrum
Chakras: according to color
Hardness: 4
Origin: England, France, Germany
Formation Process: magmatic
Purification: cold water, incense, sunlight, earth; should be cleansed after each use
Recharging: quartz cluster, sunlight

Generalities

Because it supports the learning process, fluorite is the perfect stone for students. Fluorite is also an excellent stone to counteract the effects of the electromagnetic fog produced by computers, microwaves, and televisions.

Lithotherapy

- Is highly protective, especially on a psychic level
- Purifies and stabilizes the aura
- Fosters the development of spiritual awareness by stimulating the creation and expression of the highest abstract concepts

- Heightens the spirit of invention and the process of creation on the basis of freedom of decision
- Brings awareness to repressed feelings and allows for their gradual expression
- Calms the emotions, promotes self-confidence, and dispels confusion
- Helps to eliminate rooted attitudes, obsessions, and narrow-mindedness
- Purifies, dispels, and reorganizes energies in the body
- Quickens the mental processing and organizing of information
- Stimulates learning
- Favors swift comprehension and quick thinking
- Reinforces concentration and rational thought
- Expels negative energy and stress
- Contributes to energy transmissions
- Treats deformities of the body
- Reinforces the immune system
- Stimulates the regeneration of skin and mucous membranes, especially in the lungs and respiratory tract
- Supports the body in cases of tumors, ulcers, and purulent wounds
- Fortifies bones, teeth, and cells
- Repairs damage to DNA
- Confers mobility to the body; diminishes stiffness and joint problems such as arthritis
- When placed on the affected area, gradually relieves pain until it disappears
- Enhances the activity of the nervous system, particularly that of the brain
- Relieves respiratory problems and allergies that are psychological in origin
- Facilitates the assimilation of nutrients
- Guards against anorexia
- Activates blood circulation
- Acts on muscle tone and toxin elimination, thus especially recommended for athletes
- Benefits the spleen

Placed in our living environment, fluorite enhances understanding and increases inspiration and creativity. It can also be placed directly on the skin. Fluorite has additional properties related to its particular color and may be placed on a chakra accordingly.

Blue Fluorite

Lithotherapy

· Balances the throat chakra
· Enhances creative and logical thought as well as clear communication
· Facilitates spiritual awakening
· Calms and revitalizes the biomagnetic field
· Is beneficial for eye, nose, ear, and throat problems
· Combats colds and infections
· Amplifies curative potentials by activating or intensifying dormant activities in the brain
· Reduces inflammation, such as rheumatoid arthritis

Clear Fluorite

Lithotherapy

· Stimulates the crown chakra
· Charges the aura with energy
· Aligns the chakras, allowing universal energy to penetrate the body
· Balances the mind
· Reinforces the effects of other crystals
· Improves impaired vision

Green Fluorite

Lithotherapy

· Aligns the heart chakra
· Gives access to information from the subconscious and opens the door to intuition
· Purifies the aura, the chakras, and the mind
· Anchors excessive energy
· Dissipates emotional traumas
· Reduces problems caused by asthma and regenerates lung tissue
· Absorbs negative energies from the environment
· Eliminates infections
· Relieves gastric problems and intestinal cramps

Violet or Purple Fluorite

Lithotherapy

· Stimulates the third eye
· Confers common sense and discrimination during psychic communication
· Supports meditation
· Contributes to the treatment of bones and bone marrow ailments

Yellow Fluorite

Lithotherapy

· Enhances creativity and stabilizes group energy
· Supports cooperation
· Favors intellectual activities
· Supports the treatment of disorders of the spleen or kidneys
· Eliminates toxins and soothes the liver
· Treats cholesterol imbalances

Garnet Family

Geometric alliance: cubic
Colors: black, brown, green, orange, pink, red, yellow, and sometimes purplish
Chakras: according to color
Hardness: 6.5 to 7.5
Origin: Afghanistan, Austria, Brazil, Czech Republic, India, Sri Lanka
Formation Process: metamorphic
Purification: cold water, saltwater, incense, sunlight, earth; recommended before or after each use
Recharging: quartz cluster, sunlight

Generalities

In the Middle Ages, warriors set their shields and sword hilts in garnet to protect themselves from wounds. Garnet was also worn as an amulet in order to attract happiness, wealth, and blessings.

Lithotherapy

· Illuminates the soul; sheds light and gives hope when life seems hopeless
· Instills energy and regenerates the body
· Purifies, recharges, and revitalizes the chakras
· Balances energies, generating either serenity or passion accordingly
· Fights depression
· Inspires love and devotion
· Stimulates the rise of appropriate kundalini energy and sustains virility
· Strengthens the survival instinct and transforms crisis into challenge
· Facilitates mutual assistance
· Encourages dynamism; promotes action and perseverance
· Revives awareness and memory of past lives (both related to the processes of the pituitary gland)
· Stimulates the memory
· Brings success in business (square-cut garnet)
· Helps to overcome resistance or persistent self-sabotage, and contributes to dissolving obsolete behaviors
· Removes inhibitions and taboos
· Opens the heart
· Boosts self-confidence
· Balances sexual desire and appeases emotional turmoil
· Strengthens the heart and alleviates circulation problems

Garnet can be worn as a necklace or pendant. It is important that the stone be in contact with the skin. When placed at the third eye, garnet may revive past-life memories.

ALMANDINE GARNET - red to brown, sometimes purplish

Lithotherapy

· Opens the channel between the root and crown chakras
· Confers strength and power (regenerative stone)
· Encourages taking time for ourselves
· Teaches charity and compassion
· Generates the birth of profound love
· Facilitates the absorption of iron in the intestines

- May result in harmful outcomes if used on quick-tempered or highly stressed individuals
- Treats the liver and pancreas

ANDRADITE GARNET - yellowish green

Lithotherapy

- Promotes dynamism and flexibility
- Stimulates creativity
- Attracts love affairs
- Encourages the development of masculine qualities such as courage, vigor, and force
- Purifies the aura
- Contributes to blood production
- Effective in restoring the proper functioning of the liver, gallbladder, and intestines
- Contributes to calcium, magnesium, and iron absorption
- Activates the healing process of fractures and skin disorders

GROSSULAR GARNET - dark orange to brown orange

Lithotherapy

- Reinforces our strength in times of dejection
- Helps to meet challenges and brings support during trials and tribulations
- Inspires cooperation
- Is conducive to relaxation
- Strengthens and fortifies the bone structure
- Increases fertility
- Facilitates vitamin A assimilation
- Strengthens renal function
- Contributes to the regeneration of the skin and mucous membranes
- Drains the body of encumbrances such as fat deposits

HESSONITE GARNET (VARIETY OF GROSSULARITE) - red orange to red brown

Lithotherapy

· Assists in developing self-respect
· Fosters spiritual growth
· Calms unsatisfied sexual desires
· Dissolves guilt and feelings of inferiority
· Encourages service to others
· Eliminates negative influences that undermine health
· Contributes to regulating hormone production
· Treats sterility and impotence
· Benefits the olfactory system

MELANITE GARNET - dark brown to black

Lithotherapy

· Protects and stabilizes
· Fosters honesty and candor
· Eliminates blockages in the heart and throat chakras
· Soothes heartache
· Increases strength, particularly strengthening of the spine and bones
· Facilitates the body's adaptation to medical treatment
· Collaborates with cancer treatments, eases stroke incidents, and treats rheumatism and arthritis
· When associated with carnelian, eases circulatory problems in the legs and uterus

PYROPE GARNET - blood red to red brown

Lithotherapy

· Aligns the crown and root chakras with the subtle bodies
· Stimulates the root chakra, raising earth energies to higher centers
· Inspires courage
· Intensifies charisma
· Stimulates creativity
· Confers vitality

- Favors a high quality of life
- Effective in fighting nervous breakdown and fatigue
- Improves blood circulation and blood quality
- Calms heartburn
- Soothes sore throats
- Regulates heart troubles, blood pressure, and blood circulation
- Vitalizes the sexual organs

RED GARNET

Lithotherapy

- Represents love and resonates with the heart energy
- Revives blocked feelings
- Intensifies sexuality
- Helps in anger management, most specifically when anger is aimed at ourselves

RHODOLITE GARNET - rose red, magenta to purplish

Lithotherapy

- Invites liveliness, warmth, and trust
- Generates healthy sexuality
- Stimulates the intuition and inspiration
- Reinforces the metabolism
- Treats the heart, lungs, and hips
- Excels in detoxification and treats blood poisoning

SPESSARTITE GARNET - yellow, orange, red brown

Lithotherapy

- Encourages service to others
- Inculcates the will to help others
- Eliminates feelings of guilt
- Fortifies the heart (acts as an antidepressant)

- Helps prevent nightmares and treats sexual problems, especially for women who have experienced abuse and trauma; a stone to be used in moderation
- Treats intolerance to lactose and malfunctions in calcium absorption
- Excels in the treatment of anorexia, as it revives the appetite

TSAVORITE GARNET - various shades of dark green

Lithotherapy

- Presents a very powerful yet short-lasting effect
- Relieves acute pain

UVAROVITE GARNET - emerald green with shades of green yellow

Lithotherapy

- Stimulates the heart chakra
- Promotes individuality and enthusiasm
- Fortifies spiritual relationships
- Encourages us to live in the present
- Releases emotional blockages
- Eliminates feelings of inadequacy
- Contributes to detoxification
- Acts as an anti-inflammatory
- Soothes fevers
- Treats acidosis (high acidity of the blood)
- Supports treatments of leukemia
- Stimulates low sexual libido
- Balances high blood pressure
- Supports the liver through its purifying effect on the blood

HALITE FAMILY

Geometric alliance: cubic
Colors: blue, black, clear, gray, pink, red, white, yellow, red violet
Chakras: all (according to color)
Hardness: 2 to 2.5
Origin: southwestern Africa, Algeria, Austria, Canada, China, Colombia, Ethiopia, France, Great Britain, India, Italy (Sicily), Peru, Poland, Russia (Siberia), Spain, Switzerland, United States
Formation Process: sedimentary
Purification: Not required since halite does not absorb negative energies; contact with water must be avoided to prevent disintegration.
Recharging: sunlight

Generalities

Halite is a salt stone that acts as a powerful purifier of discordant and impure vibrations, replacing them with more favorable energies. Considering its low cost, it may be used as bath salt, diffusing its beneficial properties into the water.

BLUE HALITE

Lithotherapy

Blue halite contains deep blue, violet, and white hues and therefore possesses the properties of each of these colors.

· Purifies the energy field
· Elevates the consciousness to the highest of spiritual realms
· Activates psychic abilities

Also:

· Activates the third eye and crown chakras
· Aligns energies wherever it is placed
· Releases blockages in all superior chakras, particularly the throat
· Quickly frees the mind from worries and thoughts
· Opens the door to communication with the world of spirit and with our inner guides

210

- Encourages the verbal expression of spiritual truths
- Purifies other stones and crystals
- Provides support during fasts or other types of bodily purifications
- Resonates particularly well with the lymphatic and blood systems
- Contributes to the elimination of toxins and metals from the body

CLEAR HALITE

Lithotherapy

- Purifies and illuminates the energy body
- Dissolves the energetic density that hinders the light of the soul from being integrated into the gross and subtle bodies

PINK HALITE

Lithotherapy

- Purifies the heart
- Assists in overcoming past emotional traumas
- Opens up the heart and facilitates union with the source of universal love
- Facilitates self-love and undertaking the necessary actions to accomplish this
- Supports and encourages a healthy lifestyle
- Dissolves blockages between the solar plexus and the heart
- Dissolves confusion, disappointment, and doubt
- Calms and soothes the solar plexus
- Allows us to discern the truth in a variety of situations
- Triggers an understanding of emotional patterns hidden behind life's experiences

YELLOW HALITE

Lithotherapy

- Purifies the aura
- Favors learning and improves memory
- Encourages discipline and steadfastness
- Increases the vitality of the physical body

Lapis Lazuli

Geometric alliance: cubic
Color: blue stippled with white, with pyrite inclusions
Chakras: throat, third eye
Hardness: 5 to 6
Origin: Afghanistan, Chile, Russia
Formation Process: metamorphic
Purification: cold water, incense, moonlight, sunlight, earth
Recharging: quartz cluster, moonlight, sunlight

Generalities

The ancients appreciated lapis lazuli as a bearer of truth and light. The golden particles on the surface were compared to stars in the night sky. Lapis, also known as a power stone, was one of the most esteemed and widely used stones by the pharaohs of ancient Egypt. It was worn as a protection against the evil eye and used as ornaments on royal homes.

Lithotherapy

· Favors the rebirth of our inner divine nature
· Enhances clarity of understanding and stimulates intuition
· Helps build a bridge between the spiritual and the Higher Self
· Encourages us to face our dark side, illusions, and subconscious repressions so that we may identify with our inner divinity
· Encourages mental force, clarity, and stability, which supports self-healing and contact with the soul
· Inclusions of pyrite and calcite help us to act according to higher ideals and through a more elevated view of ourselves
· Effectively counters depression, encourages recovery, and inspires idealism
· Surfaces past traumas, repressed memories, and emotional wounds to be healed and liberated
· Encourages the healthy expression of emotions
· Encourages concentration and mindfulness
· Diminishes anxiety and stress
· Stimulates communication
· Facilitates accurate diagnosis during treatment
· Grants the mental strength to support self-healing

- Purifies the subtle bodies due to inclusions of white calcite
- Reduces blood pressure (not to be used for people with low blood pressure)
- Treats eye problems such as cataracts
- Increases physical energy and strengthens the immune system
- Contributes to the proper functioning of the digestive system and the thyroid gland
- Supports us during dizzy spells

MAGNETITE

Geometric alliance: cubic
Color: black metallic, matte
Chakra: root
Hardness: 5.5
Origin: Brazil, Finland, France, Germany, Russia, South Africa, Sweden, United States
Formation Process: magmatic, metamorphic
Purification: cold water (avoid salt), sunlight, earth
Recharging: quartz cluster, sunlight

Generalities

Magnetite owes its name to the fact that it is a natural magnet. Thanks to this stone, the Chinese were able to invent the magnetic compass, which permitted many adventurous travelers to navigate with greater facility. Without this compass, the history of the world would no doubt have been quite different.

Lithotherapy

- Aligns the chakras and connects them with the nourishing aspects of the Earth, which supports the vital force and vigor of the physical-etheric body
- Grounds and anchors us to the physical plane
- Balances the meridians
- Acts as an energetic shield for the etheric body
- Neutralizes negative emotions such as fear, anger, grief, and excessive attachment

- Balances the mind and the emotions, thereby promoting a strong inner stability
- Prepares and augments our strength and resistance prior to surgery
- Transmits beneficial energies for regeneration and recovery
- Stimulates and energizes during periods of great fatigue
- Helps to eliminate toxins
- Treats cervical osteoarthritis and bone problems
- Acts as a support to physical traumas
- Eases the symptoms of asthma
- Supports the blood and circulatory system, thereby benefiting cold extremities
- Benefits the skin and hair
- Reduces inflammation and encourages cellular regeneration
- Stops nosebleeds

PYRITE

Geometric alliance: cubic
Color: golden yellow
Chakras: solar plexus, third eye
Hardness: 6 to 6.5
Origin: Italy, Peru, Spain
Formation process: magmatic, metamorphic, sedimentary
Purification: cold water, incense, sunlight, earth
Recharging: quartz cluster, sunlight

Generalities

Pyrite has been called "fire stone" for its ability to produce sparks when hit. Magical properties have been attributed to it due to the fire that is believed to inhabit its form. It is also called "fool's gold," as it is has often been confused with gold.

Lithotherapy

- Acts as an energetic shield that clears negative energy or pollutants, including infectious disease
- Eliminates inertia and feelings of mediocrity
- Stimulates the circulation of ideas

- Encourages organization, structure, and order
- Allows us to draw from personal talents and potential (useful for the creation of commercial strategies)
- Teaches how to see beyond appearances and is therefore helpful during diplomatic work
- Favors self-knowledge
- Opens the door to possible and necessary changes
- Helps us to reveal and to confront the dark and luminous aspects of our nature
- Illuminates hidden secrets and memories, thereby encouraging greater openness and honesty
- Reinforces self-confidence and feelings of virility (it may be too powerful for some personality types, who may become aggressive)
- Diminishes feelings of inferiority and the tendency to be overly submissive
- Stimulates mental activity by bringing greater blood flow to the head
- Stimulates memory (excellent during exam time)
- Enlarges and structures mental capacity, balancing instinct with intuition and creativity with analysis
- Alleviates melancholy and intense despair
- Aligns the meridians
- Increases energy and helps us to overcome fatigue
- Blocks energy leaks in the subtle bodies
- Reduces stuttering, nervous tics, and upper body spasms when regularly worn as a necklace
- Increases oxygen in the blood and fortifies the circulatory system
- Stimulates cell formation and repairs damaged DNA
- Fortifies the digestive tract and neutralizes ingested toxins
- Soothes sleep disruption due to stomach ailments
- Reduces menstrual pain
- Overcomes problems caused by asthma and bronchitis

In past civilizations, people wore pyrite amulets for their warming properties.

It is recommended to avoid wearing this stone for extended periods. It produces a black ferrous sulfide deposit when mixed with perspiration, which can irritate the skin. It is better to use this stone in meditation, during supervised treatments, or to wear it in a location where it can be checked regularly. When worn around the neck, pyrite protects the physical and subtle bodies and neutralizes malevolent energies and dangers.

SODALITE

Geometric alliance: cubic
Color: blue with black and white inclusions
Chakras: throat, third eye
Hardness: 5.5 to 6
Origin: Africa, Brazil, Canada, India
Formation Process: magmatic
Purification: cold water, incense, moonlight, earth
Recharging: quartz cluster, moonlight

Generalities

In Africa, sodalite is considered to be a stone of protection; in China and Japan, as encouraging filial gratitude.

The Celts and Greeks honored sodalite as a prophecy stone, while the Christians believed it enhanced perception.

Lithotherapy

· Aligns the superior chakras
· Contributes to awakening the third eye
· Confers humility and courage
· Builds true confidence, thus reducing the need for excessive praise for personal merits
· Encourages healthy idealism
· Instigates the search for the truth
· Inspires fidelity toward ourselves and our convictions
· Transforms the defensive or hypersensitive personality by helping the heart to release fear, guilt, and control mechanisms, which prevent us from being authentic
· Increases self-respect and reveals obscure aspects of the self, to be accepted in a nonjudgmental manner
· Color symbolizes self-confidence and loyalty
· Stimulates spiritual harmony and artistic inspiration
· Helps to balance and eventually master the emotions
· Helps calm quick-tempered personalities
· Calms anxiety and panic attacks

- Invites us to let go of obsolete and rigid mental conditioning, hence creating an opening for new possibilities
- Encourages objectivity, enhances intuitive perception, and facilitates the verbal expression of feelings
- Stimulates the brain and logical thinking
- Purifies the body, especially the mind
- Prepares the mind for intuitive knowledge and introspection
- Supports group work, stimulating confidence, camaraderie, harmony, and solidarity as well as contributing to materializing ideas and goals
- Activates the pineal gland
- Cleanses the organs and lymphatic system, activating the immune system
- Balances the metabolism
- Prevents calcium deficiency
- Protects the physical body and the psyche (with surface irradiation)
- Counteracts electromagnetic pollution (computers, etc.)
- Fights damage caused by radiation
- Treats the throat, the vocal cords, the larynx, and cases of persistent hoarseness
- Balances the thyroid gland, the nervous system, and all glandular functions
- Relieves digestive problems
- Is effective against diabetes when taken in water in the morning on an empty stomach
- Reduces fever and blood pressure
- Stimulates fluid absorption in the body

Sodalite is most beneficial when placed directly on the skin, at the wrist, heart, throat, third eye, or solar plexus.

Stones of the Hexagonal Alliance

Aquamarine

Geometric alliance: hexagonal
Colors: green to clear blue
Chakras: crown, throat, third eye
Hardness: 7.5 to 8
Origin: Brazil, India, Madagascar, Myanmar, United States
Formation Process: magmatic
Purification: cold water, saltwater, incense, sunlight, earth
Recharging: quartz cluster, sunlight

Generalities

Legend states that aquamarine changes color as a way of helping its owner distinguish true from false and friend from enemy. Ancient civilizations used it to confer well-being, stimulate memory, and awaken clairvoyant abilities. It is also said that sailors wore it for protection against drowning.

Lithotherapy

· Stimulates, activates, and purifies the throat chakra
· Opens communication with higher planes and dimensions
· Supports meditation practices
· Incites us to speak the truth and to release emotions
· Diminishes stress; calms and clears the mind
· Stimulates mental development
· Opens us up to a larger vision
· Arouses clairvoyance and mediumistic abilities
· Encourages us to be frank, straightforward, dynamic, and perseverant
· Incites tolerance, encouraging us to avoid making judgments
· Invites peace and inner serenity
· Alleviates fears, anxiety, and morose thoughts
· Prevents seasickness
· Awakens the will to achieve goals and leads us to success

- Harmonizes the pituitary and thyroid glands, regularizing growth and hormonal imbalances
- Treats sore throat
- Improves eyesight in the case of myopia (nearsightedness) or farsightedness
- Regulates the lymphatic system and blood circulation
- Reduces swelling when placed on swollen glands or worn as a necklace
- Alleviates excessive reaction of the immune system and allergies
- Relaxes the solar plexus and digestive organs when placed on the third chakra

Aquamarine can be worn at all times in contact with the skin. In the case of eyesight problems, place it directly on the closed eyes.

APATITE FAMILY

Geometric alliance: hexagonal
Colors: blue, brown, crimson, dark red, gray, green, violet, white, yellow
Chakras: heart, throat, third eye
Hardness: 5
Origin: Brazil, India, Madagascar, Myanmar, United States
Formation Process: magmatic, metamorphic, sedimentary
Purification: cold water, incense, sunlight, earth
Recharging: quartz cluster, sunlight

Generalities

Apatite is a generally massive and opaque phosphate, rarely transparent and crystalline. In the past, this stone was easily confused with other minerals such as beryl or calcite. In 1786 it was named *apatao*, the Greek word for "mislead."

Used with other stones, apatite allows for easy achievement of an expected result. It must be worn directly on the body, around the area in need.

Lithotherapy

· Balances physical, mental, emotional, and spiritual bodies as well as the chakras
· Allows for the opening of the consciousness and facilitates inner contact
· Deepens meditation
· Arouses inspiration toward humanitarian aid
· Fights against apathy
· Vivifies and acts against exhaustion, especially when overindulging in activities
· Enhances motivation and helps to mobilize energy reserves
· Overcomes emotional exhaustion
· Reduces irritability and aggressive tendencies
· Favors communication and self-expression on all levels
· Helps to overcome grief, anger, and inertia
· Stimulates creativity and intellect
· Dispels confusion
· Stimulates the appetite
· Facilitates cellular regeneration as well as cartilage formation in bones and teeth (helps with rickets, arthritis, problems of the joints, broken bones)
· Supports growth in children
· Contributes to better calcium absorption
· Is particularly beneficial for the small intestine thanks to its high mineral content
· Calms hyperactivity and stimulates when overly inert
· Soothes the eyes

Blue Apatite

Lithotherapy

· Activates the throat chakra
· Favors contact with higher spiritual planes
· Soothes heartache and emotional troubles
· Facilitates public speaking
· Intensifies group communication

YELLOW APATITE

Lithotherapy

· Activates the solar plexus
· Extracts stagnant energy, easing apathy and depression
· Increases concentration
· Calms anger
· Helps to eliminate toxins
· Relieves digestive problems
· Eliminates cellulite
· Treats the liver, pancreas, gallbladder, and spleen
· Reduces the appetite when taken as an elixir

BERYL FAMILY

Geometric alliance: hexagonal
Colors: gold (golden beryl), green, pink (morganite), red (bixbite), transparent (goshenite), yellow, yellow to blue green (heliodor)
Chakras: from the root to the crown according to colors
Hardness: 7.5 to 8
Origin: southwestern Africa, Brazil, Madagascar, Pakistan, Russia (Ural Mountains)
Formation Process: magmatic
Purification: cold water, saltwater, incense, sunlight, earth; rarely necessary
Recharging: quartz cluster, regular Sunlight

Generalities

Transparent beryl is pure, with no foreign minerals altering its composition. Colored beryl contains other minerals that grant it its particular color. For example, iron will tint it yellow, gold, and sometimes blue, while lithium and manganese will tint it red. In the past, beryl was known for its detoxifying power and for its positive effects on the eyesight. The German word for glasses, *Brille,* comes from the word *beryl.*

Golden Beryl (Heliodor)

Lithotherapy

· Stimulates the crown and solar plexus chakras
· Teaches initiative and independence
· Calms nervousness and excessive emotions due to stress or overwork
· Eases minor stomach problems and intestinal disorders
· Detoxifies the organism

Pink Beryl (Morganite)

Lithotherapy

· Draws and maintains love
· Encourages gentle thoughts and actions
· Creates space, allowing us to make the most out of life
· Provides beneficial effects on the nervous system
· Maintains stability in the emotional body during change and transition
· Oxygenates and reorganizes cells, which is beneficial against tuberculosis, asthma, emphysema, cardiac problems, dizzy spells, impotence, and lung blockages

Red Beryl (Bixbite)

Lithotherapy

· Charges and clears the root chakra
· Energizes

TRANSPARENT OR COLORLESS BERYL (GOSHENITE)

Lithotherapy

· Symbolizes protection
· Encourages determination, efficiency, multitasking, and vision
· Shows us how to accomplish what is necessary to meet our goals
· Helps with stress management
· Allows us to actualize our potential
· Fortifies courage
· Encourages positive thinking
· Discourages overanalysis and anxiety
· Relieves nervousness caused by travel or homesickness
· Instills initiative and independence
· Vivifies the will toward success
· Stimulates the elimination organs
· Fortifies the pulmonary and circulatory systems
· Enhances resistance to toxins and pollutants
· Treats the liver, heart, and stomach
· Benefits the spine and treats concussions
· Alleviates throat infections when taken as an elixir

EMERALD

Geometric alliance: hexagonal
Color: from yellowish green to blue green
Chakra: heart
Hardness: 7.5 to 8
Origin: Australia, Austria, Brazil, Colombia, India, Madagascar, Nigeria, Pakistan, Russia, South Africa, Tanzania, United States, Zambia
Formation Process: magmatic, metamorphic
Purification: cold water, incense, sunlight, earth; rarely needed as the emerald absorbs very little negative energy
Recharging: sunlight

Generalities

The ancient civilizations of Europe and India considered the emerald to be the stone that conveyed divine inspiration. In antiquity, it was used to heal the eyes, and in the Middle Ages is was known to stop illnesses. When the emerald changed color, it was indicative of infidelity.

Wearing an emerald continuously could trigger negative emotions in some individuals.

Lithotherapy

· Conveys inspiration and infinite patience
· Represents fulfilled love
· Grants domestic bliss and loyalty
· Confers frankness and the joy of living
· Acts as a guide toward our goal
· Brings clarity and alertness; encourages broad vision
· Strengthens unity, unconditional love, and partnership
· Favors friendship
· Ensures physical, emotional, and mental balance
· Eliminates negativity and inspires positive actions
· Confers strength of character to overcome obstacles
· Helps cope with misfortune
· Activates rejuvenation and recovery
· Confers the kind of wisdom that evokes discernment
· Generates mutual understanding in a group and stimulates cooperation
· Eases symptoms of claustrophobia
· Contributes to prompt recovery following an infectious disease
· Treats the sinuses, lungs, and heart
· Supports the spine and muscular system
· Improves eyesight
· Detoxifies the liver
· Relieves rheumatism and diabetes
· Is an antidote for poisons
· Alleviates epileptic attacks, Parkinson's disease, vertigo, and malignancies

Graphite

Geometric alliance: hexagonal
Color: metallic light gray to black
Chakras: throat, root
Hardness: 1.5 to 2
Origin: Canada, Finland, Germany, Madagascar, Mexico, Slovenia, United States
Formation Process: metamorphic
Purification: incense
Recharging: quartz cluster, candle flame

Generalities

The word *graphite* comes from the Greek word *graphein*, which means "to write." Like diamond, it is a form of crystalline carbon. Although in its own way it is as pure as diamond, it is very soft. Graphite is used to make pencils that are often mistakenly called "lead" pencils. Its most common domestic use is in the production of such pencils.

Lithotherapy

· Protects against negative energies
· Anchors the root chakra to the Earth
· Is a good conductor of energy
· Helps clarify ideas and thoughts
· Helps excessively spontaneous or talkative people be more reserved, and gives them some distance
· Is an excellent stone for improving the quality of communication
· Confers a sense of diplomacy, raises debates to a higher level, and clarifies discussions
· Helps drain the liver and improve blood flow
· Relieves constipation, if applied on the colon

SUGILITE (LUVULITE OR ROYAL AZEL)

Geometric alliance: hexagonal
Colors: black, translucent, violet
Chakras: all
Hardness: 6.5 to 7
Origin: Japan, South Africa
Formation Process: magmatic
Purification: cold water, saltwater, incense, sunlight, earth
Recharging: quartz cluster, sunlight

Generalities

Only two deposits of sugilite have been discovered to this day, the first being dating to 1944, which makes it a rare stone. Its therapeutic properties were recognized in 1980, when it was renowned as a New Age stone, a symbol of the Age of Aquarius, bringing to earth the numerous benefits of the violet ray.

Translucent sugilite purifies the lymphatic system and the blood. It is placed at the third eye to ease headaches and to diminish despair.

Lithotherapy

· Opens and aligns all the chakras concerned with spiritual love
· Inspires the expansion of consciousness
· Encourages living according to our own truth
· Promotes logical and determined action to deal with unpleasant situations
· Assists with conflict resolution
· Alleviates sorrow, sadness, and fear by inspiring self-forgiveness
· Inspires finding solutions that answer to everyone's needs
· Favors forgiveness by eliminating hostility
· Contributes to constructive group work
· Encourages affectionate communication
· Eases psychic tensions, paranoia, and symptoms of schizophrenia
· Surmounts learning difficulties such as dyslexia
· Soothes the nerves and brain
· Reduces intense pain and treats headaches
· Is beneficial for epilepsy and motor problems
· Eases symptoms of autism

Vanadinite

Geometric alliance: hexagonal
Color: reddish brown, orange brown, chestnut brown, light brown
Chakras: hara, solar plexus, root
Hardness: 3
Origin: Argentina, Morocco, Russia, United States
Formation Process: sedimentary
Purification: incense
Recharging: quartz cluster, avoid sunlight, moonlight

Generalities

Strongly connected to the Earth, vanadinite is excellent for people who have trouble accepting their physicality. It anchors the soul in the physical body and helps it feel at ease on the earthly plane. The vanadium contained in vanadinite takes its name from the Vanir, Scandinavian goddesses of peace, fertility, and prosperity.

Lithotherapy

· Confers strength and courage
· Is known as an incarnation and grounding stone that can promote energy realignment and the attainment of goals
· Enhances grounding in reality
· Assists meditation, silencing persistent humming in the brain
· Eliminates mind chatter, helps "empty" the mind, inspires clear vision, helps define and pursue goals
· Stimulates blood circulation
· Red vanadinite is considered an aphrodisiac
· Useful for respiratory disorders such as asthma and congested lungs
· Helps chronic fatigue
· Relieves bladder problems

ZINCITE

Geometric alliance: hexagonal
Colors: green, orange yellow, red, reddish brown, translucent
Chakras: hara, root, solar plexus
Hardness: 4
Origin: Italy, Poland, United States
Formation Process: metamorphic
Purification: distilled saltwater, cold water, incense, moonlight, sunlight
Recharging: quartz cluster, moonlight, sunlight

Generalities

Zincite was accidentally discovered in the pipes of industrial ovens destined to produce zinc in Poland. This gem is consequently considered both synthetic and natural, not having been intentionally fabricated by humans. Zincite from Poland is becoming rarer, yet it is still highly sought after on the international market.

Lithotherapy

· Activates the three lower chakras and conveys energy to the upper chakras, reenergizing them in turn
· Anchors spiritual aspirations to the physical plane
· Increases energy and vitality
· Instills courage, passion, and willpower
· Ignites the fires of creativity and arouses sexual desire
· Recharges a depleted solar plexus with energy, thus inviting determination, perseverance, and the ability to manifest intentions
· Confers the final impulse necessary for the completion of long-term projects
· Amplifies the energy of the majority of other stones
· Facilitates the acceptance of change when necessary
· Contributes to finding the cause of a phobia and to freeing ourselves from it
· Promotes group work and cooperative activity, drawing like-minded people together
· Provides support during periods of change

- Increases fertility, revives the reproductive organs, and alleviates menstrual symptoms
- Stimulates the meridians and all the systems within the body
- Stimulates the endocrine and immune systems
- Benefits the skin and hair
- Activates the organs related to assimilation and elimination
- Supports the prostate

Stones of the Monoclinic Alliance

Azurite

Geometric alliance: monoclinic
Color: deep blue
Chakras: throat, third eye
Hardness: 3.5 to 4
Origin: Australia, Brazil, Czech Republic, France, Norway, Russia, Slovenia, United States
Formation Process: sedimentary
Purification: cold water, incense, moonlight, earth
Recharging: quartz cluster, moonlight, limited amount of sunlight

Generalities

Known as the "Stone of Heaven," azurite was considered sacred to Native American people, who believed that it would facilitate contact with spiritual guides. The Mayans used this stone to raise their psychic powers.

Lithotherapy

- Activates the throat and third-eye chakras
- A powerful accelerator that brings great aid to the process of transformation
- Facilitates deep meditation
- Facilitates out-of-body experiences, stimulating the consciousness and elevating it to a higher plane
- Encourages confrontation with the reality of ourselves, piercing illusions and delusions
- Facilitates decision-making and encourages critical thinking
- Accentuates clarity of mind, creativity, inspiration, and intuition
- Provides soothing effects to a restless mind
- Motivates and guides us to face and overcome fears
- Represents the will to know and the will to change
- Enhances our sense of justice
- Reveals and liberates us from imprints of the past
- Stimulates awareness and self-knowledge
- Helps to reveal reasons for psychosomatic illnesses

- Activates and purifies the liver and gallbladder
- Aids cerebral and nerve activity
- Accelerates the scarring process
- Stimulates the thyroid gland and consequently growth
- Treats throat and spinal cord problems

AZURITE-MALACHITE

Geometric alliance: monoclinic
Color: deep blue, black, green
Chakra: throat
Hardness: 3.5 to 4
Origin: Democratic Republic of the Congo, Mexico, Morocco, Russia, Slovenia, United States
Formation Process: sedimentary
Purification: cold water, incense, earth
Recharging: quartz cluster, limited amount of sunlight

Generalities

As its name indicates, azurite-malachite is the physical association of azurite and malachite, and as such it possesses the properties of both stones. However, from a spiritual perspective, it is less effective than azurite, which is an indispensable aid to meditation.

Lithotherapy

- Neutralizes negativity and harmonizes, thereby awakening an interest for everything and everyone that surround us
- Activates openness to ourselves and others
- Encourages willingness to serve
- Has a beneficial effect on the psyche of vulnerable or unstable individuals
- Instills feelings of well-being
- Supports in times of pain and misfortune, helping to free repressed emotions, to listen to our heart, and to express innermost feelings
- Vivifies, detoxifies, defuses, and supports the immune system
- Protects against radiation
- Helps to suppress tumors

- Alleviates joint problems (arthritis and osteoarthritis) and reduces joint inflammation
- Acts against anxiety, heart disease, grief, and asthma

Azurite with malachite can be held in the hands or placed on the third eye during meditation and contemplation. It is best for this stone to have direct contact with the skin, on or around the area affected, as it will directly absorb the energies causing the problem, such as hematoma, fractured bones, sprains, rheumatism, or internal pain.

CHAROITE

Geometric alliance: monoclinic
Colors: violet purple scattered with white and deep violet
Chakra: third eye
Hardness: 5 to 6
Origin: Russia
Formation Process: metamorphic
Purification: cold water, incense, moonlight, earth
Recharging: quartz cluster, moonlight

Generalities

This new stone manifests itself when the human race needs its energy. Charoite works with the violet ray, which brings people into closer alignment with the soul.

Lithotherapy

- Creates a bridge between the crown and heart chakras, thereby purifying the aura and encouraging unconditional love
- Stimulates inner vision and spiritual intuition
- Facilitates connections with other spiritual dimensions while remaining anchored
- Purifies and transmutes negativity
- Known as a magical and mysterious stone
- Arouses profound physical and emotional healing
- Helps us to accept the present moment

- Reduces feelings of insecurity
- Increases self-confidence, stimulates the need for action, and encourages constancy
- Encourages acknowledging our faults and tolerating those of others
- Confers direction, vigor, and spontaneity
- Encourages a fresh start when necessary
- Diminishes stress and worries
- Helps to overcome compulsions and obsessions
- Encourages autonomous decision-making for those too influenced by others
- Rejuvenates following exhaustion
- Protects the skin from ultraviolet and X-ray radiation
- Strengthens the immune system
- Regularizes blood pressure
- Supports the eyes; treats the heart, liver, and pancreas
- Alleviates cramps and pain
- Relieves insomnia and grants peaceful sleep to children
- Treats autism and bipolar disorders

Known as the "Stone of Transformation" or the "Stone of the Soul," charoite is a powerful transmuter of fears. It can be worn in contact with the heart chakra, or placed directly on the skin wherever its energy is required.

CHRYSOCOLLA

Geometric alliance: monoclinic
Colors: blue turquoise, green
Chakras: third eye, throat, heart, solar plexus, hara
Hardness: 2.5
Origin: Chile, Democratic Republic of the Congo, Peru, Russia, United States (Arizona and Nevada)
Formation Process: sedimentary
Purification: cold water, incense, sunlight, earth
Recharging: quartz cluster, sunlight

Generalities

Chrysocolla is a feminine energy and is known as the younger sister to her brother, turquoise. It symbolizes beauty, love, and harmony. A force resides in its softness, acting to elevate the consciousness of those who work with it.

Lithotherapy

· Favors equanimity and self-observation
· Helps us to accept ever-changing situations and to strive toward goals
· Gives momentum when we are lethargic; calms an overactive nervous system when we are agitated
· Helps to maintain a cool head
· Helps us to discern what promotes evolution and growth of the consciousness and what retards and regresses our potential
· Eases feelings of guilt and encourages forgiveness
· Harmonizes groups and environments
· Is particularly recommended for children since it supports the formation and growth of bones
· Fights infections, in particular of the throat and tonsils
· Reduces inflammation of sinuses, tonsils, larynx, and lungs
· Detoxifies and reinforces the liver, kidneys, and colon
· Regularizes the nervous system and heart
· Balances sugar levels and treats the pancreas
· Balances the hormones and soothes premenstrual ailments and menstrual pains
· Lowers the body temperature in cases of fever
· Reduces tension and promotes relaxation
· Fortifies the muscles and alleviates cramps
· Accelerates the healing of burns
· Normalizes the functioning of the thyroid
· Alleviates digestive problems caused by stress (ulcers)

Placed on the solar plexus chakra, chrysocolla roots out negative emotions; on the heart chakra, it treats grief and sorrow and intensifies the capacity to love. Placed on the throat chakra, it improves communication while encouraging discernment. Placed on the third eye, it improves inner vision.

EPIDOTE

Geometric alliance: monoclinic
Color: green
Chakras: heart, solar plexus
Hardness: 6 to 7
Origin: Austria, Mexico, Mozambique, Norway, United States (California)
Formation Process: magmatic, metamorphic
Purification: cold water, saltwater, incense, sunlight, earth
Recharging: quartz cluster, sunlight

Generalities

Epidote amplifies the intrinsic characteristics of an individual. It fosters the development of positive attributes but also amplifies the negative aspects, forcing us to make profound changes.

Lithotherapy

· Increases personal power
· Conveys the gift of initiative
· Favors positive interaction with others
· Diminishes tendencies to criticize ourselves and others
· Facilitates the creation of realistic goals, all the while guiding us toward success
· Confers patience, optimism, and self-confidence
· Encourages acceptance of our own weakness while supporting self-esteem
· Contributes to overcoming self-destructive emotions that cause depression
· Stimulates the desire for healthy, realistic, and positive changes that will bring success
· Facilitates recovery after illness, burnout, or stress
· Regenerates and rejuvenates at all levels
· Works in favor of good health and overall well-being
· Develops and reinforces the immune system
· Assists in the proper functioning of the digestive system, especially the gallbladder, liver, and small intestine
· Relaxes the abdominal region and dissolves mucus in the respiratory system
· Relieves heartburn

- Treats the nervous system
- Reinforces the thyroid gland
- Relieves brain disorders
- Softens the skin (especially when taken as an elixir)

GEM SILICA

Geometric alliance: monoclinic
Colors: blue, turquoise, translucent green
Chakras: heart, throat, third eye
Hardness: 6 to 7
Origin: Peru, United States
Formation Process: sedimentary
Purification: cold water, incense, sunlight, earth
Recharging: rarely required—incense and quartz cluster at the user's discretion

Generalities

Gem silica is, in fact, a gem-quality chrysocolla. It is a combination of chrysocolla and quartz.

Lithotherapy

- One of the most refined stones to treat the throat chakra
- Stimulates and clears the third eye
- Encourages self-expression and allows for a clear and eloquent conveyance of truth
- Acts gently, though it possesses great power
- Encourages the locution of our inner truth
- Facilitates a concrete manifestation of feminine power by calling on the energy of the Goddess
- Possesses the ability to evoke past-life memories
- Awakens imaginative and creative abilities
- Allows us to let go of what oppresses the psyche
- Heightens inner vision and clairvoyance
- Enhances telepathic communication
- Balances and soothes the emotional body

- Increases emotional discernment, directing our focus to what is essential in life and in relationships
- Alleviates depression and feelings of self-deprecation
- Seals holes in the astral and etheric bodies, especially in the area of the heart
- Amplifies the effectiveness of prayers, chants, and mantras by augmenting the power and purity of words and sound vibrations
- Contributes to the proper functioning of the respiratory system
- Helps in case of bronchitis and asthma
- Treats diseases of the vocal cords

HOWLITE

Geometric alliance: monoclinic
Colors: blue, green, white
Chakra: third eye
Hardness: 3.5
Origin: Canada, Germany, United States
Formation Process: sedimentary
Purification: water, incense, earth
Recharging: quartz cluster, limited sunlight

Generalities

Howlite is often confused with turquoise. It is to be noted, however, that blue howlite is artificially colored.

Lithotherapy

- Allows the mind to open up to spiritual dimensions in order to develop intuition
- Supports meditation
- Facilitates out-of-body experiences into past or in-between lives
- Inspires the creation of ambitions and activates their realization
- Soothes and calms
- Acts as an antidote against insomnia caused by an overagitated mind
- Facilitates dream recollection
- Encourages patience and helps to eliminate rage and uncontrollable anger

- Contributes to diminishing selfish tendencies and negative criticism
- Reinforces positive personality traits
- Revives the memory and increases the desire for knowledge
- Calms turbulent emotions coming from past lives
- Balances calcium levels in the body
- Contributes to the healthy preservation of bones, teeth, and soft tissues

JADE FAMILY

Geometric alliance: monoclinic
Colors: white, beige brown, black, green, purple blue, red brown
Chakra: heart
Hardness: 6.5 to 7
Origin: China, Guatemala, Japan, Mexico, Myanmar, United States
Formation Process: metamorphic
Purification: cold water, saltwater, incense, sunlight, earth
Recharging: quartz cluster, sunlight

Generalities

In ancient times, jade was considered a sacred stone that brought good luck, prosperity, and long life.

Lithotherapy

- Preserves loving sentiments
- Facilitates dream interpretation
- Helps to resolve problems
- Instills compassion
- Contributes to spiritual realization
- Allows us to see ourselves as a spiritual being
- Generates spontaneity in the organization of our life
- Awakens hidden knowledge
- Invigorates passive individuals
- Stimulates ideas and the need for action
- Purifies all of the body and eliminates bodily toxins
- Treats the adrenal glands and the kidneys
- Balances the metabolism and reduces fever

· Accelerates the healing of an injury and prevents scarring
· Favors fertility and supports labor and delivery
· Stabilizes bodily fluids
· Is beneficial for general heart problems
· Balances the nervous system
· Soothes irritation

Jade can be worn as jewelry or placed directly on the body. It collaborates with the dream process when placed on the forehead. According to Chinese tradition, jade transmits its virtues to whomever holds it in his or her hand.

JADE (JADEITE)

Purification: saltwater
Recharging: quartz cluster, sunlight

Lithotherapy

· Represents the earthly manifestation of the cosmic male principle
· Inspires virtue
· Confers tolerance
· Prolongs life
· Regulates the activity of the kidneys and urinary system
· Treats back pain

LAVENDER JADE

Purification: saltwater
Recharging: quartz cluster, sunlight

Lithotherapy

· Brings inner peace
· Contributes to delineating our limits
· Alleviates emotional pain and trauma

Magnetite Jade

Purification: cold water, incense, moonlight, sunlight, earth; requires more frequent purification than other kinds of jade
Recharging: quartz cluster, sunlight, moonlight

Lithotherapy

· Confers a prosperous life
· Attracts success
· Brings good fortune and is favorable in games of chance
· Benefits the kidneys and bladder

Nephrite Jade

Purification: saltwater, cold water
Recharging: quartz cluster, sunlight

Lithotherapy

· Regulates the kidneys, the urinary system, and the adrenal glands
· Contributes to eliminating kidney stones
· Reduces incontinence and soothes cystitis

Kunzite

Geometric alliance: monoclinic
Colors: clear, gray, green, pink violet, purple, yellow
Chakras: heart, throat, third eye
Hardness: 6 to 7
Origin: Afghanistan, Brazil, Madagascar, Myanmar, Pakistan, United States (California)
Formation Process: magmatic
Purification: cold water, saltwater, incense, earth; requires little purification
Recharging: quartz cluster, no sunlight

Generalities

Kunzite is one of the best stones to offer as a gift as it opens the heart to divine love, self-love, and love for others and of humanity, animals, plants, and minerals.

Lithotherapy

- Stimulates the heart chakra
- Urges forgiveness
- Brings suppressed emotions to the surface, allowing us to face them
- Balances and calms emotions
- Allows us to be focused and calm when surrounded by many distractions
- Encourages wisdom and just actions
- Favors loving thoughts and communication while allowing suppressed feelings to be expressed in a constructive way
- Calms anxiety and panic attacks
- Its lithium content can be beneficial in treating bipolar disorders
- Frees us from emotional dependency
- Facilitates maturity and encourages tolerance
- Encourages receptivity and connection to others
- Provides a protective shield against undesired energies
- Encourages healthy love and self-respect
- Creates openness toward unconditional love
- Purifies the subtle bodies and facilitates profound meditation
- Helps in the treatment of drug and alcohol addiction
- Reinforces the physical heart muscles and supports the lungs
- Regulates the thyroid gland and balances hormones
- Encourages healthy blood circulation
- Facilitates proper functioning of the sciatic nerve; reduces joint pain
- Balances calcium and magnesium levels in the body

LEPIDOLITE

Geometric alliance: monoclinic
Colors: pink to violet pink, with pearly and translucent luster
Chakras: heart, third eye
Hardness: 2.5 to 3
Origin: Italy, Madagascar, Russia, United States
Formation Process: magmatic
Purification: cold water, saltwater, incense, minimal sunlight, earth; should be purified after each use
Recharging: quartz cluster, minimal sunlight

Generalities

Due to the lithium content in its composition, lepidolite is a stone that invites tranquility and balance. It is one of the most powerful stones for soothing strong traumatic emotions, such as anxiety, fear, grief, and stress, as well as for calming negative and anxious thoughts.

Lithotherapy

· Favors the elevation of consciousness in overly materialistic and Cartesian individuals
· Alleviates insomnia
· Offers protection against nightmares
· Favors autonomy: helps us to fix objectives and to realize them without help from others
· Protects from outer influences and helps to preserve our identity in a crowd
· Eliminates electromagnetic pollution from computers
· Favors objective evaluation and just decisions
· Motivates us to concentrate on what is essential and to avoid distractions
· Calms obsessive thoughts and anxieties
· Helps to overcome any type of emotional or mental addiction, such as anorexia, drug addictions, etc.
· Frees and reorganizes psychological models and old behaviors
· Stimulates the intellect and analytical capacities
· Offers support for those suffering form bipolar disorder

- Alleviates nervous pains, sciatic nerve pain, and other neuralgic or articulation troubles
- Detoxifies and stimulates the purification processes of the skin and of the connective tissues
- Reinforces back muscles
- Strengthens the kidneys and the liver
- Eases the symptoms of epilepsy
- Supports those with Alzheimer's disease
- Alleviates menopausal symptoms

MALACHITE

Geometric alliance: monoclinic
Color: green with black
Chakras: heart, solar plexus
Hardness: 4
Origin: Australia, Chile, Democratic Republic of the Congo, United States, Zimbabwe
Formation Process: sedimentary
Purification: cold water, incense, sunlight, earth; avoid using salt, which could damage the stone's surface
Recharging: quartz cluster, sunlight, olive oil (very absorbent, must be cleansed after each use)

Generalities

Malachite has always been associated with femininity, and in many cultures it was dedicated to the Goddess. It symbolizes the muse of the arts, beauty, curiosity, aesthetics, seduction, and sensuality.

Lithotherapy

- Brings old traumas and negative past experiences to the surface
- Powerfully transforms
- Facilitates comprehension by stimulating concentration
- Unerringly indicates what is blocking spiritual growth
- Purifies the physical and emotional bodies
- Acts as a protector from unwanted energies

- Eases anxiety
- Soothes heartache due to breakups
- Vibrates to the female sexual organs
- Eases sexual discomfort
- Facilitates the understanding of complex concepts
- Increases mental powers of observation
- Releases inhibitions and diminishes fears
- Encourages verbal expression
- Develops a sense of beauty, sensuality, friendship, and justice
- Increases the thirst for knowledge
- Encourages us to take risks and to change
- Encourages empathy
- Fights heart diseases and asthma
- Eases pain, sprains, fractures, and bruises
- Strengthens the liver and purifies it from toxins
- Benefits the spleen and pancreas
- Diminishes tissue acidity
- Evacuates excess urea, which causes rheumatism
- Rebalances the thyroid and parathyroid glands
- Diminishes inflammation and pain caused by arthritis and osteoarthritis
- Eases menstrual cramps, acting as an antispasmodic
- Known as the "midwife stone," it facilitates childbirth
- Promotes growth and brings strength
- Lowers blood pressure
- Alleviates motion sickness and vertigo
- Treats tumors and the pancreas
- Strengthens the optic nerves
- Eases symptoms of diabetes when worn at the waist level
- Fortifies the immune system
- Favors regeneration
- Protects against radiation
- Absorbs pollutants from the atmosphere as well as the body
- Harmonizes DNA and the cellular structure

In order to benefit from the properties of malachite, it must be in direct contact with the skin. It stimulates visualization and psychic vision when placed on the third eye. It absorbs negative emotions and blockages at the solar plexus. When placed at the heart, it brings balance and harmony, opening us to unconditional love.

244

Moonstone Family

Geometric alliance: monoclinic
Colors: of the rainbow, gray, peach, white
Chakras: crown, third eye
Hardness: 6 to 6.5
Origin: Australia, India, Madagascar, Myanmar, Sri Lanka, United States
Formation Process: magmatic
Purification: cold water, saltwater, incense, moonlight, sunlight, earth
Recharging: quartz cluster, abundant sunlight and moonlight

Generalities

The name "moonstone" comes from its polished appearance and its blue-white color produced by its thin-layered structure. It is still considered sacred in India.

Lithotherapy

· Inspires softness, sensitivity, and harmony
· Encourages patience and tolerance
· Awakens the intuition, guiding us to the right action at the right moment
· Balances emotions
· Reduces anxiety, including fears about the future
· Helps clarify feelings
· Guides women to be more balanced in their true feminine expression, with the potential to reveal the nature and power of the Goddess aspect within
· Balances the feminine and masculine polarities in women as well as in men
· Promotes enthusiasm, love of life, and a youthful attitude even at an advanced age
· Supports us during regression therapy
· Deepens our meditation practice
· Increases fertility
· Balances hormones and menstrual cycles
· Supports pregnancy and labor
· Reduces water retention
· Supports the lymphatic system and strengthens the immune system
· Soothes stomach pains and calms hyperacidity

Cat Eye Moonstone

Lithotherapy

· Favors clarity of mind and inner vision
· Facilitates concentration when meditating or accessing altered states of consciousness
· Encourages understanding of life lessons and emotional patterns
· Balances yin and yang polarities
· Supports the central nervous system
· Eases symptoms of asthma
· Diminishes stress
· Treats and protects the liver

New Moonstone

Lithotherapy

· Helps us to see beyond the veil of illusion
· Facilitates the travel of clairvoyants and shamans into other dimensions
· Holds the power of the new moon, in which everything exists in potentiality

Peach Moonstone

Lithotherapy

· Emits a sweet and loving energy, which sustains the heart while stimulating the mind
· Encourages the perception and celebration of the positive aspect of all situations, the divine love that sustains all moments
· Alleviates worry and anxiety by emitting a calming energy that soothes the emotional body
· Encourages sensitivity and intuition in children

246

Rainbow Moonstone

Lithotherapy

· Acts as a prism that shines throughout the whole aura
· Purifies the psychic senses and the mind
· Infuses the auric field with joyful energy
· Encourages clarity when working on intuitive planes
· Provides protection, particularly against psychic attacks, due to its ability to dissipate negative energies before they enter into the energetic field
· Purifies the emotional body and soothes traumas

White Moonstone

Lithotherapy

· Represents the power of the moon at its peak
· Stimulates all aspects of psychic perception
· Contributes to the study of dreams
· May magnify emotional states, as does the full moon itself
· Balances emotions and helps us to be more receptive

Selenite Family

Geometric alliance: monoclinic
Colors: beige, brown white, greenish, pink, transparent (rare, gem quality)
Chakras: according to color
Hardness: 2
Origin: France, Great Britain, Greece, Mexico, Poland, Russia, United States
Formation Process: sedimentary
Purification: incense, abundance of sunlight, avoid water and salt
Recharging: quartz cluster, frequent and abundant sunlight

Generalities

Placing a significant piece of selenite in a home will ensure a serene atmosphere. Selenite also acts as a protective stone when a piece is placed in the corner of each room.

Lithotherapy

· Enhances telepathy due to its purity
· Aligns all the bodies
· Relaxes and clarifies the mind
· Encourages expansion of consciousness
· Anchors the body of light on Earth
· Instills a deep sense of peace (meditation stone)
· Allows us to contact past and future lives
· Helps us develops intuition and discernment
· Eliminates disorientation
· Allows us to perceive subtleties
· Brings a conscious understanding to the unconscious
· Activates and stimulates the memory and intellect
· Generates a sense of physical well-being
· Soothes the nervous system and eases spasms
· Aligns the spine
· Confers flexibility
· Eases symptoms of epilepsy
· Neutralizes mercury poisoning caused by dental fillings
· Strengthens bones and teeth
· Produces a positive effect on the brain
· Improves concentration and clarity of mind
· Benefits the stomach
· Strengthens body tissues and restores the skin's elasticity
· Stimulates cellular regeneration, which may prolong life
· Benefits the prostate
· Fortifies the uterus and supports the organs of the abdomen during pregnancy
· Supports during breast-feeding

It is preferable to avoid placing selenite in water or in a humid environment as it tends to dissolve in such conditions.

Blue Selenite

Lithotherapy

· Calms the mind when placed on the third eye
· Allows us to ignore mental chatter during meditation
· Rapidly reveals the root of a problem

Desert Rose Selenite

Lithotherapy

· Promotes powerful psychic communication
· Promotes communication with wise ancestors, angels, and guides as well as accesses cosmic archives
· Encourages all forms of communication
· Dissolves obsolete programming or replaces it with the more appropriate
· Allows us to see through lies and behind facades
· Stimulates dream recall and past lives
· Reinforces affirmations relating to specific goals

Fishtail Selenite

Lithotherapy

· Facilitates contact with the angelic realm
· Treats illnesses of the nervous system
· Soothes and stabilizes the emotions
· Dissolves tension

Green Selenite

Lithotherapy

· Motivates us to act for the greater good
· Encourages self-acceptance
· Acts as prevention against aging of the skin and skeletal system

Orange Brown Selenite

Lithotherapy

· Anchors angelic energies
· Contributes to the healing of the Earth

Seraphinite

Geometric alliance: monoclinic
Colors: brown, green with a silver gleam, red, yellow, occasionally white
Chakras: all
Hardness: 4
Origin: Russia
Formation Process: metamorphic, sedimentary
Purification: quartz cluster, green clay, cold water, sunlight, earth
Recharging: quartz cluster, sunlight

Generalities

As its name suggests, seraphinite resonates with the order of angels closest to God and most luminous, the Seraphs. Seraphim signifies "the one who sets ablaze" and who purifies using the divine flame and lightning. It is said that seraphinite is an essential healing stone in this new era. It is also considered the stone of angels due to its elevated vibration.

Lithotherapy

· Facilitates the opening of the heart and crown chakra
· Protects, especially the heart chakra
· Amplifies the beneficial properties of other stones
· Activates contact with the higher angelic realm
· Inspires the desire to live consciously and to develop intuition
· Purifies the two principal energy channels, ida and pingala
· Balances yin and yang
· Encourages transformation and transmutation
· Powerfully regenerates and strengthens

- Acts against the growth and reproduction of cancer cells; one of the best stones for this
- Fights addictions
- Reduces chills
- Eliminates muscular tension in the neck and heart
- Supports the nerves and brain cells
- Purifies the blood and eliminates toxins in the kidneys and liver
- Contributes to weight loss

Note that when placed at the crown chakra, seraphinite balances and aligns all the chakras.

Serpentine

Geometric alliance: monoclinic
Colors: pale green to yellowish green
Chakras: heart, throat
Hardness: 2.5 to 4
Origin: Afghanistan, China, England, Europe (the Alps), France (Armorican and Central Massif regions), Italy, the Pyrenees in France and Spain, New Zealand, Norway, Russia, South Africa, United States, Zimbabwe
Formation Process: metamorphic
Purification: cold water, incense, earth
Recharging: quartz cluster, avoid sunlight

Generalities

In ancient Assyria, serpentine was worn to attract benedictions from gods and goddesses. It was also used to repel illness and counter witchcraft.

Lithotherapy

- Balances mood swings
- Directs a curative energy toward mental and emotional imbalances
- Conveys a peaceful attitude in the midst of conflict
- Appeases nervousness and stress
- Instills a sense of mastery over life

- Communicates peace and gentleness to the emotional body, thereby encouraging the release of the fear of change and adversity
- Grounds during meditation and spiritual exploration
- Stimulates visualization during meditative exercises
- Protects while traveling
- Restores depleted energy reserves
- Fortifies the heart and lungs
- Soothes headaches and calms the nervous system
- Favors calcium and magnesium absorption
- Strengthens the kidneys, bladder, stomach, and intestines
- Calms cramps and eases menstrual pains
- Treats hypoglycemia and diabetes

Stones of the Quadratic Alliance

Apophyllite

Geometric alliance: quadratic (tetragonal)
Colors: blue green, clear, white, yellowish
Chakras: heart, crown, third eye
Hardness: 4.5 to 5
Origin: Australia, Brazil, Czech Republic, Great Britain, India, Italy, Norway, Slovenia
Formation Process: magmatic
Purification: cold water, incense, sunlight, earth
Recharging: quartz cluster, sunlight

Generalities

Apophyllite is a stone rich in water, which confers a superior energetic conductivity than other phyllosilicates. A highly spiritual stone, it allows us to reach a deeper state of relaxation and receptivity.

Placed on the throat, apophyllite soothes asthma attacks; it soothes the eyes when placed directly on them.

Lithotherapy

· Favors an examination of our own behavior
· Encourages the discovery of our true self
· Instills tranquility and calm
· Helps alleviate depression and psychological blockages
· Known as the "Stone of Truth," it encourages honesty and sociability
· Facilitates remaining true to ourselves at all times
· Alleviates fears and oppressive feelings
· Releases repressed emotions
· Incites us to overcome problems and insecurities
· Brings light to difficult times
· Helps to release fixations and rigid thought patterns
· Encourages feeling at ease in our body
· Soothes respiratory problems

- Stimulates the heart by increasing the intake of oxygen, which helps eliminate toxins
- Regenerates tissues and blood vessels
- Favors regeneration of the skin and mucous membranes
- Neutralizes allergies and asthma

CHALCOPYRITE

Geometric alliance: quadratic (tetragonal)
Colors: golden metallic sheen, sometimes with orange nuances and multicolored iridescence on the surface
Chakras: crown, third eye
Hardness: 3.5 to 4
Origin: South Africa, Spain, United States
Formation Process: magmatic, metamorphic, sedimentary
Purification: cold water, incense, sunlight, earth
Recharging: quartz cluster, abundant sunlight

Generalities

Chalcopyrite is a stone that is dynamic and stimulating for the mind and in harmony with spiritual energies.

Lithotherapy

- Powerful general disinfectant
- Soothes rheumatism
- Alleviates hepatic or abdominal pains
- Improves blood irrigation

Rutile

Geometric alliance: quadratic (tetragonal)
Colors: dark gray with metallic shine, generally gilded and occasionally orange red
Chakras: crown, root
Hardness: 6 to 6.5
Origin: Brazil, Madagascar, United States (Arkansas)
Formation Process: magmatic
Purification: cold water, saltwater, incense, sunlight, earth
Recharging: quartz cluster, abundance of sunlight

Generalities

Rutile acts as an antenna that can be synchronized to divine frequencies. Thus it not only enhances psychic abilities but also amplifies emotions, whether they are positive or negative.

Lithotherapy

· Inspires hope
· Encourages integrity, truthfulness, and independence
· Confers a noble spirit
· Is an effective mood enhancer
· Acts as an antidepressant
· Dissipates hidden and buried fears
· Encourages the adoption of a new and more positive lifestyle
· Symbolizes the truth
· Enlarges the vision
· Stabilizes the emotions
· Protects against psychic attacks
· Stimulates self-healing and eliminates mental blocks
· Balances the thyroid gland
· Relieves breathing problems and chronic bronchitis by reducing inflammation
· Activates cell regeneration, regulates the nervous system, and boosts the immune system
· Stimulates physical growth as well as the proper flow of energy in the body

- Promotes sound, restful sleep
- Helps with sexual problems such as impotence, premature ejaculation, and sterility

Vesuvianite (Idocrase)

Geometric alliance: quadratic (tetragonal)
Colors: ocher, olive green to orange brown
Chakras: hara, solar plexus
Hardness: 6.5 to 7
Origin: Canada, Italy, Russia, United States
Formation Process: metamorphic
Purification: cold water, incense, sunlight, earth
Recharging: quartz cluster, abundance of sunlight

Generalities

Vesuvianite is a stone that offers support in the personal battle between the ego and the self. It serves as a guide on the path to achieving our true life purpose.

Lithotherapy

- Balances and strengthens the heart chakra
- Contributes to healing past lives and to liberating us from mental and emotional prisons
- Liberates us from feelings of confinement
- Gently dissipates anger and neutralizes negative thought patterns
- Acts as a support to combat fear and melancholy
- Broadens the mind and stimulates us to take action
- Stimulates creativity and the need for discovery
- Alleviates symptoms of depression
- Facilitates the assimilation of nutrients
- Restores the sense of smell
- Fortifies tooth enamel
- Combats chronic illnesses caused by environmental pollutants such as lead or mercury
- Supports convalescence after a long illness
- Benefits the kidneys and bladder

Wulfenite

Geometric alliance: quadratic (tetragonal)
Colors: from honey yellow to orange yellow, vermilion red
Chakras: hara, solar plexus
Hardness: 3
Origin: Austria, Democratic Republic of the Congo, Mexico, Morocco, Namibia, Slovenia, United States
Formation Process: sedimentary
Purification: cold water, incense, sunlight, earth
Recharging: quartz cluster, abundance of sunlight

Generalities

Wulfenite's properties are similar to those of amber in that it possesses the power to gently activate the chakra on which it is placed. It can also be programmed to initiate contact with our soul group.

Lithotherapy

· Prevents discouragement
· Benefits those in a state of imbalance
· Supports the recognition and integration of the shadow side of the self
· Acts as a mirror for those who have become superficial or false, thereby allowing for correction of these very aspects
· Favors rejuvenation and fights aging
· Preserves energy
· Activates the renal functions and treats the pancreas
· Alleviates chronic throat problems

Zircon

Geometric alliance: quadratic (tetragonal)
Colors: blue, brown, clear, orange yellow, red
Chakras: hara, third eye
Hardness: 7.5
Origin: Australia, Brazil, Cambodia, France, Madagascar, Myanmar, Tanzania, Thailand, Vietnam
Formation Process: magmatic
Purification: cold water, saltwater, incense, sunlight, earth
Recharging: quartz cluster, sunlight

Generalities

Zircon is not recommended for those prone to stress or anger. The presence of hafnium, thorium, and uranium (up to ten percent) may render this stone radioactive. In antiquity, it was believed that zircon could heal madness.

Lithotherapy

- Encourages reflection on the meaning of existence
- Contributes to overcoming feelings of grief
- Helps us to become conscious of the transitory nature of things
- Invites reflection on what is truly important in life
- Helps those who are too materialistic
- Stimulates the liver and the gallbladder
- Eases pain and prevents water retention
- Relieves abdominal cramps caused by digestive problems and blockages in the intestines
- Relieves colds and all bronchial and chest infections
- Alleviates asthma and allergy-related problems
- Stimulates the metabolism and regulates blood pressure
- Treats menstrual problems

Stones of the Rhombic Alliance

Alexandrite (Variety of Chrysoberyl)

Geometric alliance: rhombic (orthorhombic)
Colors: violet in artificial light, green reflections in the sunlight
Chakra: solar plexus
Hardness: 8.5
Origin: Brazil, Madagascar, Myanmar, Russia, United States
Formation Process: metamorphic
Purification: saltwater in low light, cold water, incense, sunlight, earth; rarely necessary
Recharging: quartz cluster, sunlight

Generalities

It was named in honor of Alexander II, czar of Russia. It became the national stone of Russia due to its red and green, colors associated with the Russian army. Alexandrite is a very rare, expensive stone. Interestingly, it can change color according to whether it is exposed to sunlight or artificial light.

Lithotherapy

· Imparts balance between force and gentleness, and between power and humility
· In sunlight it is green, the color of peace and love; in artificial light it is red, the color of strength and willpower.
· Awakens willpower and a dynamic attitude, particularly when the task is stressful, as it alleviates nervousness and stimulates creativity and intelligence
· Facilitates strategic thought and planning
· Acts as an anti-inflammatory
· Improves blood circulation, protects against heart attacks, and regulates blood flow to the brain
· Regenerates the liver
· Awakens the power to heal ourselves
· Confers longevity and protection

- Promotes self-respect and self-esteem
- Creates inner harmony, joy, and enthusiasm
- Has an effect on the nervous and glandular systems
- Helps alleviate stomach, spleen, and pancreatic disorders
- Relieves tension in the muscles and neck

ANDALUSITE

Geometric alliance: rhombic (orthorhombic)
Colors: brown, gray, from green-yellowish shades to green brown, red brown
Chakras: heart, root, solar plexus
Hardness: 7.5
Origin: Brazil, Canada, Russia, Spain, United States
Formation Process: magmatic, metamorphic
Purification: cold water, saltwater, incense, sunlight, earth; rarely necessary
Recharging: quartz cluster, sunlight

Generalities

Because of its shape, andalusite is often confused with tourmaline. Unlike its sister stone, chiastolite, it doesn't have a central cross-like pattern.

Lithotherapy

- Grants great protection
- Transforms chaos and conflict into harmony
- Contributes to the transition from one situation to another
- Neutralizes conditioning and programming
- Stabilizes emotions and helps us to remain centered
- Releases fears, particularly the fear of insanity, and eliminates feelings of guilt
- Soothes the nervous system
- Reinforces the intuition in order to achieve professional objectives
- Guides toward the expression of our authentic self, aligned with our life mission
- Fortifies analytical abilities

- Encourages psychological maturation and independence
- Dissipates illusions
- Gives a sense of reality and objectivity, encouraging detachment
- Instills balance between the material world and our spiritual selves
- Eases the transition at the time of death
- Encourages moderation in all things
- Facilitates astral journeys and the comprehension and exploration of immortality
- Alleviates hyperacidity, rheumatism, and gout
- Fortifies nerves during weakened states, diminished cognitive capacities, and reduced mobility
- Alleviates paralysis of the nerves, muscles, and joints
- Regulates sleep
- Balances the immune system

GREEN ANDALUSITE

Lithotherapy

- Provides balance
- Purifies the heart
- Releases emotional hang-ups, particularly those caused by anger and old emotional traumas
- Used in psychotherapy sessions

ARAGONITE

Geometric alliance: rhombic (orthorhombic)
Colors: blue, brownish red, golden yellow, green, greenish brown, white, yellow
Chakras: according to color
Hardness: 3.5 to 4
Origin: Great Britain, Namibia, Spain
Formation Process: magmatic, sedimentary
Purification: cold water, incense, abundant sunlight
Recharging: quartz cluster, sunlight

Generalities

Aragonite is a stone that anchors us to the Earth and reinforces our connection with Mother Earth. It accompanies us into the past, helping to resolve conflicts and issues that keep us from moving forward.

Lithotherapy

- Increases vibrations and anchors us to the physical body in meditation
- Helps prevent nightmares and sleepwalking
- Stabilizes and balances
- Alleviates stress and banishes anger
- Stimulates communication on higher planes of consciousness
- Teaches patience and tolerance
- Helps to maintain a state of well-being and acceptance during periods of great responsibility
- Awakens powers of discrimination for those who give too much of themselves
- Encourages a peaceful and pleasant mood and quite comportment
- Teaches us to delegate when necessary
- Favors reliability
- Keeps us practical and grounded
- Encourages us to feel at ease in our body
- Reduces hypersensitivity
- Reduces chills and helps to warm the extremities
- Alleviates vitamin A and D deficiencies
- Promotes healthy bone formation and good joint mobility due to its high calcium content
- Helps prevent hair loss, wrinkles, and callused feet

BARITE (BARYTINE)

Geometric alliance: rhombic (orthorhombic)
Color: colorless, white, pale yellow
Chakra: crown
Hardness: 3 to 3.5
Origin: France, Germany, Switzerland
Formation Process: magmatic, sedimentary
Purification: incense, sunlight; avoid water
Recharging: quartz cluster, abundant sunlight

Generalities

Barite is a powerful protective stone. Its name derives from the Greek word *barys*, meaning "heavy." North American native people used it in their rituals to enter spirit worlds. It is also one of the main sources of barium.

Lithotherapy

- Confers effective protection against negative energies, evil spells, and radiation
- Is ideal for relationships because it wards off negative influences
- Protects us from ourselves by encouraging us to focus on what is essential in life
- Helps alleviate depression
- Lowers high blood pressure by calming agitation and promoting inner flexibility
- Alleviates skin damage (acne, burns, sunburn, inflammation, and irritation)
- Treats fungal infections of nails and teeth
- Helps counter addictions, agoraphobia, and compulsive behavior
- Balances brain chemistry and enhances the mechanical function of cells and brain synapses
- Alleviates chronic fatigue
- Reduces extreme sensitivity to cold

Cat's Eye (Cymophane)

Geometric alliance: rhombic (orthorhombic)
Colors: brownish green to yellow with a light iridescent stripe on the surface that moves according to the direction of light
Chakras: heart, solar plexus
Hardness: 8.5
Origin: Brazil, China
Formation Process: magmatic, metamorphic
Purification: cold water, saltwater, incense, moonlight, sunlight, earth
Recharging: quartz cluster, moonlight, sunlight

Lithotherapy

· Helps find solutions to apparently unsolvable problems
· Attracts good fortune
· Offers protection against negative energies
· Contributes to freeing ourselves from harmful behaviors
· Awakens courage
· Favors creativity
· Calms impulsiveness
· Elevates the spirits and communicates joy
· Inspires forgiveness
· Encourages flexibility, versatility, and adaptability
· Leads to professional, financial, and emotional success
· Encourages philosophical reflection
· Confers energy, suppleness, and audacity
· Increases precision and speed in body reflexes and movements
· Calms stress
· Supports athletes who must make short but intense efforts, such as sprinting and jumping
· Alleviates hearing problems
· Facilitates night vision
· Regulates and protects the liver, gallbladder, pancreas, and bowels
· Relieves the bronchial tubes and lungs and treats asthma
· Assists the body when low in minerals and vitamins
· Supports the central nervous system
· Eliminates toxins

CELESTITE

Geometric alliance: rhombic (orthorhombic)
Colors: blue, red, reddish brown, white, yellow
Chakras: heart, throat
Hardness: 3 to 3.5
Origin: Egypt, Great Britain, Lebanon, Madagascar, Mexico, Peru
Formation Process: sedimentary
Purification: cold water, incense, earth
Recharging: quartz cluster, sunlight

Generalities

Known as an exceptional healing stone, celestite dissolves pain and instills love. Bearer of the energy of maternal love, this stone provides great support for children.

Lithotherapy

· Encourages spiritual growth
· Stimulates clairvoyance, dream recall, out-of-body travel, and contact with the angelic realm
· Cultivates purity of heart
· Balances yin and yang energies
· Helps to maintain an atmosphere of harmony during stressful times
· Improves difficult relationships through negotiation
· Increases artistic creativity
· Favors deep peace, allowing us to open up to new experiences
· Teaches us to trust in divine wisdom
· Soothes fiery emotions
· Helps the healing of wounds
· Sustains clear ideas and flowing communication
· Radiates maternal love
· Reduces anxiety and relieves insomnia
· Alleviates pain caused by excess tension
· Regulates the menstrual cycle

Chiastolite

Geometric alliance: rhombic (orthorhombic)
Color: brown, gray, pink with black cruciform inclusions, yellowish green
Chakras: heart, solar plexus, root
Hardness: 6.5 to 7.5
Origin: Australia, Bolivia, Canada, Chile, Spain, United States, numerous deposits worldwide
Formation Process: metamorphic
Purification: saltwater, incense
Recharging: quartz cluster, sunlight

Generalities

The word *chiastolite* comes from the Greek *khiastos,* which means "arranged crosswise" (180 degrees). Long known at Santiago de Compostela in Spain, where its resemblance to the Greek letter χ was noted, chiastolite is a variety of andalusite with black carbon inclusions in the form of a cross. It was used to make religious artifacts such as cross stones and in ancient times was recognized for its power to ward off evil spells.

Lithotherapy

· Stimulates the development of spiritual consciousness, intuition, and creativity
· Is the gateway to out-of-body travel, understanding, and the exploration of immortality
· Grounds us in concrete reality
· Centers and stabilizes
· Is recognized as a powerful protective stone, able to transmute chaos and conflict into harmony
· Eases the transition beyond death
· Strengthens analytical faculties
· Eliminates feelings of guilt and provides emotional stability
· Dissipates illusions and calms fears, enabling us to face reality
· Helps us recognize the various facets of our personality and achieve balance

- Helps us understand that even though self-sacrifice may be a good thing, it is not an obligation
- Strengthens the nerves and improves weakness, diminished perception, and reduced mobility
- Alleviates excess acidity, rheumatism, and gout
- Stimulates lactation in nursing mothers

CHRYSOBERYL

Geometric alliance: rhombic (orthorhombic)
Color: yellow to brownish green
Chakras: solar plexus
Harness: 8.5
Origin: Brazil, Madagascar, Myanmar, Russia
Formation Process: magmatic, metamorphic
Purification: saltwater, cold water, incense, earth, sunlight
Recharging: quartz cluster, abundant sunlight

Generalities

Chrysoberyl is a powerful stone that encourages us to exceed our limits. Cat's eye is a variety of chrysoberyl that awakens knowledge and spiritual vision.

Lithotherapy

- Bestows strength, authority and leadership
- Encourages ambition, self-discipline, and self-control
- Combats fears and eliminates nightmares
- Is considered useful in stressful situations and reducing lethargy
- Helps us do what has to be done without being overwhelmed by our fears and feelings
- Stimulates strategic thinking
- Helps regulate the liver, gall bladder, pancreas, and intestines
- Stimulates a sluggish nervous system
- Promotes self-healing
- Eliminates negative thoughts and encourages optimism, kindness, and tolerance

Danburite

Geometric alliance: rhombic (orthorhombic)
Colors: colorless, light blue, light pink, translucent gold
Chakras: heart, crown
Hardness: 7 to 7.5
Origin: Japan, Madagascar, Mexico, Myanmar, United States
Formation Process: magmatic
Purification: cold water, incense, early morning sunlight, earth
Recharging: quartz cluster, early morning sunlight

Generalities

Danburite is a stone that holds spiritual virtues. It lends assistance to our inner path of growth and awareness.

Lithotherapy

· Aligns the heart chakra with the higher chakras
· Acts on the heart energy
· Endowed with a very pure vibration
· Activates the intellect and higher consciousness, helping us to connect to the angelic realm
· Bridges heaven and heart, linking us to the divine consciousness
· Liberates from karmic cycles and helps with the process of transformation
· Balances the brain hemispheres
· Alleviates blockages in the meridians
· Invites light into the aura and favors lucid dreams
· Opens the heart and incites self-love (pink danburite)
· Treats liver and gallbladder problems
· Eliminates bodily toxins
· Alleviates allergies and eases chronic conditions
· Favors weight gain if necessary
· Fortifies muscular and motor functions

When placed near the bed, danburite accompanies a dying person through his or her journey beyond death, allowing for a conscious spiritual transition. To stimulate lucid dreaming, it is recommended to place a danburite under our pillow. To prevent different types of illness, place it wherever it is needed.

Iolite

Geometric alliance: rhombic (orthorhombic)
Colors: blue, gray, violet, yellow
Chakra: third eye
Hardness: 7 to 7.5
Origin: Brazil, India, Madagascar, Myanmar, Sri Lanka, United States
Formation Process: magmatic
Purification: quartz cluster, cold water, saltwater, incense, abundance of sunlight, earth
Recharging: quartz cluster, abundance of sunlight

Generalities

Iolite has a particular affinity with the era of the Knights Templar, the Cathari, and the legend of King Arthur. It is a stone of high spirituality and vision.

Lithotherapy

· Activates the third eye
· Enhances visualization and intuition
· Facilitates access to inner wisdom
· Contributes to the integration of common thinking with intuitive knowing
· Possesses the capacity to unlock the gateways of memory in order to integrate lessons and information acquired in past lives
· Offers support during out-of-body travels
· Encourages the creative expression of spiritual ideas and ideals
· Dissolves the fear of the unknown and repressed aspects of the psyche
· Produces an electrical jolt that heightens the vibrational level of the auric field
· Aligns the subtle bodies
· Brings an understanding and a release of the causes of addictive behaviors
· Encourages free expression of the higher self, regardless of what others may say or think
· Clarifies thoughts
· Eases discord in relationships
· Promotes responsibility
· Alleviates codependency in intimate relationships

- Strengthens the body structure
- Eliminates fat deposits from the body
- Diminishes the side effects of alcohol
- Detoxifies and regenerates the liver
- Fights malaria and fever
- Supports the pituitary gland, the sinuses, and the respiratory system
- Treats eye problems
- Alleviates migraines
- Eliminates unhealthy bacteria

MARCASITE

Geometric alliance: rhombic (orthorhombic)
Color: pale greenish yellow
Chakra: solar plexus
Hardness: 6 to 6.5
Origin: Italy, Peru, Spain
Formation Process: magmatic, sedimentary
Purification: cold water, incense, earth, sunlight
Recharging: quartz cluster, sunlight

Generalities

For many years, marcasite and pyrite were easily confused because they have so much in common: the same composition, hardness, and appearance. They are also both found in iron mines. In fact, the only difference is that marcasite belongs to the rhombic alliance, whereas pyrite is associated with the cubic alliance.

Lithotherapy

Using marcasite in lithotherapy isn't recommended because it can decompose into iron sulfate particles, which are harmful to our health, when it comes in contact with damp or wet skin. Marcasite also oxidizes on contact with air, producing sulfuric acid and iron sulfate. However, there is no reason not to wear it in jewelry when it is lacquered or varnished to prevent oxidation.

- Is appropriate for architects and builders as it is considered a stone of creativity and inspiration
- Promotes friendship
- Enhances energy, dynamism, and charisma
- Soothes the nerves
- Strengthens eyesight

Marcasite shouldn't be used if it is even only slightly damaged. When it oxidizes, it produces sulfuric acid and iron sulfate.

PERIDOT (OLIVINE OR CHRYSOLITE)

Geometric alliance: rhombic (orthorhombic)
Colors: from pale green to yellowish green to olive green
Chakras: heart, solar plexus
Hardness: 6.5 to 7
Origin: Australia, Brazil, Democratic Republic of Congo, Egypt (Zabargad Island), Myanmar, Norway, South Africa, United States
Formation Process: magmatic
Purification: cold water, saltwater, incense, sunlight, earth; rarely necessary, as peridot is very resistant to negative energies
Recharging: quartz cluster, sunlight

Generalities

Peridot, or olivine, is a protective stone and a symbol of the olive tree and olive oil, which are recognized for their nourishing and purifying aspects.

Lithotherapy

- Facilitates understanding of the necessity for change and growth
- Reveals negative habits hindering us from reaching what is necessary to evolve
- Stimulates and purifies the solar plexus and the heart, bringing openness and acceptance
- Contributes to regulating the cycles of life in the physical, emotional, and mental bodies

- Protects against outside influences and prevents them from affecting our balance
- Helps heal injured egos by attenuating anger, resentment, envy, and jealousy
- Inspires us to be happy and to rejoice in the unique expression of our own life
- Increases energy
- Harmonizes and balances emotions
- Brings joy and stimulates the mind
- Attracts wisdom and friendship
- Provides freedom from self-reproach
- Increases confidence and assurance without awakening aggressiveness
- Encourages self-forgiveness and the acceptance of personal faults
- Purifies the subtle bodies and the mind
- Reinforces the etheric body
- Diminishes stress
- Eliminates toxins from the body and neutralizes them on all planes
- Prevents dehydration
- Stimulates the liver and bile production
- Activates the metabolism (tonic effect)
- Provides relief of skin ailments, especially warts
- Helps to overcome fatigue
- Facilitates proper functioning of the intestines
- Reinforces the heart, thymus, spleen, and lungs

PREHNITE

Geometric alliance: rhombic (orthorhombic)
Colors: light green to yellowish green
Chakras: heart, solar plexus, third eye
Hardness: 6 to 6.5
Origin: Australia, China, Scotland, South Africa, United States
Formation process: magmatic
Purification: cold water, incense, sunlight, earth
Recharging: quartz cluster, sunlight

Generalities

Prehnite is said to be a stone of unconditional love that will "heal the healer." Meditating with it allows us to connect to the energetic framework of the universe. It establishes a link with the archangel Raphael and facilitates a connection to other spiritual and extraterrestrial beings.

Lithotherapy

- Increases psychic abilities and intuition
- Enhances the visualization process and motivates us toward deep meditation in which the higher self can be contacted
- Pinpoints the way to spiritual evolution
- Prepares us for any eventuality
- Favors a tranquil environment that brings peace and protection
- Seals the aura with a protective shield of divine energy
- Teaches how to be in harmony with nature and the elements
- Helps to eliminate what is no longer useful to personal growth, whether it be possessions or ties with others
- Contributes to dissolving escape and repression mechanisms
- Supports us when facing repressed memories and the associated liberation of emotions
- Speeds up the processing of sensory information
- Increases the capacity to receive
- Favors understanding by analysis
- Alleviates phobias, nightmares, and deep fears
- Facilitates the discovery of the root cause of certain problems or illnesses
- Activates the metabolism
- Stimulates all renewal processes in the body
- Speeds up the elimination of toxins accumulated in body fat
- Treats thymus, shoulder, chest, and lung problems
- Helps with urinary incontinence by treating the kidneys and bladder

STIBNITE

Geometric alliance: rhombic (orthorhombic)
Color: metallic gray
Chakra: root
Harness: 2
Origin: Bolivia, France, Japan, South Africa
Formation Process: magmatic
Purification: incense
Recharging: quartz cluster, moonlight

Generalities

Stibnite is mainly found in the form of wands several inches long.

Lithotherapy

- Considered a powerful stone that shields the etheric body by acting as an impenetrable barrier
- Protects against involution as it provides confidence in combating lower astral forces
- Enhances meditation through providing protection when entering unknown zones
- Strengthens weak immune systems, cleanses the lymphatic system
- Encourages discernment and wisdom
- In lithotherapy, relieves pain when directed toward a painful area
- Strengthens the liver
- Can be a valuable aid for tendinitis, torn muscles, rheumatism, muscle cramps, and certain eye problems
- Treats esophageal and stomach disorders (heartburn, nausea, vomiting)
- Relieves skin problems (dryness, rashes, eczema, itching)
- Diminishes inflexible behavior

SULFUR

Geometric alliance: rhombic (orthorhombic)
Colors: bright yellow, sometimes slightly brownish or brownish green
Chakra: solar plexus
Hardness: 1.5 to 2
Origin: Indonesia, Italy, Japan, United States
Formation Process: magmatic, sedimentary
Purification: incense, sunlight
Recharging: quartz cluster, sunlight

Generalities

For many years, sulfur was an object of fear, but it's now time to get to know it better. Its relationship to the body is that of the sun to our universe—an endless source of energy, power, and light.

Lithotherapy

· Provides powerful protection against evil spells
· Has the ability to absorb negative energies
· Facilitates connection to our inner light
· Inspires a genuine change of self by shedding new light on obstacles blocking our transformation
· Brings joy and good humor; helps alleviate depression
· Reduces stubbornness
· Enhances creativity
· Stimulates the desire and will to be cured when used with citrine
· Purifies the blood, intestines, and urine
· Fights bacteria and parasites; is a strong cleanser
· Relieves fever and inflammation
· Reduces allergies and viral epidemics
· Combats colds and the flu
· Calms rashes

Tanzanite (Blue Zoisite)

Geometric alliance: rhombic (orthorhombic)
Color: indigo, purplish blue, bluish violet
Chakras: throat, third eye, crown
Hardness: 6.5 to 7
Origin: Kenya, Tanzania
Formation Process: metamorphic
Purification: saltwater
Recharging: quartz cluster, limited sunlight, abundant moonlight

Generalities

A blue variety of zoisite, this stone was discovered in Tanzania in 1967. Most tanzanites on the market have been heated to produce or enhance their color.

Lithotherapy

· Has a high vibration
· Facilitates and deepens meditation
· Stimulates the imagination, intuition, and creativity
· Sharpens therapists' intuition in treating their patients
· Activates the connections between the chakras and facilitates contact between the physical and higher mental levels
· Purifies and clarifies the spirit
· Stimulates our mental faculties to serve our hearts
· Has a soothing effect, promoting calm restorative sleep
· Strengthens the memory (Alzheimer's); stimulates curiosity
· Very beneficial for vision and hearing
· Promotes cellular healing
· Supports healing after surgery
· Promotes the absorption of calcium
· Treats dyslexia, varicose veins, painful and tired limbs, cataracts, glaucoma, bone problems, and incontinence

Topaz Family

Geometric alliance: rhombic (orthorhombic)
Colors: blue, clear brown, golden yellow, green, reddish pink
Chakras: heart, crown, throat, third eye
Hardness: 8
Origin: Australia, Brazil, Japan, Madagascar, Mexico, Myanmar, Nigeria, Russia, Sri Lanka, United States
Formation Process: magmatic
Purification: cold water, saltwater, incense, sunlight, earth
Recharging: quartz cluster, abundance of sunlight

Generalities

Topaz is considered to be the stone of Jupiter. Ancient civilizations therefore recognized its ability to grant us the power to control our lives. Golden topaz is associated with the sun, while blue topaz spreads this solar fire throughout the sky.

Lithotherapy

- Guides toward self-realization in tune with filial desires
- Brings to light our own inner wealth
- Encourages truth, candor, and honesty
- Removes doubt and uncertainty toward our inner being
- Confers joy, abundance, and health
- Purifies the aura
- Induces relaxation by eliminating tension
- Inspires self-confidence
- Encourages a philanthropic attitude
- Sharpens and reinforces the intellect
- Facilitates the expression of ideas
- Aligns and recharges the meridians
- Facilitates digestion
- Fights anorexia
- Activates the metabolism
- Promotes the process of recovery and regeneration following surgery
- Improves blood circulation, thereby warming cold extremities
- Treats varicose veins as well as cardiovascular problems

- Fights exhaustion and insomnia
- Revitalizes the liver
- Stimulates the taste buds
- Fortifies the nerves

BLUE TOPAZ

Lithotherapy

- Connected to the angelic realm, particularly the angels of truth and wisdom
- Enhances meditation
- Stimulates artistic inspiration
- Contributes to living life according to our true aspirations
- Improves verbal expression
- Eases ailments of the throat
- Stimulates the renal functions
- Treats head injuries and general afflictions of the head and skull
- Alleviates occipital pains, jaw clenching, and migraines

CLEAR TOPAZ

Lithotherapy

- Reveals the karmic consequences of our actions
- Purifies negative emotions
- Facilitates insight and realizations
- Dissipates stagnant energies

GOLD TOPAZ (IMPERIAL TOPAZ)

Lithotherapy

- Revitalizes the body and mind
- Augments faith and optimism
- Balances mood swings
- Encourages harmony with the higher forces
- Facilitates access to akashic archives
- Contributes to the recognition of our own faculties

- Improves confidence
- Inspires us to overcome limitations
- Regenerates cellular structures
- Facilitates recovery from nervous exhaustion and burnout
- Aids with the assimilation of nutrients
- Treats the liver and gallbladder and balances the endocrine glands

PINK TOPAZ

Lithotherapy

- Restores hope
- Gently eliminates uneasiness
- Offers the possibility to perceive the face of the divine

VARISCITE (UTAHITE)

Geometric alliance: rhombic (orthorhombic)
Colors: colorless, gray, green
Chakras: heart, throat
Hardness: 4 to 5
Origin: Australia, Germany, Unites States
Formation Process: sedimentary
Purification: distilled water, avoid salt
Recharging: quartz cluster, sunlight

Generalities

The properties of variscite vary according to its color. Sometimes they are similar to those of chrysoprase and other times to those of chrysocolla. A stone of encouragement, variscite helps improve understanding and dialogue and promotes self-confidence.

Lithotherapy

- Considered a stone of encouragement, hope, and courage
- Stimulates intuition
- Encourages authenticity and truthfulness
- Dissolves illusions so that we can show our true selves to the world

- Opens the heart chakra and allows unconditional love to enter
- Increases self-confidence and confidence in the future
- Contributes to self-expression and the communication of ideas
- Encourages restful sleep and calms the spirit when placed under the pillow
- Restores depleted energy reserves, thereby helping in cases of chronic fatigue
- Calms nervousness and inner agitation; reduces stress
- Neutralizes excess acidity and is beneficial for gout, hyperacidity, stomach ulcers, and rheumatism

ZOISITE

Geometric alliance: rhombic (orthorhombic).
Colors: brownish green with red (ruby), green
Chakras: heart, root, third eye
Hardness: 6.5 to 7
Origin: Australia, Cambodia, India, Kenya, Madagascar, Russia, South Africa, Sri Lanka, Tanzania
Formation Process: metamorphic
Purification: cold water, incense, sunlight, earth
Recharging: quartz cluster, sunlight

Generalities

In moments of indecisiveness, zoisite inspires the capacity to make enlightened and authentic choices. It is recommended to work with zoisite on a consistent basis, as it is known to take time before demonstrating its effect.

Lithotherapy

- Transforms negative energies into positive ones
- Encourages breaking free from the influence of others
- Allows us to reconnect with true desires and intentions, thereby allowing for the attainment of authentic dreams and goals
- Enhances creativity
- Transforms destructive attitudes into a more constructive lifestyle

- Eliminates lethargy
- Uncovers suppressed emotions to allow for their expression
- Encourages rest and recovery following an illness or difficult circumstances
- Increases fertility and stimulates sexual energy
- Is considered a protective stone during pregnancy
- Treats testicular and ovarian conditions
- Strengthens the immune system and detoxifies
- Detoxifies and neutralizes hyperacidity and inflammation

Stones of the Triclinic Alliance

Amazonite

Geometric alliance: triclinic
Color: blue green
Chakras: all, but mainly heart, third eye, and throat
Hardness: 6 to 6.5
Origin: Brazil, India, Russia, South Africa, United States (Colorado)
Formation Process: magmatic, sedimentary, metamorphic
Purification: cold water, incense, sunlight, earth
Recharging: quartz cluster, abundant sunlight (rapidly discharges)

Generalities

According to legend, amazonite was the stone of the Amazons, a group of female warriors who lived in a community without men.

Lithotherapy

· Encourages loving communication
· Contributes to the development of intuition
· Facilitates self-expression
· Encourages self-sufficiency and connection to our inner power
· Encourages confidence, triggers vitality, and stimulates joy in living
· Treats depression and reduces anxiety when placed on the third chakra
· Balances thyroid glands
· Strengthens weakened muscles
· Renews energy during periods of general fatigue
· Regularizes the metabolism (liver)
· Encourages relaxation during childbirth, thus facilitating the opening of the cervix
· Fortifies nerves
· Alleviates some brain ailments
· Relieves headaches and migraines when worn as a necklace (is effective for migraines when an amazonite necklace is in direct contact with the skin)

- Harmonizes the pituitary gland and thymus as well as the autonomic nervous system and internal organs
- Alleviates cardiac pain due to grief
- Resolves calcium deficiencies
- Has a beneficial influence on osteoporosis and tooth decay
- Soothes cramps and muscular spasms
- Helps relieve stress, tension, and pain, including neuralgia
- Emits a strong soothing energy, which harmonizes the nervous system by dissipating worry, fear, and anger and by balancing mood swings
- Promotes restorative sleep when placed under the pillow

Amazonite also protects against electromagnetic waves produced by microwave ovens and computers. For this purpose, it may be worn directly on the body or set near the microwave oven or beside the computer. It is also possible to attach it to a cell phone.

KYANITE (CYANITE, DISTHENE)

Geometric alliance: triclinic
Colors: black, blue and white, gray, green, pink, yellow
Chakras: throat, third eye
Hardness: 4 to 5 in length; 7 in width
Origin: Brazil
Formation Process: metamorphic
Purification: cold water, incense, moonlight, earth
Recharging: quartz cluster, moonlight

Generalities

Kyanite builds bridges of light between all aspects of experience. It particularly encourages connecting the head with the heart.

Lithotherapy

- Strengthens the throat chakra
- Instantaneously aligns the chakras and the subtle bodies, purifying meridians and other etheric channels
- Dissolves sorrow and makes life worth living again

- Favors creative expression, communication, and is helpful when learning other languages
- Powerfully transmits and amplifies high-frequency energies stimulating intuition and psychic abilities
- Removes the veils of ignorance to reveal spiritual and psychological truths
- Encourages awareness of the illusion behind blind fate or implacable karma
- Helps us to face the past with a balanced view
- Eases the transition during the dying process
- Calms anxious thoughts and feelings
- Produces positive energy, sharpens concentration, and promotes relaxation
- Favors a peaceful and pleasant mood
- Releases frustrations
- Encourages the assertion of truth and surmounting of fears and obstacles
- Inspires rational and logical thought and reinforces memory
- Balances yin and yang energies
- Benefits psychological problems and depressive tendencies
- Reduces complexes
- Invites us to act spontaneously and with certainty when necessary
- Wards off confusion
- Dissipates blockages, illusions, anger, frustration, and stress
- Encourages healthy curiosity
- Helps the mind to be of service to the heart
- Treats the brain, particularly reinforcing the proper functioning of the cerebellum and of the motor nerves, thereby improving mobility and agility
- Treats eye and hearing problems; improves the sense of smell
- Supports the throat, thyroid, and parathyroid glands
- Eases muscle pains
- Reinforces the urogenital system and adrenal glands
- Diminishes fever and high blood pressure
- Acts as a natural analgesic and treats infections

Kyanite has a penetrating energy that acts rapidly. It improves the therapist's intuition during treatment. It is advisable not to leave it in sunlight, as it will lose its color and energy.

Labradorite (Spectrolite)

Geometric alliance: triclinic
Colors: grayish to black, with slight blue, green, red and yellow reflections
Chakras: all
Hardness: 6 to 6.5
Origin: Australia, Canada, Madagascar, Mexico, Russia, United States
Formation Process: magmatic
Purification: cold water, saltwater, incense, early morning sunlight, earth
Recharging: quartz cluster, abundant early morning sunlight

Generalities

Labradorite is indispensable for those who work in public service. It is known to provide a protective barrier, allowing us to serve wisely without losing too much energy or taking on the problems of those who are in need.

Lithotherapy

- A highly mystical stone
- Provides powerful protection
- Elevates the consciousness
- Acts as a bridge to universal energies
- Prevents energy leaks
- Provides a powerful protector, forms a barrier against undesirable energies
- Helps calm quick-tempered personalities
- Dissolves illusions
- Clearly deploys all our objectives and intentions
- Stimulates intuition and psychic gifts
- Allows forgotten memories to resurface
- Provides a deepening of sentiments
- Stimulates imagination
- Encourages contemplation and internalization
- Helps us to manifest childlike enthusiasm and favors an abundance of ideas
- Facilitates friendship
- Nourishes those who feel alone

- Provides support during periods of change
- Transmits strength and perseverance
- Balances body temperature, thereby reducing chills
- Alleviates bone problems, including rheumatism, arthritis, gout, spinal disorders, and worn-out joints
- Reduces tension and soothes
- Benefits eye and brain problems
- Balances hormones and relieves menstrual tension
- Stimulates the thymus and regulates the immune system
- Powerfully regenerates us when we're exhausted

Labradorite counters electromagnetic effects on the body that can come from devices such as televisions, microwave ovens, and computers.

LARIMAR (PECTOLITE, DOLPHIN STONE)

Geometric alliance: triclinic
Colors: blue, gray or red with white, green blue
Chakras: heart, crown, throat, third eye
Hardness: 4.5 to 5
Origin: Dominican Republic
Formation Process: magmatic
Purification: cold water, incense, sunlight, earth
Recharging: quartz cluster, sunlight

Generalities

Larimar is a feminine power stone that calls upon the energy of the Goddess, thereby facilitating access to the divine feminine aspect within us, whether male or female.

Lithotherapy

- Frees us from self-imposed chains and from slavery to the materialistic world
- Breaks down ingrained patterns, opens up to new ways of thinking and acting, protects against negative energies
- Stimulates a more profound understanding of our place in this world

- Dissolves the martyr complex
- Helps us to acknowledge our errors
- Brings peace and honesty
- Develops a capacity to see beyond the point of view of the personality
- Eliminates fear and excessive emotions
- Encourages us to stay calm during dramatic situations
- Stimulates creative and constructive thinking
- Allows us to let events happen without feeling the need to control or manipulate situations
- Motivates self-healing
- Strengthens the bones; often used to treat growing children
- Is beneficial for arthritis, hardening of the arteries and muscles, the sciatic nerve, and lumbago
- Alleviates scalp problems
- Diminishes pain, in particular foot discomforts
- Soothes sore throats
- Dissolves energy blockages in the chest, head, and neck
- Balances and purifies the meridians

RHODONITE

Geometric alliance: triclinic
Colors: red with mottled black, pink
Chakra: heart
Hardness: 5.5 to 6.5
Origin: Australia, Canada, India, Madagascar, Mexico, Russia, South Africa, Sweden, United States
Formation Process: metamorphic
Purification: cold water, incense, sunlight, earth
Recharging: quartz cluster, sunlight.

Generalities

As with other pink stones, rhodonite emanates the energy of unconditional love. Like its cousin rhodochrosite, rhodonite encourages loving without barriers, always for the benefit of those who cross our paths.

Lithotherapy

- Stimulates, liberates, and activates the heart chakra
- Confers emotional balance
- Balances the yin and yang
- Encourages love and brotherhood
- Heals self-destructive emotions as well as deep-rooted emotional wounds
- Dissolves resentment, anger, and suffering caused by abuse, betrayal, and abandonment
- Encourages forgiveness and neutralizes vengeance
- Allows us to see the solution to seemingly insoluble problems, hence giving more meaning to life
- Spurs insightfulness during conflicts (often caused by a lack of self-love)
- Encourages attention to details in relationships
- Diminishes the impact of emotional shock; dissipates panic attacks
- Alleviates primitive fears and phobias
- Calms during frustrating situations
- Activates the pineal gland by stimulating intuitive vision
- Helps cope with changes such as a separation, a new job, a move, or a long journey
- Helps in passing exams and preventing mental blocks
- Relieves wounds and insect bites
- Helps prevent scarring
- Treats arthritis
- Soothes stomach ulcers
- Treats emphysema and streptococcal infections of the throat
- Eases the symptoms of multiple sclerosis
- Alleviates hearing problems
- Reinforces the immune system and protects against allergies
- Stimulates fertility in both males and females
- Corrects cardiac problems in their early stages and stimulates the respiratory passages and the lungs
- Known as the "first aid" stone

SUNSTONE

Geometric alliance: triclinic
Colors: brown, yellow, orange, peach, pink, red with shimmering inclusions of goethite or hematite
Chakras: throat, hara, solar plexus, root
Hardness: 6 to 6.5
Origin: Canada, India, Norway, Russia, United States
Formation process: magmatic
Purification: cold water, incense, sunlight, earth
Recharging: quartz cluster, sunlight

Generalities

The name "sunstone" originates from the very nature of its properties, known to communicate joy and to transmit light.

Lithotherapy

· Has a close affinity with the solar plexus
· Has a very positive effect on the psyche
· Brings peace and contentment
· Eliminates anger and helps overcome feelings of rage
· Dispels stress, anxiety, and fear
· Facilitates positive self-affirmations and teaches how to say no
· Communicates the art and joy of living, warmth, and good humor
· Fights depression and seasonal mood disorders
· Diminishes feelings of inferiority
· Transmits a sense of self-worth and self-confidence
· Promotes optimism and the will to act
· Reveals new perspectives to the most inveterate pessimists
· Encourages healthy detachment
· Stimulates the autonomic nervous system as well as autoimmunity
· Ensures harmonious cooperation between the organs
· Eases chronic sore throats
· Relieves gastric ulcers and all digestive disorders
· Facilitates weight loss
· Helps with sexual problems and disorders of the reproductive organs
· Purifies the kidneys, bladder, and intestines

- Eases problems of the spinal column
- Relieves rheumatism, arthritis, and general difficulties related to cartilage

This stone is especially effective when used outside in the sun.

TURQUOISE

Geometric alliance: triclinic
Colors: blue, green, turquoise
Chakras: all, although mainly the heart, throat, hara, solar plexus, and third eye
Hardness: 5 to 6
Origin: Afghanistan, Austria, China, Iran, Israel, Tanzania
Formation Process: sedimentary
Purification: cold water, incense, earth
Recharging: quartz cluster, limited sunlight

Generalities

To this day, turquoise is known to possess a protective power against malicious forces. It is recognized as an ancient stone of power.

Lithotherapy

- Aligns, balances, and fortifies all the chakras and meridians
- Purifies the throat chakra, thereby activating effective oral and written communication and allowing for the expression of true emotion
- Possesses a strong capacity to regenerate and protect, providing overall health and strength
- Balances mood swings
- Calms the nervous system
- Prevents panic attacks
- Assists in recovery following depression
- Transmits the message that we are responsible for our own happiness
- Eliminates the martyr complex
- Revitalizes by providing strength and drive when we are exhausted or discouraged
- Provides endurance and self-confidence

- Protects from unhealthy external influences or atmospheric pollutants
- Provides for a consistent inner tranquility while awakening vivacity and the desire to take action
- Awakens the intuition
- Strengthens the meridians and energy fields
- Neutralizes hyperacidity
- Relieves symptoms of gout and rheumatism
- Helps fight viral infections
- Increases muscular strength
- Generates inner heat in order to warm the body
- Regenerates tissues
- Stimulates cerebral activity as well as sensory perception
- Fortifies the blood and stimulates circulation
- Balances cholesterol levels
- Eases respiratory conditions
- Soothes stomach problems
- Detoxifies, thereby acting as an analgesic, antispasmodic, and anti-inflammatory agent

Turquoise is often worn as an amulet for protection, and it has been known to change color as a warning of impending danger. Placed on the third eye, it increases intuition and intensifies meditation. Turquoise is beneficial wherever it is worn, especially at the throat, the third eye, and the solar plexus.

STONES OF THE TRIGONAL ALLIANCE

AGATE FAMILY

Geometric alliance: trigonal (rhombohedral)
Colors: blue, brown, green, red, yellow
Chakras: according to color
Hardness: 6.5 to 7
Origin: Brazil, India, Madagascar, Uruguay
Formation Process: magmatic
Purification: cold water, saltwater, incense, earth
Recharging: quartz cluster, sunlight

Generalities

In ancient times, agate was considered a lucky charm and a stone of protection. In India, Nepal, and Tibet it is worn as an amulet and is still known for its virtues.

Lithotherapy

· Balances and harmonizes the body, mind, and spirit
· Cleans and stabilizes the aura, removing all negativity
· Stimulates and reinforces analytical abilities
· Reinforces powers of concentration and brings clarity of thought
· Revives inspiration and facilitates access to spiritual worlds
· Helps to discern the truth and to accept reality
· Gives strength and courage
· Stabilizes body energies
· Calms and balances both mother and child during pregnancy and labor
· Prevents the descent of the uterus and stimulates tissue regeneration of the uterus after childbirth
· Alleviates eye diseases such as conjunctivitis
· Treats gastritis and stomach tumors
· Reduces bladder and colon inflammation
· Facilitates digestion and excretion
· Reinforces blood vessels and tissues
· Eases skin ailments
· Purifies the lymphatic system and pancreas

Placed on the heart, agate treats emotional turmoil that prevents us from accepting love; placed on the stomach, it stimulates the digestion process.

BLUE LACE AGATE

Lithotherapy

· Activates and balances the throat chakra
· Encourages a positive attitude
· Neutralizes anger, infections, inflammations, and fever
· Calms the mind, encourages peace and tranquility, and elevates the consciousness
· Reduces inflammation and diminishes deformities caused by arthritis
· Fortifies the skeletal structure and treats broken bones
· Relieves irritated red eyes and inflamed irritated skin
· Treats shoulder and neck problems
· Alleviates thyroid and lymphatic deficiencies
· Calms throat infections
· Facilitates the functioning of the pancreas

FIRE AGATE

Lithotherapy

· Has an affinity with the root chakra
· Helps to ground the self and to establish a connection of power with the Earth
· Creates a shield around the body represents a great protective force
· Incites destruction and transmutation of the "old"
· Helps eliminate obstacles to radical change
· Calms fears and instills a profound feeling of security
· Revitalizes and energizes when we are exhausted
· Eliminates envy and destructive desire
· Treats addiction and dependency
· Fortifies night vision and clarifies inner vision
· Increases vitality at all levels, including the libido
· Eases stomach problems
· Balances the endocrine and nervous systems
· Treats circulatory problems
· Alleviates hot flashes and lowers body temperature

Moss Agate

Lithotherapy

· Stabilizes and balances
· Awakens a love of nature
· Known as a stone of abundance; attracts wealth
· Alleviates pain during childbirth and favors easy delivery
· Speeds up recovery, especially after a long illness
· Used as an anti-inflammatory
· Purifies the circulatory system
· Facilitates lymphatic circulation
· Activates the immune system
· Prevents hypoglycemia
· Contributes to the production of phlegm, which prevents dry cough, and reduces sensitivity to climatic conditions

Amethyst

Geometric alliance: trigonal (rhombohedral)
Colors: deep violet to pale lavender, almost to the point of being clear
Chakras: crown, third eye
Hardness: 7
Origin: Brazil, Canada, East Africa, Great Britain, India, Madagascar, Mexico, Russia (Siberia), Sri Lanka, United States, Uruguay
Formation Process: magmatic
Purification: saltwater, cold water, incense, earth
Recharging: quartz cluster, sunlight (for short periods only, or it may lose its luster)

Generalities

In ancient times amethyst was known for its sobering effects and its ability to clear the mind. In the Middle Ages it was recognized that this form of quartz instilled courage and banished negative thoughts, encouraging kindness and understanding.

Lithotherapy

· Has an affinity with the third eye and crown chakra
· Embodies the alchemical violet ray of transformation
· Offers powerful protection
· Brings clarity of mind
· Increases paranormal and mediumistic abilities
· Stimulates inspiration and intuition
· Reinforces a sense of justice and proper discrimination
· Encourages honesty and openness
· Calms an overactive inner dialogue
· Contributes to finding deep inner peace and to discovering inner wisdom
· Helps to overcome grief from mourning
· Aids visualization and clarifies dreams
· Calms passions, violent emotions, and anger
· Alleviates general pain and provides relaxation
· Eases addictions, such as to drugs or alcohol
· Help with diseases of the ectoderm of all organs
· Soothes nervous problems
· Calms the lungs and afflictions of the respiratory system
· Clears skin impurities such as boils and eases maladies of the skin and cases of swelling
· Soothes intestinal disorders and regularizes flora, even in the presence of parasites
· Reinforces the endocrine and immune systems
· Purifies the blood
· Activates the functioning of the right side of the brain and of the pituitary and pineal glands
· Relieves headaches and migraines

Placed under a pillow, amethyst encourages deep sleep, alleviates nightmares, and allows for a clearer comprehension of dreams. For optimal affect on the mind, it is best to wear amethyst on the body for a long period of time. For a particular ailment on a specific area of the body, such as an organ, it is recommended to place amethyst close to the affected area.

Ametrine

Geometric alliance: trigonal (rhombohedral)
Colors: violet, yellow
Chakras: solar plexus, third eye
Hardness: 7
Origin: Brazil, Bolivia, Uruguay
Formation Process: magmatic
Purification: cold water, saltwater, incense, sunlight, earth
Recharging: quartz cluster, sunlight

Generalities

Ametrine is a quartz with delimited zones of amethyst and citrine, bringing together characteristics and properties of both stones.

Lithotherapy

· Encourages confident and well-considered action
· Contributes to bringing together apparent opposites, for example, feminine and masculine energies
· Awakens optimism and arouses inner well-being
· Is recognized as a source of great creativity with powerful energy
· Encourages taking charge of our life
· Facilitates acceptance of others, creating greater compatibility and cooperation in order to avoid passing judgment
· Raises the mind to higher levels of awareness
· Brings comprehension as to the causes of chronic illnesses
· Protects during astral voyages
· Protects against psychic attacks
· Eliminates stress and balances energies in the mind, allowing for better concentration during meditation
· Brings clarity of mind and better concentration
· Dissolves harmful emotional programming
· Facilitates transformation
· Dissipates negativity in the aura
· Purifies the blood and revitalizes the body
· Purifies cellular metabolism and tissues
· Harmonizes interactions between internal organs

- Activates functions of the autonomic nervous system
- Regenerates the physical body
- Reinforces the immune system
- Sustains people suffering from chronic fatigue, depression, and problems linked to stress
- Releases blockages in the physical, emotional, and mental bodies

AVENTURINE

Geometric alliance: trigonal (rhombohedral)
Color: shimmering nuances of green
Chakra: heart
Hardness: 7
Origin: Brazil, India, Russia
Formation Process: magmatic, metamorphic, sedimentary
Purification: cold water, saltwater, incense, sunlight, earth
Recharging: quartz cluster, sunlight

Generalities

The name "aventurine" comes from the term *a ventura* in Italian, which means "by chance." The name is also derived from the darker fragments scattered randomly within its core.

Lithotherapy

- Benefits the heart chakra
- Arouses deep relaxation and great satisfaction
- Fulfills those who do not feel loved or who find it difficult to open their hearts
- Strengthens leadership qualities
- Favors empathy and compassion
- Inculcates perseverance
- Stimulates creativity
- Balances masculine and feminine energies
- Grants courage to live our truth from the heart
- Brings comfort and balance and calms emotional stress, especially when combined with rose quartz

- Encourages new ideas
- Encourages tolerance toward others
- Creates a network of connections protecting against geopathic stress around gardens and homes
- Absorbs electromagnetic fog and protects against environmental pollution; protects from electromagnetic emissions when attached to a cell phone
- Regularizes growth from birth to age seven
- Relieves insomnia, headaches, and migraines
- Reinforces, stabilizes, and regenerates the heart
- Treats skin diseases caused by nervous tension
- Exercises a beneficial influence on the thymus, conjunctive tissue, and nervous system
- Balances the blood pressure and stimulates metabolism
- Reduces cholesterol and helps prevent arteriosclerosis and heart attacks
- Produces an anti-inflammatory effect in cases of skin rashes
- Soothes pain
- Calms nausea
- Supports the adrenal glands and the urogenital and muscular systems
- Treats the lungs, throat, and sinuses
- Alleviates stuttering and severe neuroses
- Supports us during treatment of malignant diseases

Aventurine can be worn as a pendant or a necklace, held in the hand for a certain period, or in some acute cases, placed on the region concerned.

BULL'S EYE OR OX EYE

Geometric alliance: trigonal (rhombohedral)
Colors: shimmering nuances of red and reddish brown
Chakras: solar plexus, root
Hardness: 7
Origin: Australia, Brazil, Unites States
Formation Process: sedimentary
Purification: quartz cluster, cold water, saltwater, incense, sunlight, earth
Recharging: quartz cluster, sunlight

Generalities

The bull's eye is actually red tiger eye with a red or chestnut-brown predominance. Just as good a protector as the tiger eye, it is, however, more aggressive and specifically employed to obtain strength and courage.

Lithotherapy

· Energizes and clears the root chakra, grounding us to the physical plane
· Allows for regulation and balance of earth energies into the root chakra
· Brings suppleness to the human psyche
· Encourages setting goals for ourselves and persevering without dispersing energy
· A great protector due to its mirroring qualities, it repels negative energies from the auric field and sends them back to their source
· Wards off unnecessary obstacles in daily life
· Protects against theft of material goods
· Stimulates the survival instinct
· Brings warmth, force, and physical dynamism
· Supports in business affairs and projects
· A stone for physical suppleness, it is useful for any problem related to the back
· Reinforces the whole body structure from the base of the spine and is therefore particularly recommended for athletes
· Gives the necessary energy to sustain physical effort until the goal is reached

CALCITE FAMILY

Geometric alliance: trigonal (rhombohedral)
Colors: almost all colors
Chakras: according to color
Hardness: 3
Origin: found throughout the world
Formation Process: magmatic, sedimentary
Purification: cold water, incense, sunlight, earth
Recharging: quartz cluster, sunlight

Generalities

Calcite was formerly used in the form of lime to treat skin problems, tumors, warts, and infectious wounds.

Lithotherapy

- Balances emotions and stabilizes feminine and masculine polarities
- Calms fears, reduces stress, and quiets the mind
- Provides stability, self-confidence, and constancy
- Brings joy and lightheartedness
- Provides stability, self-confidence, and constancy
- Accelerates the development of those who no longer believe their lives can take a positive turn
- Symbolizes clarity and mental growth
- Encourages efficiency and swift action
- Improves judgment and reinforces memory
- Calms excessive energy
- Increases the potential for astral travel
- Is a powerful purifier and potent amplifier with the ability to swiftly increase our vital energy
- Repels negative energies and intensifies personal energy
- Treats the kidneys, pancreas, and gallbladder
- Stimulates immunity and encourages growth in children
- Treats skin ailments
- Relieves intestinal problems
- Encourages coagulation and favors regeneration of tissues and bones
- Normalizes the heartbeat and fortifies the heart
- Purifies the elimination organs
- Favors absorption of calcium in the bones while destroying calcifications and fortifying the skeletal system and joints

Calcite can be held in the hand or placed on the body, on or around the distressed area. It can also be placed on the chakra, according to its color.

Black Calcite

Lithotherapy

· Stimulates recall of past memories or the purpose of healing and letting go
· Grounds the energy body to the physical body following trauma or great stress
· Alleviates depression
· A useful companion during existential crises and profound transitions and changes

Blue Calcite

Lithotherapy

· Has an affinity with the throat chakra
· Favors clear communication
· Reduces stress and anxiety
· Supports us during channeling
· Encourages recuperation and relaxation
· Absorbs negative energy, filters it, and returns it to the transmitter
· Soothes the throat and lungs; reduces thyroid inflammation
· Regulates blood pressure

Clear Calcite

Lithotherapy

· Refines and aligns all chakras
· Powerfully purifies and disinfects
· Provides deep soul healing
· Revitalizes the subtle bodies
· Improves and sharpens inner and outer vision

Gold or Yellow Calcite

Lithotherapy

- Generally placed at the crown chakra and the solar plexus
- Stimulates willpower
- Raises the spirits
- Intensifies meditation, inducing a profound state of relaxation
- Purifies the elimination organs
- Emits a very expansive energy that encourages mental agility by anchoring superior mental energies within the physical form

Green Calcite

Lithotherapy

- Beneficial to the heart chakra
- Dissipates rigid beliefs
- Helps to release attachments to what may seem familiar and comfortable, yet is actually stagnating and useless
- Calms distress caused by anger
- Stimulates the thymus
- Reinforces the immune system
- Relieves bacterial infections and absorbs negativity
- Alleviates arthritis and muscle and ligament strain
- Soothes fevers, burns, and inflammations
- Supports the adrenal glands
- Restores balance to the nervous system
- Reduces stress and calms heart palpitations
- Reinforces the heart and regulates its rhythm

Optical Calcite

Lithotherapy

- Helps us to understand the double meaning of words
- Purifies the subtle bodies
- Amplifies images and soothes eye problems
- Diminishes tension-caused migraines

ORANGE CALCITE

Lithotherapy

· Vibrates with the solar plexus due to its warm and welcoming energy
· Increases energy and purifies the lower chakras
· Balances emotions
· Dissipates fear
· Alleviates depression, helping us to maximize our full potential
· Treats problems related to the reproductive system
· Stimulates the libido
· Supports the gallbladder and purifies the kidneys
· Eases intestinal problems such as constipation, diarrhea, and irritable bowel syndrome
· Eliminates mucus

PINK CALCITE

Lithotherapy

· Known as the "stone of the heart" that works closely with the kingdom of devas
· A "stone of forgiveness," it frees us from that which imprisons the heart, such as fear and sorrow
· Favors inner awareness
· Encourages self-acceptance
· Treats nervous problems, eliminating tension and anxiety
· Prevents nightmares
· Dissolves resistance
· Supports those who suffer from trauma

RED CALCITE

Lithotherapy

· Vibrates well with the root chakra
· Increases energy and willpower, raises spirits, and opens the heart chakra
· Transmits a love of life
· Eliminates stagnant energy

- Relieves constipation
- Eases lower back and sciatic nerve pain as well as hip, leg, and knee problems
- Treats the reproductive system
- Purifies and stimulates the genitals
- Treats infertility

CARNELIAN

Geometric alliance: trigonal (rhombohedral)
Color: orange, red, brownish orange, brownish red
Chakras: hara, root
Hardness: 6.5 to 7
Origin: Brazil, Czech Republic, Egypt, England, India, Peru, Romania, Slovenia, Uruguay
Formation Process: magmatic
Purification: cold water, saltwater, incense, sunlight, earth
Recharging: quartz cluster, abundant sunlight

Generalities

Carnelian has evolved with the terrestrial cycle and has become one of the power stones of the Age of Aquarius. It symbolizes the force and beauty of our planet.

Lithotherapy

- A stone of courage, it instills self-confidence and encourages standing up for ourselves
- Banishes negative emotions such as fear, rage, envy, jealousy, and resentment
- Energizes and rejuvenates
- Gives momentum when we are lethargic
- Stimulates the mind and clears mental confusion
- Favors concentration and constructive problem solving
- Alleviates depression and awakens inner joy
- Restores trust and communicates love following abuse and trauma
- Aligns the etheric with the physical body

- Facilitates connection with the higher self
- Enhances fertility
- Helps to clear physicoenergetic blockages in reproductive organs that cause sterility and impotence
- Stimulates the libido and creativity
- Activates the assimilation of vitamins, nutrients, and mineral salts in the small intestine
- Improves the quality of blood and stops hemorrhaging
- Ensures the proper elimination of toxins from the organs and tissues
- Relieves lower back problems, rheumatism, arthritis, and neuralgia
- Contributes to the proper functioning of the digestive system
- Benefits the bladder

Carnelian attracts abundance and acts as a guardian against unwanted energies and visitors when placed near the entrance of a home. In the past, it was used to protect the dead during their journey into the next life. It may be worn as jewelry or placed directly on the skin as needed.

CHALCEDONY FAMILY

Geometric alliance: trigonal (rhombohedral)
Colors: great variety of colors
Chakras: according to color
Hardness: 6.5 to 7
Origin: Austria, Brazil, Czech Republic, Great Britain, India, Madagascar, Mexico, Morocco, New Zealand, Norway, Russia, Slovakia, United States, Turkey
Formation Process: magmatic, sedimentary
Purification: cold water; saltwater to be used in moderation, as chalcedony is a porous stone; incense; sunlight; earth
Recharging: quartz cluster, sunlight

Generalities

In past civilizations, chalcedony was associated with air and water elements and was therefore used to influence atmospheric conditions. It was also used to heal ailments caused by weather conditions, such as cold temperatures. Chalcedony was sculpted into drinking bowls as an antidote to poisonous liquids.

Lithotherapy

· Instills a sense of belonging to a group
· Increases goodwill toward others
· Supports us during telepathic communication
· Prevents nightmares and negative thoughts and emotions
· Absorbs negative energies and suppresses them in order to prevent propagation
· Encourages kindness and generosity
· Diminishes hostile feelings and doubt toward ourselves
· Encourages inner reflection
· Transforms melancholy into joy and enthusiasm
· Harmonizes the physical, emotional, and mental body with the spiritual self
· Purifies open wounds
· Helps to develop maternal instinct and activate milk production in the mammary glands
· Encourages mineral assimilation while preventing deposits in the veins
· Increases physical energy
· Soothes the eyes
· Treats the gallbladder and spleen
· Supports the blood, bones, and circulatory system

BLUE CHALCEDONY

Lithotherapy

· Stimulates the throat and third-eye chakras
· Encourages the ability to listen and understand others and to express ourselves correctly
· Instills understanding and appreciation of life from all kingdoms: human, animal, plant, and mineral
· Stimulates telepathy and communication with invisible worlds
· Useful for therapists as it encourages the healthy awareness of subconscious truths that are difficult to access
· Helps us to accept new situations without feeling lost
· Excels in supporting diplomats and orators
· Confers the ability to speak other languages: the diplomat's stone
· Brings lightness and optimism; gives momentum

- Stimulates awareness of our feelings, desires, and needs
- Calms the emotional body and the mind
- Reduces anxiety and relieves panic attacks
- Activates the memory, eliminates stress, and increases efficiency; ideal for students
- Reinforces vocal organs and prevents irritation
- Treats throat problems and infections
- Helps to overcome difficulties of the respiratory system
- Alleviates harmful consequences caused by tobacco
- Acts as an anti-inflammatory
- Ensures good circulation of organic fluids such as lymph and blood
- Treats edema
- Fortifies the immune system
- Regularizes production of insulin and is therefore useful in early stages of diabetes
- Contributes to the balanced secretion of the endocrine glands

DENDRITIC CHALCEDONY

Lithotherapy

- Helps to differentiate real objectives from opinions or the influence of others
- Releases the mind from unconscious habits and memories from the past
- Clarifies confused thoughts
- Invites calm during stressful times
- Favors tolerant interaction without judgment
- Encourages living in the present moment and grants the courage to face unpleasant situations
- Supports us during chronic illness
- Diminishes effects of nicotine addiction
- Increases assimilation of copper in the body
- Treats the liver
- Diminishes inflammation of female sexual organs

PINK CHALCEDONY

Lithotherapy

- Inspires kindness, empathy, cordiality, and vivacity
- Encourages active listening and understanding in order to help others overcome difficulties
- Instills inner peace and profound trust
- Favors curiosity and childlike wonder
- Awakens the desire to always learn more
- Fortifies the heart and immune system
- Activates lymphatic circulation
- Treats psychosomatic diseases

RED CHALCEDONY

Lithotherapy

- Confers vigor and necessary persistence to reach goals
- Incites wisdom and discrimination as to when to fight and when to give in
- Favors an open mind
- Reinforces motivation and trust
- Suppresses hunger
- Stimulates blood coagulation and circulation without increasing blood pressure
- May inhibit nutrient absorption within the intestines
- May cause nausea; it is therefore recommended to be used for short periods

CHRYSOPRASE

Geometric alliance: trigonal (rhombohedral)
Colors: lemon, clear green to deep green, apple green
Chakras: heart, solar plexus
Hardness: 6.5 to 7
Origin: Australia, India, Madagascar, Russia, South Africa, United States
Formation Process: sedimentary
Purification: cold water, saltwater, incense, abundant sunlight, earth
Recharging: quartz cluster, sunlight

Generalities

Chrysoprase is the stone of spring and of new life cycles. Known as a "stone of truth," it allows perception into hidden motives behind speech and actions.

Lithotherapy

· Activates foresight and flexibility
· Provides a sense of security and trust
· Diminishes anger, jealousy, envy, miserliness, and egotism
· Acts to stimulate and purify the heart chakra, helping us to heal from past relationships
· Balances masculine and feminine polarities
· Favors nonjudgment, stimulating acceptance of ourselves and others
· Helps to eliminate negative attitudes by directing attention to positive events
· Contributes to freeing ourselves from feelings and attitudes of superiority or inferiority
· Develops self-confidence and clarity of mind
· Stimulates appreciation of beauty and art
· Opens the mind to new ways of doing things in a variety of situations
· Favors a profound state of meditation
· Encourages the cultivation of a compassionate nature
· Stimulates the liver and detoxifies the body
· Reinforces the reproductive organs
· Increases fertility
· Helps to treat gout and skin ailments
· Fortifies the thymus and lungs and treats heart problems
· Fights against hypertension as well as physical and mental exhaustion

CITRINE

Geometric alliance: trigonal (rhombohedral)
Color: yellow
Chakra: solar plexus
Hardness: 7
Origin: Brazil, Madagascar, Russia
Formation Process: magmatic
Purification: cold water, saltwater, incense, sunlight, earth
Recharging: quartz cluster, sunlight

Generalities

Citrine is known to attract wealth, abundance, and prosperity. Authentic citrine is becoming more and more difficult to find, and much of it is actually radiated amethyst. The key to distinguishing the real from the false is the color. Pure citrine is a light yellow crystal, whereas heated amethyst is far darker and more opaque. The properties of heated amethyst are similar to those of real citrine, though less effective.

Lithotherapy

· Purifies the aura by filling the dark spaces with light and joy
· Stimulates the brain and reinforces the intellect
· Is especially effective for children suffering from attention deficit disorder
· Encourages new ideas and stimulates creativity in order to resolve problems more easily
· Favors the expression of individuality
· Grants confidence, courage, and dynamism
· Stimulates the desire for change, new experiences, and self-realization
· Encourages a joy of living and elevates the spirits
· Soothes family or group discord
· Contributes to overcoming depression and oppressive influences
· Encourages extroversion and favors self-expression
· Enhances the capacity for rapid understanding
· Vibrates an energy of wealth and abundance in order to attract what is naturally our due
· Protects from snake venom and negative thoughts
· Supports sensitive and vulnerable people

- Generates inner heat within the body
- Stimulates digestion and the proper functioning of the stomach, spleen, and pancreas
- Alleviates diabetes
- Relieves bladder infections
- Reinforces the nerves and the immune system
- Relieves constipation and dissolves cellulite

A citrine that points downward invites the golden ray of the spirit into the physical realm. It is recommended to place a citrine in a corner of a room, preferably in the left corner that is the most distant from the door, as this is known as the corner of wealth.

DIOPTASE

Geometric alliance: trigonal (rhombohedral)
Colors: dark blue, emerald green
Chakra: heart
Hardness: 5
Origin: Chile, Democratic Republic of the Congo, Iran, Namibia, North Africa, Peru, Russia, United States
Formation Process: sedimentary
Purification: cold water, saltwater, incense, sunlight, earth (required before each treatment)
Recharging: quartz cluster, sunlight

Generalities

Legend has it that dioptase is related to Venus and thus symbolizes beauty. This stone, also called "copper emerald," was formerly considered a stone of wealth and abundance.

Lithotherapy

- Opens the higher heart chakra and heals the energies of the heart
- Draws in a new vibration of love at all levels
- Assists in reaching a higher state of consciousness

- Encourages us to live in the present while also activating memories of past lives
- Supports the awareness of our own inner wealth
- Facilitates service to others
- Helps to emphasize innate faculties and guides us toward self-realization
- Invigorates imagination and creative ideas
- Has the power to change negative into positive in all aspects of life
- Guides us toward the direction we need, especially when we don't know where to go
- Clarifies and purifies thoughts
- Lessens the tendency to control others
- Contributes to healing the emotional wounds of the inner child
- Dissolves and heals feelings of grief, betrayal, sadness, and abandonment
- Draws in a new vibration of love
- Teaches that difficulties in relationships are the reflection of an inner separation from the higher self
- Activates liver regeneration
- Eases pain, cramps, nausea, and chronic headaches
- Regularizes cellular disorders
- Activates T cells and the thymus
- Contributes to relieving arterial hypertension
- Treats cardiac problems
- Improves the libido
- Fights dependency and stress
- Heals trauma and nervous shock

HAWK EYE

Geometric alliance: trigonal (rhombohedral)
Colors: shimmering nuances of blue gray and green gray blue
Chakras: throat, third eye
Hardness: 7
Origin: Australia, Brazil, India, Myanmar, South Africa, United States
Formation Process: magmatic
Purification: cold water, saltwater, incense, moonlight, sunlight, earth
Recharging: quartz cluster, moonlight, sunlight

Generalities

The asbestos fibers contained within the hawk eye create a silky reflection that resembles an eye. During the Middle Ages, this stone was thought to protect its bearer and allow him or her to perceive impending danger. Hence it was worn as an amulet to protect against evil spells and the evil eye.

Lithotherapy

· Purifies and energizes the root chakra
· Activates the throat chakra and facilitates oral expression
· Awakens the appreciation for knowledge and research
· Opens the mind to new ideas and modes of thinking
· Confers a keen and alert mind
· Conveys a broad vision for projects
· Increases observation skills
· Encourages active listening and understanding
· Supports the capacity to see with precision and sustained attention
· Provides a clear view of complicated situations
· Assists with decision making
· Eliminates doubts
· Reinforces self-confidence by activating the will
· Generates enthusiasm
· Grants luck and abundance
· Eliminates nightmares
· Protects from harmful influences
· Provides an understanding of the "greater plan" in reference to our own
· Reveals repressed emotions and pains from present and past lives
· Exposes the source of emotional blockages
· Promotes healthy detachment from our emotions
· Helps to disengage us from the negativity that causes mood swings
· Tempers pessimism and eliminates the desire to blame others for our problems
· Contributes to healing the Earth and aids us to remain anchored to the physical plane
· Develops intuition and facilitates clairvoyance
· Reveals the psychosomatic causes of certain physical maladies
· Treats inflammatory eye problems, visual fatigue, conjunctivitis, and cataracts

- Relieves migraines
- Balances the thyroid gland
- Regulates breathing and purifies the bronchial tubes
- Eases pain
- Alleviates ailments related to the voice
- Calms nervousness and trembling
- Treats hyperstimulation of the hormonal glands
- Calms an overactive libido

HEMATITE

Geometric alliance: trigonal (rhombohedral)
Color: metallic gray
Chakra: root
Hardness: 5 to 6
Origin: Brazil, United States
Formation Process: magmatic, metamorphic
Purification: cold water, incense, sunlight, earth
Recharging: quartz cluster, sunlight

Generalities

Hematite was used in ancient Egypt to facilitate the development of red blood cells and to stop hemorrhaging. For this reason, it inherited the name "blood stone" during the Middle Ages.

Lithotherapy

- Eliminates and transmutes negative energies in the root chakra
- Grounds and reinforces the connection with the Earth
- Confers feelings of safety and confidence
- Provides strength, courage, stamina, and vitality
- Encourages spontaneity and joy in living
- Protects from the negativity of others
- Alleviates anxiety
- Reinforces the physical and etheric bodies
- Encourages optimism and increases personal magnetism
- Facilitates healthy blood regeneration

- Stops hemorrhaging
- Increases blood quality and reduces blood pressure
- Treats anemia
- Stimulates iron absorption in the small intestine as well as red blood cell formation
- Improves oxygen absorption and stabilizes the health
- Alleviates insomnia, restlessness, stress, and anxiety
- Decreases body temperature during a fever
- Relieves muscular pain due to skeletal problems
- Treats problems related to the skeletal system, such as arthritis, leg cramps, and fractures
- Assists in purifying the blood in the kidneys
- Regenerates tissues

Hematite is to be avoided in the case of active inflammation, as it may worsen this condition. It facilitates alignment of the spinal column when one piece is placed at the top of the spine. It is advisable to place or maintain hematite directly on the skin, depending on the need. It is, however, not advisable to use it for prolonged periods of time.

HERKIMER DIAMOND

Geometric alliance: trigonal (rhombohedral)
Color: colorless, sometimes with inclusions of rutile, silicate, etc.
Chakras: all
Hardness: 7.5
Origin: Mexico, Spain, Tanzania, United States
Formation Process: magmatic
Purification: saltwater, rinse under running water; must be cleansed after each use that requires it to be reprogrammed
Recharging: quartz cluster, abundance of morning sunlight

Generalities

Herkimer crystals vibrate with blissful energy. In Native American tradition, Herkimer diamonds are considered sacred stones of wisdom and clairvoyance that enhance the ability to enter a trance and enable the spirit to soar, see the invisible, and awaken consciousness.

Herkimer is quartz that can be naturally and easily programmed. It strengthens willpower and possesses a crystal memory that can store a wealth of information for later retrieval.

Lithotherapy

- Opens and activates the crown and third eye chakras
- When placed at the crown chakra, it creates a fusion with the divine and contributes to understanding our life mission
- Removes energetic blockages and eliminates debris in the energetic field due to its clarity, brilliance, and high vibration
- Stimulates telepathy, clairvoyance, and other psychic abilities
- Promotes creativity
- Activates our connection to the higher self, angels, and higher spiritual realms
- Facilitates spiritual transformation while focusing on the soul's purpose
- Confers access to information from past lives, hence revealing the source of blockages that may impede spiritual growth
- Enhances concentration in meditation and inner vision
- Promotes dream recall, conscious and premonitory dreaming, and communication with higher dimensions
- Harmonizes the therapist and the client
- Increases the effectiveness of other stones
- Removes energetic blockages and eliminates debris in the energetic field
- Corrects cellular disorders and metabolic imbalances
- A powerful regenerator, it accelerates the healing process
- Eliminates stress and muscular tension
- Fortifies the muscles
- Neutralizes the effects of radiation

Jasper Family

Geometric alliance: trigonal (rhombohedral)
Colors: black, brown, green, red, yellow
Chakras: according to color
Hardness: 6.5 to 7
Origin: Brazil, France, Germany, India
Formation Process: sedimentary
Purification: cold water, saltwater, incense, sunlight, earth
Recharging: quartz cluster, sunlight

Generalities

In ancient Egypt, jasper was used to make amulets on which scarab beetles were carved. In the Middle Ages, this stone was recognized as the stone of the warrior.

Lithotherapy

· Purifies and aligns the chakras
· Is known as the "supreme protector"
· Absorbs negative energies
· Assists in shamanic journeys
· Facilitates the recall of dreams when placed under the pillow
· Confers courage and determination, encouraging a warrior spirit
· Favors self-honesty and candor
· Kindles mutual assistance
· Supports us in times of conflict
· Facilitates rapid reflection
· Contributes to the development of organizational abilities
· Stimulates imagination
· Transforms ideas into actions
· Reenergizes the body
· Anchors energies within the body
· Absorbs electromagnetic and environmental pollution
· Supports us during periods of stress or during long-lasting illness
· Benefits the digestive system, especially the gallbladder and liver
· Fortifies the circulatory system
· Supports the bladder and sexual organs
· Balances the mineral content of the body

Jasper is a stone that imparts an earthy, physical vibration and is a powerful therapeutic companion. It must be placed directly on the skin for effective results. Its energy is less intense and slower to act and may therefore be worn for long periods of time.

BLACK JASPER (1st Chakra)

Lithotherapy

· Grounds us to reality
· Protects us from negative energies

BLOOD OR HELIOTROPE JASPER (1st and 4th Chakras)

Lithotherapy

· Promotes the connection between the first and fourth chakra
· Stimulates kundalini energy
· Calms irritation, aggressiveness, and impatience
· Revitalizes the physical body, a powerful healer
· Purifies the physical body and blood
· Increases oxygen
· Strengthens the heart, spleen, bones, spinal column, and liver as an iron stabilizer
· Excellent in treating infections, inflammations, and poisoning
· Strengthens the immune system when placed on the thymus
· Activates the lymph flow in the metabolism
· Reabsorbs abscesses
· Detoxifies and neutralizes excess acidity
· Revitalizes energy in cases of exhaustion and fatigue

BROWN JASPER

Lithotherapy

· Embodies the energy of Mother Earth
· Brings comfort and reduces fear
· Instills a sense of right proportion
· Inspires harmony

· Favors the unveiling of hidden feelings
· Stimulates the immune system
· Purifies the kidneys

GREEN JASPER (4th Chakra)

Lithotherapy

· Balances the heart chakra
· Reinforces the immune system
· Detoxifies the body
· Provides an anti-inflammatory effect for the entire body
· Protects against pollution
· Treats the lungs

RED JASPER (1st and 2nd Chakras)

Lithotherapy

· Balances and anchors the root chakra
· Conveys courage and will
· Is an excellent protection during travel
· Inspires physical vitality
· Stimulates fertility
· Strengthens the legs
· Activates circulation and increases energy

YELLOW JASPER (3rd Chakra)

Lithotherapy

· Stimulates the solar plexus chakra
· Calms the nerves
· Helps us to persevere
· Eliminates toxins
· Treats the stomach and overall digestion
· Revives the endocrine system
· Is very helpful for women in menopause
· Reinforces the immune system

Magnesite

Geometric alliance: trigonal (rhombohedral)
Color: creamy white
Chakras: heart, third eye, crown
Hardness: 4 to 4.5
Origin: Austria, Brazil, France, Italy
Formation Process: sedimentary, rarely magmatic
Purification: saltwater, cold water, sunlight, earth
Recharging: quartz cluster, sunlight

Generalities

Discovered in the thirteenth century, magnesite was called "pure talc." It was later renamed following the discovery of its chemical properties.

Lithotherapy

· Encourages a positive attitude
· Realigns inverse and unbalanced energy currents within the body and the Earth
· Aligns the meridians
· Invites self-acceptance and self-love
· Transmits a profound calm
· Tones and stabilizes the mind, balancing the brain hemispheres
· Reduces tension, fear, and irritation
· Balances magnesium deficiencies
· Detoxifies and neutralizes body odor
· Eases spasms and acts as a muscle relaxant
· Soothes headaches and migraines
· Eases symptoms of epilepsy
· Calms menstrual and gastrointestinal cramps
· Treats liver problems
· Slows blood coagulation
· Activates the metabolism of fats and the breakdown of cholesterol
· Prevents the calcification of arteries and tissues
· Acts as a preventive as well as supports the treatment of arteriosclerosis and angina
· Acts as a prophylactic for heart conditions

Onyx

Geometric alliance: trigonal (rhombohedral)
Color: black
Chakra: root
Hardness: 6.5 to 7
Origin: Brazil, Madagascar
Formation Process: magmatic
Purification: cold water, saltwater, incense, moonlight, sunlight, earth
Recharging: quartz cluster, moonlight, sunlight

Generalities

During the Middle Ages, onyx was seen as an instigator of conflict and discord. Nowadays, it is said that wearing it for an extended period may cause listlessness and melancholy. Onyx is a black variety of agate. Pregnant women should avoid using it. However, it does have some very interesting properties.

Lithotherapy

· Increases concentration and revives the memory
· Refines judgment, allowing us to make better decisions
· Stimulates analytical thinking and logic
· Encourages humility
· Inspires studiousness and self-control
· Confers a sense of responsibility
· Gives support to people who are too easily influenced, thereby helping them to reach their true objectives
· Grounds and anchors
· Absorbs negativity while letting through positive vibrations
· Protects against accidents
· Balances the yin and yang energies
· Helps us to accept conflict
· Treats inner-ear conditions
· Improves eyesight
· Reinforces the immune system and protects against risks of infection
· Improves the condition of the skin, nails, and hair
· Strengthens the heart

· Is effective against fungal infections, inflammation, and even sunburn (make a compress with onyx water)
· Treats ulcers
· Improves the functioning of the sensory and motor nerves

PETRIFIED WOOD (XYLOID)

Geometric alliance: trigonal (rhombohedral) or buddhic
Colors: brown, yellow, reddish
Chakras: solar plexus, root
Hardness: 7
Origin: Argentina, Egypt, United States (Arizona)
Formation Process: sedimentary
Purification: cold water, incense, sunlight
Recharging: quartz cluster, abundant sunlight

Generalities

Petrified wood is about 200 million years old and dates back to the first conifer tree, Araucaria, from the Jurassic period.

Petrified wood is classified according to its transformation process. It belongs to the trigonal alliance when the cavity of the wood becomes lined with quartz; this transformation is the most common. However, when the cavities are lined with opal, which occurs less frequently, petrified wood belongs to the buddhic alliance.

Lithotherapy

· Relaxes, calms, and encourages, making time for reflection and contemplation
· Grounds and anchors
· Facilitates the creation of a positive environment
· Encourages us to live simply
· Acts as a link to the Earth and its energy
· Communicates a feeling of being at home here on Earth
· Excels against all kinds of physical problems
· Activates the metabolism

- Calms the nerves
- Confers a feeling of well-being
- Favors the physical and intellectual growth of children
- Diminishes preoccupations and grants strength to sort through irritating details
- Revives the memory and gives support to distracted people
- Supports us in the case of excess weight, which is often caused by a lack of connection to the Earth
- Reinforces bone structure and treats broken bones
- Offers protection against intestinal parasites
- Purifies the liver and the blood
- Balances the liver and the gallbladder
- Treats the hair when taken as an elixir

PHENACITE

Geometric alliance: trigonal (rhombohedral)
Colors: colorless, very pale yellow, very pale pink
Chakras: heart, crown, solar plexus, third eye
Hardness: 7.5 to 8
Origin: Africa, Brazil, France, Norway, Russia, Switzerland, United States
Formation Process: magmatic
Purification: cold water, saltwater, incense, sunlight, earth
Recharging: quartz cluster, sunlight

Generalities

The name "phenacite" comes from the Greek word *phenax*, meaning "deceiver" or "imposter," because it can easily be confused with crystals like quartz, topaz, or even tourmaline.

Lithotherapy

- Has high vibrations that promote communication with higher frequencies
- Helps free us from the influence and constraints of the past, expand our vision, and be reborn
- Activates and purifies the energy of the etheric body

- Stimulates the memory, counters intellectual laziness, and eliminates forgetfulness and carelessness among young and old
- Acts on the central nervous system
- Contributes to the functional reeducation of the body and synchronizes movement in the case of physical disabilities that are nervous in origin
- Relaxes the muscles and relieves muscle cramps
- Acts on the nose (sneezing and nose bleeds) the sinuses (decongestion and nasal drip) and improves the sense of smell

PIETERSITE (TEMPEST STONE)

Geometric alliance: trigonal (rhombohedral)
Colors: golden brown to blue gray with black traces
Chakras: throat, heart, solar plexus, third eye
Hardness: 7
Origin: Namibia, South Africa
Formation Process: sedimentary
Purification: cold water, distilled saltwater, incense, moonlight, sunlight, earth
Recharging: quartz cluster, moonlight, sunlight

Generalities

The discovery of this stone is relatively recent. It is composed of jasper, hawk eye, tiger eye, and possibly onyx.

Lithotherapy

- Stimulates the third eye
- Favors subtle spiritual visions
- Dispels spiritual illusions
- Stimulates intuition and extrasensory faculties
- Fortifies and engenders a positive attitude
- Supports us during chaotic situations
- Encourages mastery over charged memories and unresolved inner conflicts
- Allows us to keep a certain distance without becoming indifferent
- Opens the mind to original ideas

- Facilitates communication and stimulates eloquence
- Inspires impeccability in times of rapid and boisterous personal or collective change and the creation of a new order from chaos
- Releases us from deep-rooted habits
- Helps to distinguish truth from falsehood
- Dispels blockages caused by an overly stubborn attitude
- Encourages the ability to stay loyal to principles
- Leads us to speak out and to explore all that can block the way to the truth
- Activates an understanding of impressions and helps to keep the mind in a receptive state
- Offers the opportunity to remain focused and contemplative in the midst of distractions
- Invigorates the mind
- Eliminates mental and verbal conditioning imposed by authority figures
- Connects the day-to-day consciousness to the spiritual consciousness
- Anchors the etheric body to the physical body
- Helps with hearing disorders and tinnitus
- Treats and clears vocal cords
- Helps the healing of wounds
- Balances hormones
- Harmonizes digestive functions, especially the liver and intestines
- Purifies and energizes the meridians
- The golden brown variety eases suicidal tendencies and depression
- Provides the necessary resistance to avoid professional burnout
- Fights illnesses caused by stress, anxiety, and burnout
- Supports the lungs and treats respiratory ailments
- Stimulates the pituitary gland, thereby balancing the endocrine system, which stimulates the hormone production that governs metabolism, blood pressure, growth, sexuality, and body temperature
- Benefits the legs and feet
- Facilitates the assimilation of essential nutrients in food
- Provides relief during chronic illness

Quartz

Angel Aura Quartz

Geometric alliance: trigonal (rhombohedral)
Color: clear crystal with pink, yellow, and blue iridescent reflections
Chakras: crown, superior chakras up to the crown
Hardness: 7
Origin: artificially modified quartz
Formation Process: magmatic
Purification: cold water, saltwater, incense, sunlight, earth
Recharging: quartz cluster, sunlight

Generalities

This crystal has been bonded with a fine dust of silver, platinum, and other metals that give off colorful reflections reminiscent of angel wings. Its fiery aura inspires its name.

Lithotherapy

· Purifies the chakras and the aura
· Has an energetic connection to the angelic kingdom
· Inspires the possibility to communicate with spiritual beings, angels, and divinities
· Uplifts the spirit and stabilizes moods
· Allows access to our "inner temple," a place of rest and purification
· Creates an atmosphere of tranquility and a sense of satisfaction
· Encourages unity with the beauty present everywhere, as much in nature as within ourselves
· Activates light on the physical and energy levels
· Helps eliminate programmed beliefs and erroneous mental attitudes
· Protects us from people who tend to deplete energy
· Brings joy, light, and optimism
· Deepens meditation
· Contributes to integrating new knowledge acquired in meditation
· Encourages practitioners of meditation to move into the higher realms of meditation, visions, and achievements
· Inspires us to go beyond illusions
· Instills force and courage in those who truthfully desire to reach realization

Aqua Aura Quartz

Geometric alliance: trigonal (rhombohedral)
Color: blue, from pale to dark
Chakras: throat, third eye
Hardness: 7
Origin: Brazil, Madagascar, United States (Arkansas), artificially created quartz
Formation Process: magmatic
Purification: cold water, saltwater, incense, sunlight, earth
Recharging: quartz cluster, sunlight

Generalities

The aqua aura is quartz that has gone through a laboratory process of irradiation with pure gold. The result is radiant blue quartz with rainbow reflections.

Lithotherapy

· Stimulates the throat chakra
· Activates the third eye, bringing concentration and clarity of mind
· Helps develop clairvoyance and clairaudience
· Purifies the aura
· Encourages sincere communication
· Calms and balances the emotional body
· Attenuates aggressiveness and feverishness; releases stress
· Reinforces the curative properties of other stones
· Protects against psychic and psychological attacks and negative intrusions
· Reinforces and supports the thymus and immune system

Faden Quartz (Healing Quartz)

Geometric alliance: trigonal (rhombohedral)
Color: clear with a fine white line running through it
Chakras: all
Hardness: 7
Origin: Brazil, Pakistan
Formation Process: magmatic
Purification: cold water, saltwater, incense, sunlight, earth
Recharging: quartz cluster, sunlight

Generalities

Faden quartz is usually flat, elongated, or tabular shaped. A white line or filament runs through the middle of the quartz parallel to the direction of the layers. This line is usually straight, varying in width from approximately 0.04 to 0.96 inch. Esoterically, it represents the *antahkarana*, the bridge of light that connects us to the soul.

Lithotherapy

· Carries a strong healing force in its cellular memory because it has injured and healed itself on many occasions during its development. As a result, being in harmony with a faden stone enables us to access our own healing power, which is activated and strengthened.
· Helps contact the soul
· Teaches us to understand the lessons to be learned in different incarnations
· Is strongly linked to the angelic realm and has the ability to bridge the gap between this realm and earthly reality
· Promotes relations, connections, and communication with others
· Activates the energy of the nervous system
· Contributes to postoperative healing in the case of fractures, torn muscles, injured blood vessels, lesions in nervous tissue, and even severed nerves
· Reduces scarring, strengthens the spine, and alleviates vertebral pain
· Is an excellent protection during air travel

Pure intentions are essential to invoke the protection, guidance, and healing energies of the angels through the support of faden quartz

Rose Quartz

Geometric alliance: trigonal (rhombohedral)
Colors: pale pink to dark pink
Chakra: heart
Hardness: 7
Origin: Brazil, Madagascar, United States (Arkansas)
Formation Process: magmatic
Purification: cold water, saltwater, incense, sunlight, earth
Recharging: quartz cluster, sunlight

Generalities

Rose quartz is the stone of unconditional love and inner peace.

Lithotherapy

· Harmonizes with the heart chakra
· Transmits unconditional love for ourselves and for others
· Calms worries and preoccupations
· Supports us in moments of emotional shock
· Encourages forgiveness and trust
· Confers gentleness, infinite tenderness, absolute calm, and a connection to our spiritual self
· Soothes emotional pain and heartache by reinforcing self-love and acceptance, thereby reinforcing the capacity to love others
· Inspires harmony in chaotic situations
· Balances all the systems in the body
· Enhances discernment
· Favors service, openness to others and to life, and the desire to create favorable surroundings
· Helps to maintain a satin-like complexion
· Protects against television and computer electromagnetic radiation
· Strengthens the heart
· Reinforces the sexual organs
· Increases fertility
· Treats the kidneys and adrenal glands
· Attenuates vertigo
· Eliminates impurities from bodily fluids

- Helps to counter depression
- Relieves insomnia
- Assists individuals affected by Alzheimer's, Parkinson's, or senile dementia
- Relieves arthritis pain
- Soothes burns

Rose quartz is often worn next to the heart. Placed on the thymus, it can heal chest and lung disorders. A rose quartz cluster brings tranquility and peace when placed in a child's room.

RUTILATED QUARTZ (VENUS HAIR)

Geometric alliance: trigonal (rhombohedral)
Color: light with copper-red or gold fibers
Chakras: gold at the crown, copper-red at the root and the solar plexus
Hardness: 7
Origin: Brazil, Madagascar, United States (Arkansas)
Formation Process: magmatic
Purification: cold water, saltwater, incense, sunlight, earth
Recharging: quartz cluster, sunlight

Generalities

In ancient times, rutilated quartz was said to represent sunlight.

Lithotherapy

- Heightens the energy impulse of quartz
- Stimulates the circulation of energy
- Purifies and energizes the aura
- Protectively absorbs negative energies and dissolves the barriers to spiritual development
- Helps draw off damage from former lives, eradicating past ills and shedding light on previous events that affect the present, revealing their causes and consequences
- Encourages forgiveness at all levels
- Helps us to be conscientious and get to the root of a problem
- Supports the development of new ways of life; clarifies thought

- Has a stabilizing effect on the emotions, bringing strength, resilience, and energy, and enhances our inner vital force and spiritual radiance
- Acts as an antidepressant, improves dark moods, reduces phobias, calms anxiety, dissolves hidden unconscious fears, and releases inhibitions
- Activates cellular regeneration
- Stimulates growth
- Relieves respiratory disorders, particularly chronic bronchitis
- Stabilizes the thyroid
- Is excellent for physical burnout and loss of energy
- Alleviates sexual problems, including impotency

SMOKY QUARTZ

Geometric alliance: trigonal (rhombohedral)
Color: brown to black
Chakra: root
Hardness: 7
Origin: Brazil, Madagascar, United States (Arkansas)
Formation Process: magmatic
Purification: cold water, saltwater, incense, sunlight, earth
Recharging: quartz cluster, sunlight

Generalities

Smoky quartz calls on the inner warrior in each of us. It challenges those who use it, encouraging them to leave their less useful traits behind and open the path to their creative potential.

Lithotherapy

- Is considered a stone of transformation
- Promotes grounding in the material world
- Sustains us to face reality and the demands and responsibilities of day-to-day life
- Provides strong protection against negative energies; penetrates their inner core and then neutralizes them
- Effectively dissolves blockages in the etheric body
- Helps uncover the causes of self-destructive habits such as tobacco or alcohol addiction

· Provides effective support for depression and suicidal tendencies
· Increases the workload we can bear
· Helps us accomplish what we need to do
· Provides the support needed in troubled times
· Boosts self-confidence
· Improves stress management; teaches us how to take the time to live
· Relieves pain and cramps
· Is an excellent stone for the lower back

Because of the powerful properties they possess, crystals should be used with care. If we persevere and seriously try to free ourselves from harmful patterns, a real transformation can occur. However, we must understand that healing and growth have their own rhythms and cycles. Attempting to make a radical change too quickly, whether consciously or unconsciously, could cause conflict with the self, which may not be ready for such a dramatic change and could result in rebellion or regression.

RHODOCHROSITE

Geometric alliance: trigonal (rhombohedral)
Color: from pale to bright pink, in irregular layers, often with white or pale gray bands; may be orange or dark orange red if it is gem quality
Chakras: heart, solar plexus
Hardness: 4
Origin: Argentina, Russia, South Africa, United States, Uruguay
Formation Process: sedimentary
Purification: cold water, incense, sunlight; frequent purification is recommended
Recharging: quartz cluster, sunlight

Generalities

The name "rhodochrosite" comes from the Greek word *rhodon,* which means "rose." Rhodochrosite is considered to be an altruistic stone.

Lithotherapy

- Possesses a particular affinity with the heart chakra
- Awakens impersonal and universal love
- Is considered a stone of love and passion; attracts our soul mate
- Due to its overall calming effect, promotes greater ease of movement and facilitates the breathing process
- Encourages greater mastery over the emotions
- Alleviates stress and emotional turmoil
- Facilitates emotional healing in cases of sexual abuse
- Confers a positive attitude and enthusiasm toward life
- Consoles those who feel unloved
- Encourages spontaneity and emotional expression
- Stimulates creativity and innovation
- Awakens, stimulates, and motivates us to take action
- Confers the courage to face fears
- Improves awareness of personal worth
- Relieves gastric ulcers due to its antistress qualities
- Purifies the blood and stimulates blood circulation
- Restores elasticity in the blood vessels, thereby regulating blood pressure and relieving migraines
- Invigorates sexual activity by revitalizing the sexual organs
- Fights osteoarthritis
- Fortifies the heart by diminishing palpitations
- Stabilizes the pulsation of the spleen
- Treats skin allergies
- Balances the thyroid gland
- A good remedy for chronic migraines, to be used over a long period
- Relieves kidney and intestinal problems
- Detoxifies the body and is effective for skin problems such as acne
- Absorbs the irritants that can be found in the respiratory tract, thus alleviating asthma and other breathing difficulties
- Improves vision
- Alleviates symptoms of depression
- Revives the memory

Rhodochrosite can be placed directly on the body, the wrist, the heart, or the solar plexus.

Ruby

Geometric alliance: trigonal (rhombohedral)
Color: red
Chakra: root
Hardness: 9
Origin: Brazil, Cambodia, India, Kenya, Madagascar, Mexico, Myanmar, Russia, Sri Lanka, Thailand
Formation Process: magmatic, metamorphic
Purification: cold water, saltwater, incense, sunlight, earth
Recharging: quartz cluster, abundant sunlight

Generalities

Ruby is endowed with one of the most powerful vibrations of the mineral kingdom. According to an ancient Burmese legend, inserting a ruby under the skin could render a man invincible. The ruby was considered a stone of power and royalty for a long time and by many cultures.

Lithotherapy

- Stimulates and balances the heart chakra
- Constitutes a powerful shield against psychic attacks and against "vampires" of the heart energy
- Instills energy, balance, and dynamism
- Awakens enthusiasm
- Confers vigor and passion for life
- Increases motivation
- Encourages the establishment of realistic goals
- Facilitates positive dreaming and visualization
- Grants long-lasting wealth and passion as a stone of abundance
- Unveils anger and negativity so that it can be resolved
- Encourages dynamic leadership
- Instills a positive and courageous state of mind
- Offers strong inner stability during debates and situations of conflict
- Activates the pineal gland
- Stimulates the libido
- Calms hyperactivity
- Fortifies the immune system and repels infectious diseases

- Helps cure eye infections, even when worn as jewelry
- Combats low blood pressure
- Strengthens the heart and circulation
- Detoxifies the blood, the body, and the lymphatic system

SAPPHIRE

Geometric alliance: trigonal (rhombohedral)
Colors: black, blue, colorless, yellow
Chakras: throat, third eye
Hardness: 9
Origin: Australia, Brazil, Czech Republic, India, Kenya, Sri Lanka
Formation Process: magmatic, metamorphic
Purification: cold water, saltwater, incense, moonlight, earth
Recharging: quartz cluster, moonlight

Generalities

The word "sapphire" draws its name from the Sanskrit word *sani,* meaning "Saturn"; the ancients from India and Europe identified it as the stone of Saturn. The sapphire is also acknowledged as a stone of wisdom, as it favors the desire for knowledge.

Lithotherapy

- Helps us to wisely evaluate our life
- Known as the stone of prosperity, attracts gifts and blessings
- Awakens faith and love for the truth
- Calms the mind and repels intrusive thoughts
- Promotes objectivity and an analytical mind
- Enhances the power of intention and the will in order to encourage the rapid manifestation of ideas and thoughts
- Invites peace and inner serenity
- Aligns the physical, mental, and spiritual bodies, conferring a better balance
- Dissipates spiritual confusion
- Calms hallucinations
- Stimulates concentration
- Diminishes frustration

- Facilitates self-expression
- Encourages the will to heal
- Fights depression
- Stimulates the appetite
- Relieves psychological illnesses
- Regularizes the functioning of the glands, especially the thyroid
- Calms overactive physiological systems
- Relieves eye troubles
- Improves the elasticity of the veins and strengthens them
- Reduces fever
- Aids the circulatory system, treats illnesses of the blood, and calms hemorrhages
- Benefits the vagus nerve
- Supports the intestines
- Assists with problems of the nervous system—the brain and nerves

SARDONYX

Geometric alliance: trigonal (rhombohedral)
Color: pale to dark orange
Chakra: root
Hardness: 6 to 7
Origin: Brazil, India, Madagascar
Formation Process: magmatic
Purification: cold water, saltwater, incense, sunlight, earth
Recharging: quartz cluster, sunlight

Generalities

Sardonyx takes its name from a combination of two stones that belong to the chalcedony family, sard and onyx. It is called the "stone of virtue."

Lithotherapy

- Brings stability and lasting happiness
- Encourages friendliness and helpfulness
- Protects against negative influences of all kinds
- Enhances our understanding of life; helps us in our search for the meaning of existence and encourages positive thinking

- Increases willpower, strength of character, and self-confidence
- Relieves depression
- Improves the absorption and comprehension of information
- Boosts sensory perception
- Calms quick-tempered personalities
- Reinforces the immune system by activating bodily fluids
- Improves the absorption of nutrients in the intestine and the elimination of waste
- Helps prevent bronchitis and respiratory-system infections
- Relieves back and liver problems

SMITHSONITE (BONAMITE)

Geometric alliance: trigonal (rhombohedral)
Crystal System: trigonal
Colors: brown, green to blue, lavender, pink, purple, white to gray, yellow
Chakras: according to color
Hardness: 5
Origin: Greece, Italy, Mexico, Namibia, Spain, United States
Formation Process: sedimentary
Purification: cold water, avoid salt, earth
Recharging: moonlight

Generalities

It is said that the vibration of smithsonite resonates with Kwan Yin, the feminine bodhisattva of compassion. Kwan Yin is frequently called on for her healing qualities as well as her capacity to dissolve interpersonal conflicts and relationship problems. Smithsonite is a stone of absolute gentleness that eases feelings of loneliness. Wearing smithsonite is somewhat like having a compassionate friend at our side.

Lithotherapy

- Activates the heart through the crown chakra, inspiring greater comprehension of emotions
- Liberates us from feelings of grief and soothes broken hearts
- Stimulates the understanding of universal love

- Enhances sensitivity to subtle energies emanating from other dimensions
- Facilitates friendship by encouraging inner harmony and harmony with others
- Contributes to dissolving negative energies and blockages in the energy fields
- Forms a protective shield against unnecessary obstacles
- Encourages profound relaxation, thereby calming the mind and instilling a deeper meditative state
- Is an important emotional healer that calms anger and resentment
- Provides relief from mental exhaustion and intense stress
- Allows us to see the brighter side, even in moments of depression
- Contributes to reestablishing awareness of the Unity of the Whole
- Is beneficial for those or who feel unloved or unwanted, or who have had a difficult childhood experience
- Heals the inner child, alleviating the negative effects of abuse and psychological neglect
- Favors gentleness, stimulates compassion, and encourages us to support others
- Confers courage
- Accentuates psychic powers, telepathic communication, and conversation with beings of the angelic realm
- Supports those who suffer from alcoholism
- Treats osteoporosis
- Regulates weight
- Augments physical energy
- Aids the reproductive organs
- Balances the endocrine system
- Benefits the sinuses
- Helps with digestive problems
- Restores elasticity to the veins and muscles
- Strongly supports the immune system

The bond between client and therapist may be greatly improved during a lithotherapy session when both wear smithsonite. This may also enhance the connection to their respective guides.

Tiger Eye

Geometric alliance: trigonal (rhombohedral)
Colors: shimmering nuances of golden yellow and brown
Chakras: hara, solar plexus, root
Hardness: 7
Origin: Australia, Brazil, United States
Formation Process: sedimentary
Purification: cold water, saltwater, incense, sunlight, earth
Recharging: quartz cluster, sunlight

Generalities

In the Middle Ages, tiger eye was worn in the form of an amulet in order to ward off evil spells, demons, and the evil eye.

Lithotherapy

· Resonates with the energy of the solar plexus
· Unites the energies of heaven and Earth (anchors and elevates)
· Protects and dissipates fear and anxiety
· Balances mood swings and stabilizes the emotions
· Confers strength, will, courage, and self-confidence
· Supports us during challenging times
· Protects and guards against harmful influences and unwanted energies
· Stabilizes confusing and complicated situations
· Confers the power to make decisions with a clear mind unclouded by emotions
· Improves the capacity to objectively perceive a problem or difficulty
· Aids hypochondriacs
· Alleviates psychosomatic illnesses, headaches, and migraines
· Treats ailments of the neck, throat, and eyes
· Benefits the reproductive organs
· Strengthens the spine by releasing toxins and easing pain
· Assists with the treatment of broken bones
· Relieves asthma and treats bronchial problems
· Soothes hyperstimulated nerves
· Calms overactivity of the adrenal glands

In order to fully benefit from the virtues of tiger eye, it is recommended to be worn or placed directly on the skin. To anchor spiritual energies, it is suggested to be placed in the navel area. To benefit from its protective force, it can be placed on the solar plexus.

TIGER IRON (TIGERITE)

Geometric alliance: trigonal (rhombohedral)
Colors: layered aggregates of red jasper, black and metallic gray iron oxides (magnetite, hematite), and golden-brown tiger eye
Chakras: hara, solar plexus, root
Hardness: 7
Origin: Australia, Brazil, India, South Africa, United States
Formation Process: metamorphic
Chemical Composition: iron and silicon oxide
Purification: quartz cluster, cold water, incense, moonlight, sunlight, earth; avoid salt unless the stone has been polluted by a highly negative energy
Recharging: quartz cluster, moonlight

Generalities

Tiger iron possesses the qualities of red jasper, hematite, and tiger eye. The properties of iron are concentrated and channeled by the tiger eye.

Lithotherapy

· Recharges the solar plexus
· Embodies force, audacity, and energy
· Revitalizes apathetic and despondent people
· Encourages facing our fears
· Stimulates the mind and intellectual acuity
· Develops a sense of constructive self-criticism
· Energizes the body
· Rejuvenates and invigorates in cases of great fatigue
· Eases traumas that cause depression
· Reinforces and purifies the bloodstream, thereby acting as a prevention to illnesses of the blood
· Stimulates blood flow

- Diminishes sensations of heaviness in the legs
- Regulates the heart rate
- Recommended for athletes who must make arduous and sustained efforts
- Reinforces the muscular structure
- Contributes to healthy scarring of the tissues
- Stimulates the taste buds
- Helps to reinstate equilibrium following shock or trauma

TOURMALINE FAMILY

Geometric alliance: trigonal (rhombohedral)
Colors: blue, black, green, pink, yellow
Chakras: according to color
Hardness: 7 to 7.5
Origin: Australia, Brazil, India, Italy, Madagascar, Myanmar, Russia, United States
Formation Process: magmatic
Purification: cold water, saltwater, incense, sunlight, earth
Recharging: quartz cluster, sunlight

Generalities

Tourmaline will transmit its beneficial effects to various parts of the body according to its particular color. Its natural ridges act as conductors of high-frequency energy, which make it an ideal stone for treatment, whether it is used to direct a particular energy to an area in need or to gradually dissipate certain blockages. Multicolored tourmaline is a superb transmitter that unites the properties of each of its respective colors.

Lithotherapy

- Balances the chakras and the meridians
- Creates a protective shield around the bodies
- Purifies the aura
- Considered to be a symbol of clear wisdom, unveils all forms of injustice and wrong action
- Helps to build the bridge between the soul and the mental, astral, and physical bodies to create a harmonious working unity

- Awakens creativity and incites wisdom
- Supports imagination, visualization, and creative dreams
- Develops the capacity for assimilation and imagination
- Cleanses, purifies, and transforms any dense energy into a lighter vibration
- Carries and increases the quantity of light and energy anywhere it is used
- Removes blockages
- Eliminates the feeling of being a victim
- Invites inspiration, compassion, tolerance, and prosperity
- Transforms negative thoughts into positive ones
- Stimulates the metabolism, hormonal glands, and the immune system
- Detoxifies and successfully treats digestive disorders
- Treats vertigo, pain of all kinds, and injuries of the nervous system
- Balances the cerebral hemispheres
- Calms paranoia and treats dyslexia

BLACK TOURMALINE (SCHORL)

Lithotherapy

- Anchors and grounds, being especially useful following a treatment as it helps those who have not fully integrated into their body
- Protects from negative energies
- When used with mica, reflects negative energies back to the person responsible to be worked out by that person
- Neutralizes the effects of radiation
- Deflects harmful vibrations coming from electrical equipment (cell phones, computers, televisions, etc.)
- Relieves pain and redirects unbalanced bodily energies
- Confers neutrality and serenity by activating clear and logical reasoning
- Stabilizes mental deviations and digressions, thereby helping to prevent insanity
- Alleviates problems caused by scarring
- Alleviates stress and tension caused by an excessive workload
- Regenerates the female reproductive system, thereby aiding menstrual problems such as cramps and ovarian cysts

BLUE TOURMALINE (INDICOLITE)

Lithotherapy

- Activates the throat and third eye chakras
- Enhances communication and intuition necessary for contact with other worlds
- Appeases and dissipates sadness and suppressed emotions
- Intensifies the aspiration toward freedom of mind
- Increases tolerance and the sense of responsibility
- Calms mental agitation and incessant thoughts
- Aligns the mental processes
- Treats throat, lung, and eye problems
- Ensures the equilibrium of the organic fluids
- Regenerates the kidneys and bladder
- Soothes burns and prevents scars
- Eases skin problems of a psychosomatic nature
- Alleviates sinusitis
- Supports the brain and balances the brain hemispheres
- Treats the heart and lungs
- Stimulates the thymus and strengthens the immune system
- Benefits the throat and thyroid, which may encourage weight loss
- Treats bacterial infections

GREEN TOURMALINE (VERDELITE)

Lithotherapy

- Encourages love and compassion as it possesses an affinity with the heart chakra
- Known as the "stone of universal healing," thereby benefiting the body and the mind
- Reveals emotional issues and facilitates their release
- Confers patience and openness, permitting us to perceive many solutions in any given situation
- Liberates us from past-life traumas
- Dissolves stress and fears, thereby conferring tranquility
- Conveys joie de vivre and renders us grateful for the miracles of life
- Promotes peaceful sleep

- Strengthens the nervous system, hence providing greater resistance to stress and fatigue
- Develops the sense of touch and smell; restores the taste buds
- Tones the heart
- Detoxifies the body, favoring elimination
- Relieves constipation and diarrhea
- Benefits hyperactive children

PINK TOURMALINE (RUBELLITE)

Lithotherapy

- Intimately tuned to the heart chakra, it communicates joy and unconditional love
- Generates profound relaxation
- Communicates peace and security
- Supports those who have been abused
- Comforts us during periods of grief
- Benefits the heart and lungs
- Eases skin problems
- Stimulates the desire to face life and relationships with enthusiasm and joy, without fears or barriers
- Inspires love on contact
- Helps heal past emotional pain; provides assurance that it is safe to love
- Encourages us to be targeted but still flexible enough to determine the validity of our goals and change direction if necessary; inspires us to devote ourselves body and soul to a task
- Improves the flow of energy in the physical and subtle bodies and ameliorates nerve conduction

WATERMELON TOURMALINE

Lithotherapy

- Activates the heart chakra through its gentle potency as well as its power
- Transmits its energies lightly and harmoniously, thus being particularly favorable for children
- Grants love, tenderness, and friendship
- Instills patience

344

- Encourages tact and diplomacy
- Facilitates the comprehension of situations and the expression of our intentions
- Relieves stress and promotes inner security
- Encourages finding joy in every situation
- Facilitates liberation from old emotional wounds
- Alleviates depression and soothes fears
- Activates nerve regeneration, especially in cases of paralysis or multiple sclerosis

Yellow Tourmaline (Dravite)

Lithotherapy

- Regenerates the solar plexus
- Stimulates simple and imaginative creativity
- Sharpens the intellect
- Confers mental clarity
- Instills a sense of courage and personal power
- Activates a sense of community, service, and social commitment
- Sharpens and strengthens manual skills
- Supports those involved in business endeavors
- Benefits the stomach, liver, spleen, gallbladder, and kidneys
- Revives the regenerative power of cells, tissues, and organs

Stones of the Buddhic Alliance

Amber

Geometric alliance: buddhic
Colors: milky white, light yellow to brown, black, red, green tones, rarely blue
Chakras: throat, solar plexus
Hardness: 2 to 2.5
Origin: Canada, Dominican Republic, France, Myanmar, Romania
Formation Process: sedimentary
Purification: quartz cluster, incense, earth
Recharging: quartz cluster; amber should be gently wiped with a chamois cloth.

Generalities

Although amber is actually resin, it is considered the first "precious stone" in the history of humanity. It has been used for more than 7,000 years for its therapeutic benefits; it has similar properties to penicillin.

Lithotherapy

· Possesses great wisdom
· Is the secret guardian of the Earth
· Awakens inner memories
· Allows the body to balance and heal itself
· Provides a cheerful, gentle, and easygoing yet confident nature
· Encourages spontaneity, openness, and respect
· Purifies the body, mind, and spirit
· Treats and regenerates the nervous system
· Balances the brain hemispheres
· Helps treat asthma and allergies
· Acts on stomach, spleen, and kidney disorders
· Relieves skin illnesses caused by liver disorders, accumulation of bile, and dysfunctional metabolism
· Helps with joint problems such as formation of cartilage
· Alleviates rheumatism and strengthens the heart muscle
· Fights epilepsy
· Soothes acute dental pain in young children

346

Amber has powerful therapeutic properties. It acts effectively if worn often and over long periods of time. When treating infants and children with amber, it is recommended that the piece be worn by the mother in advance.

JET

Geometric alliance: buddhic
Color: black
Chakra: root
Hardness: 2.5 to 4
Origin: France, Great Britain, Spain, United States
Formation Process: sedimentary
Purification: quartz cluster, cold water, incense, moonlight, earth
Recharging: quartz cluster, moonlight

Generalities

Jet is known to be a powerful protector. Due to its texture and its light weight, jet is sometimes referred to as "black amber."

Lithotherapy

· Grounds and strengthens our connection to the Earth
· Sustains us during periods of mourning and solitude
· Protects against negative forces and curses
· Repels negative thoughts and renews courage
· Stimulates the awakening of the kundalini
· Absorbs inflammation caused by arthritis and rheumatism
· Prevents inflammation in the respiratory system
· Relieves toothaches and migraines
· Eases symptoms of epilepsy
· Soothes stomach pains and menstrual cramps
· Diminishes or eliminates foot swelling if applied where the swelling predominates
· Confers elasticity to the body

Moldavite (Tektite Family)

Geometric alliance: buddhic
Color: green
Chakras: heart, crown, throat, third eye
Hardness: 5.5
Origin: Czech Republic, Slovenia
Formation Process: metamorphic
Purification: quartz cluster, cold water, incense, moonlight, sunlight, earth
Recharging: quartz cluster, moonlight, sunlight

Generalities

Moldavite was formed when a meteorite impacted the Earth's surface. The violence of the shock itself and the heat produced from it generated a mix that was propelled many miles from the impact zone. This material settled on the shores of the Vltava River in the Czech Republic, called the Moldau in German, hence its name.

Lithotherapy

· Grants access to higher spiritual realities due to its significantly elevated vibration
· Redirects focus to our main purpose in life, thereby encouraging transformation and expansion of consciousness
· Restores harmony and instigates self-healing
· Favors clairvoyance
· Brings understanding to the meaning of life and of humanity's mission on Earth
· Reinforces the capacity for empathy
· Grants guidance in work, relationships, and lifestyle, thereby promoting loyalty to our life mission
· Eradicates old outdated patterns
· Held in the left hand, guides the therapist in his or her work
· Clears and purifies the meridians
· Inspires creativity and good ideas

Due to the powerful vibration of this stone, it is advisable to use moldavite in moderation for cases of high blood pressure, heart problems, and vertigo. It is also recommended to use it with an effective grounding stone in order to remain anchored while working with such high energies.

Obsidian Family

Geometric alliance: buddhic
Colors: black, brown, glints of silver, gold, or multicolored
Chakra: root
Hardness: 5 to 5.5
Origin: Mexico, United States
Formation Process: magmatic
Purification: quartz cluster, cold water, incense, moonlight, sunlight, earth
Recharging: quartz cluster, moonlight, sunlight

Generalities

Obsidian is a "mirror" stone that emphasizes truth, compelling us to face who we really are.

Lithotherapy

· Provides an anchoring link from the root chakra down to the center of the Earth
· Purifies the atmosphere of negative influences
· Acts as a shield against psychic attacks
· Provides protection for hypersensitive people
· Dissipates fear, shock, and trauma
· Expands consciousness and helps us to change
· Confers mental clarity
· Clears confusion and rigid beliefs
· Sharpens the senses
· Unveils hidden aspects of the unknown
· Attenuates pains and tension and dissolves energy blockages
· Eases vascular constrictions
· Treats trauma to the cellular structure caused by injury

- Relieves pain in the joints, as with arthritis, as well as in the muscles
- Improves blood circulation; warms the hands and feet
- Accelerates healing
- Stops hemorrhaging
- Eliminates toxins from the body
- Absorbs environmental pollution
- Has a positive effect on the stomach and bowels

Obsidian is produced by the rapid cooling of lava, which categorizes it as a noncrystallized stone and part of the buddhic alliance. Obsidian acts rapidly and with great force. Its mirroring qualities emphasize truth, thereby helping us to face the darker sides of our being, such as profound fears, negative traits, and blocked energies. It must therefore always be used with caution and awareness. Placed on the navel, obsidian anchors spiritual energy in the body. Placed on the third eye, it breaks through mental barriers and dissolves mental conditioning.

APACHE TEAR OBSIDIAN

Lithotherapy

- Anchors and purifies the root chakra
- Acts with more moderation than black obsidian
- Gently reveals the darker aspects of our nature
- Eases sadness by revealing its source
- Lightens long-standing grief
- Favors forgiveness
- Pushes away self-imposed limitations
- Increases spontaneity

GOLDEN OBSIDIAN

Lithotherapy

- Guides us to access knowledge pertaining to the future
- Supports us during inner struggles with the ego
- Balances the energetic fields
- Treats allergies
- Stabilizes mood swings

Mahogany Obsidian

Lithotherapy

· Acts with more moderation than black obsidian
· Vibrates with the Earth
· Anchors and protects
· Stimulates our life objective
· Eliminates energy blockages
· Facilitates growth in all aspects
· Strengthens the aura
· Restores the normal rotational direction of the hara and solar plexus chakras
· Relieves pain
· Improves circulation

Rainbow Obsidian

Lithotherapy

· Acts with more moderation than all other forms of obsidian
· Provides powerful protection
· Reveals our spiritual nature
· Gently removes the "hooks" left in our aura by a partner
· Absorbs negative energy
· Calms stress and anxiety

Silver Obsidian

Lithotherapy

· Intensifies meditation
· Acts as a mirror to our inner being
· Allows access to purity and humility in the search for truth
· Confers patience and perseverance

Snowflake Obsidian

Lithotherapy

· Calms and soothes, thereby encouraging receptivity
· Teaches us to appreciate errors as well as successes
· Instills purity
· Balances the body, the mind, and the spirit
· Favors impartiality and inner poise

Opal Family

Geometric alliance: buddhic
Colors: see specific types
Chakras: according to type
Hardness: 5.5 to 6.5
Origin: Australia, Brazil, Guatemala, Japan, Mexico, Peru, United States
Formation Process: sedimentary
Purification: quartz cluster, a lot of water, incense, moonlight, sunlight, earth, avoid salt
Recharging: Quartz cluster, water, moonlight, sunlight, olive oil; it is suggested that the opal be rubbed gently with a high-quality vegetable oil once a month, as this will nourish it and help prevent dehydration.

Generalities

Opal's reputation demands respect because it is known to carry the power to bring luck or to take it away. Its high percentage of water—up to twenty percent—makes it a tool that can soothe or amplify emotions. It must therefore always be worn with an awareness of its potential and with a certainty of its positive effects. In case of doubt, refrain from wearing it.

BLACK OPAL (1st and 7th Chakras)

Generalities

Using a black opal in lithotherapy first requires determining the intentions behind the desire to use it, particularly if they are linked to emotions. It is worth noting that black opal, a very powerful stone, can support positive as well as negative intentions. We must always remain aware and in control of our thoughts and emotions while working with this stone; benevolent intentions are a must. Here's a proverb linked to the black opal: "Beware of what you ask for; you might actually get it."

Lithotherapy

· Stimulates the root chakra and links it with the crown chakra
· A stone of mystery and magic
· Helps to integrate our spiritual aspirations to everyday life
· Strongly amplifies intent
· Contains the power of manifestation when the will is linked to a precise goal
· Supports those who have undertaken profound inner work
· Favors letting go of negative experiences that create certain karmic patterns
· Frees us from traumatic memories governing certain periods of life (it is helpful to have the aid of an experienced guide for this work.)
· Supports us when facing the darkest fears
· Helps to overcome phobias and panic attacks
· Makes it possible to visit the dark aspects of being while staying connected to the light
· Supports those who help lost souls by directing them toward more luminous worlds
· Contributes to diminishing tumors and cysts

FIRE OPAL (1st Chakra) Yellow orange to fluorescent red

Lithotherapy

· Has a strong effect in the hara chakra region
· Reinforces personal power
· Awakens the inner fire

- Protects us from danger
- Encourages a spontaneous and impulsive character
- Inspires risk taking
- Gives hope
- Awakens us to the joy of being alive
- Stimulates the libido
- Transforms sexuality into spontaneous pleasure
- Allows us to quickly seize reality and to act accordingly
- Helps us to overcome emotional problems caused by mistreatment and injustice
- Frees us from the past and from the risk of discordant behavior caused by strong recurring emotional patterns
- Clears up feelings of sadness stemming from present and past lives
- Contributes to the proper functioning of the kidneys and adrenal glands, such as production of adrenaline
- Prevents exhaustion
- Fortifies blood circulation
- Aids digestion by regulating acid and enzymes in the stomach
- Soothes menstrual pains caused by hormonal imbalances

HYDROPHANE OPAL (1st Chakra) Opaque white

Lithotherapy

- Contributes to the exteriorization of certain qualities repressed due to lack of self-confidence
- Enhances connection with the spiritual level because of its water content
- Stabilizes moods
- Supports us during out-of-body transitions
- Teaches us that the body is a temporary vehicle for the soul

NOBLE OPAL (7th Chakra) Milky white with multicolor iridescence

Lithotherapy

- Symbolizes purity in sentiments, fidelity, shared confidences, and loving kindness
- Favors sleep

White Opal (4th Chakra)

Lithotherapy

· Stimulates originality and dynamic creativity
· Alleviates worries, chronic stress, and depression
· Communicates the joy of living on Earth
· Reinforces the will to live
· Brings mental clarity and spontaneity
· Soothes emotions and encourages a positive attitude
· Helps heal broken hearts
· Is associated with love, passion, desire, and eroticism
· Comforts those who have lived through abuses of all kinds
· Fights exhaustion
· Contributes to the treatment of Parkinson's disease
· Fights infections and fever
· Improves memory
· Regulates insulin levels
· Eases symptoms of premenstrual syndrome
· Reinforces eyesight when taken as an elixir

Petrified Wood (Xyloid)

Geometric alliance: buddhic or trigonal (rhombohedral)
Colors: brown, yellow, reddish
Chakras: solar plexus, root
Hardness: 7
Origin: Argentina, Egypt, United States (Arizona)
Formation Process: sedimentary
Purification: cold water, incense, sunlight, earth
Recharging: quartz cluster, abundant sunlight

Generalities

Petrified wood is about 200 million years old and dates back to the first conifer tree, Araucaria, from the Jurassic period.

Petrified wood is classified according to its transformation process. It belongs to the trigonal alliance when the cavity of the wood becomes lined with quartz; this transformation is the most common. However, when the cavities are lined with opal, which occurs less frequently, petrified wood belongs to the buddhic alliance.

Lithotherapy

· Encourages trust in the rhythm of life and in what is needed to evolve
· Guides us slowly but surely toward spiritual transformation
· Gives the impression of being at the right place at the right moment
· Stimulates inner images and past lives
· Helps to recognize and to release emotional patterns transmitted from our family history
· Relaxes, calms, and encourages, making time for reflection and contemplation
· Facilitates the creation of a positive environment
· Excels against all kinds of physical problems
· Activates the metabolism
· Calms the nerves
· Confers a feeling of well-being
· Favors the physical and intellectual growth of children
· Reinforces bone structure and treats broken bones
· Offers protection against intestinal parasites
· Purifies the liver and the blood
· Balances the liver and the gallbladder
· Treats the hair when taken as an elixir

TEKTITE

Geometric alliance: buddhic
Colors: black, brown black
Chakra: root
Hardness: 5 to 5.5
Origin: Czech Republic, Slovenia, Tibet
Formation Process: metamorphic
Purification: quartz cluster, occasionally cold water, incense, sunlight, earth
Recharging: quartz cluster, sunlight

Generalities

As with most black stones, Tibetan tektite is known to provide reliable protection. It is considered a cousin of obsidian, and it works harmoniously with lapis lazuli, all types of quartz, jasper, chalcedony, and opal. Petrified wood has been known to contribute to grounding the strong energies of tektite without overpowering its positive effects.

Lithotherapy

- Stabilizes the flow of energy when placed on the chakras
- Purifies the lower chakras, allowing us to remain grounded while maintaining a greater awareness
- Possesses a particularly elevated vibration
- Increases the quality of the vibration of the auric field when it is worn
- Helps the body integrate high-frequency energies (right to the cellular level) that have proven vital for the evolution of humanity
- Holds the power to increase communication with other dimensions
- Encourages the feeling of being home here on Earth for those who feel they originate from elsewhere and have a difficult time integrating here
- Elevates the consciousness beyond the vibration of the physical plane
- Facilitates the emotional release of undesirable events and assists in the assimilation of the lessons learned by focusing our mind on what contributes to spiritual growth
- Guides us to the heart of a problem or a difficulty so as to understand its true cause and undertake the necessary actions to remedy it
- Expels energetic residues, hence freeing the energy body and making it more receptive
- Balances the masculine and feminine energies
- Reduces fever
- Strengthens the capillaries and improves circulation
- Helps to prevent the transmission of infectious disease

INDEX

REFERENCES

D.D.D. *Knots of Eternity: Paradoxes from Dadi to Daughter,* Volume I. Montreal: Orange Palm Publications, 2007.

The Group of 5. *Crystals and Stones: A Complete Guide to their Healing Properties.* Berkeley, CA: North Atlantic Books, and Montreal: Paume de Saint-Germain Publishing, 2010.

Jung, C. G. *Man and His Symbols.* Garden City, NY: Doubleday, 1964.

Karta, Etbonan. "Seven Studies of the Soul's Earthly Pilgrimage of Service upon the Seven Cosmic-Physical Rays." *The Divine Concordance of Light: A Handbook from Heaven to Progression Earth, the Seven Rays of God.* Montreal: Magnificent Magus Publications, 2000.

Sri Adi Dadi. *The Spiritual Science of Essential Yoga: Techniques of Meditation, Mantrams and Invocations,* Volume I. Montreal: Paume de Saint-Germain Publishing, 2004.

Sri Adi Dadi. *The Spiritual Science of Essential Yoga,* Volume II. Montreal: Orange Palm Publications, forthcoming.

ABOUT THE AUTHORS

Collaborating in this present work are the members of The Group of 5. This name, The Group of 5, evokes the five-branch star symbolizing the perfect person, drawn by Leonardo da Vinci, a visionary of his time. It also refers to therapists affiliated with the Medicine Buddha Mandala Institute of Applied Alternative Therapies. We are united within this star and form a working unity in service to all.

These are the names of those who have collaborated in the present volume: Klaire D. Roy, Lisa C. Bergeron, Richard Frappier, André Lavoie, Johanne Marier, François Nicol, Sylvain Plante, Kristiane Roy, Jacqueline Sylvain, Marcel Tardif, and Gisèle Thifault.

Paume de Saint-Germain Publishing©
Division of Orange Palm and Magnificent Magus Publications Inc.©
235 Rene Levesque Boulevard East, Suite 310
Montreal, Quebec, Canada H2X 1N8
Telephone: 514 255-8700
Facsimile: 514 255-0478
E-mail: info@palmpublications.com
Website: http://www.palmpublications.com